THE FINE ART OF SMUGGLING:
King's Cutters vs Smugglers - 1700-1855

by

E. Keble Chatterton

Fireship Press
www.FireshipPress.com

The Fine Art of Smuggling: King's Cutters vs. Smugglers - 1700-1855 - Copyright © 2008 by Fireship Press

>All rights reserved. No part of this book may be used or reproduced by any means without the written permission of the publisher except in the case of brief quotation embodied in critical articles and reviews.

ISBN-13: 978-1-934757-19-2
ISBN-10: 1-934757-19-5

BISAC Subject Headings:
>HIS027150   HISTORY / Military / Naval
>HIS015000   HISTORY / Europe / Great Britain

This work is based on the 1912 edition of *King's Cutters and Smugglers 1700-1855* by E. Keble Chatterton, London: George Allen & Company..

1.0

THE FINE ART OF SMUGGLING:
King's Cutters vs Smugglers -
1700-1855

ABOUT CONTEMPORIZED CLASSICS™

Books from the Victorian era and earlier were written quite differently than today's works. The paragraphing, sentence structure, terminology, spelling and other factors are not what we're used to seeing. As a result, too often they jar the reader into putting the book down—or not picking it up at all. They simply do not "read right" to the modern eye.

We have taken a different approach in producing our "Contemporized Classics." Each book in this series has been edited so that long rambling sentences and paragraphs are divided into shorter ones, some sentence structures are updated, and so forth. The idea is to present a work that looks and reads in a more modern, more familiar, style. These are *not* abridged works in the usual sense. If wording has been altered or cut, it is only to enhance modern readability. Indeed, great care has been taken to make sure that meaning has in no way been altered.

In many respects this process is similar to the "colorization revolution" which recently took place in the film industry. With the development of digital technology in the late 1970's, filmmakers and historians were able to re-issue a large number of classic black and white films in a modern color format. The process gave these films new life by making them more acceptable to the modern viewer.

As with the colorization of films, we're sure there will be some who will consider this effort some kind of literary sacrilege. If so, they are free to read these books in their original form. There are plenty of those volumes around.

For everyone else, welcome to the world of Contemporized Classics. If you can read these books and have the impression that they were written only yesterday, then we will have done our job.

Read them again for the first time... and enjoy!

Contents

Preface

1. Introduction	1
2. The Earliest Smugglers	7
3. The Growth of Smuggling	19
4. The Smugglers' Methods	27
5. The Hawkhurst Gang	38
6. The Revenue Cruisers	49
7. Cutters and Sloops	63
8. Preventive Organization	71
9. Cutters' Equipment	81
10. The Increase in Smuggling	95
11. The Smugglers at Sea	105
12. The Work of the Cutters	115
13. The Period of Ingenuity	126
14. Some Interesting Encounters	137
15. A Tragic Incident	147
16. Administrative Reforms	157
17. Smuggling by Concealments	169
18. By Sea and Land	181
19. Action and Counter-Action	193
20. Force and Cunning	203

Appendices

Appendix I - Sloops or Cutters	215
Appendix II - A List of Cruisers Employed in the Customs Service for the Year 1784	217
Appendix III - A List of Cruisers Employed in the Customs Service for the Year 1797 (up to June 27th)	221
Appendix IV - A List of Revenue Cruisers Built Between July 18, 1822 and October 1, 1838	225
Appendix V - Specification for Building a Cutter for the Revenue Service of Thirty-Five Tons (As built in the Year 1838)	231
Appendix VI - Dimensions of Spars of Revenue Cutters	237
Appendix VII - A List of the Cruisers in the Revenue Coast Guard of the United Kingdom in the Year 1844	239
Appendix VII - The Relationship between the Royal Navy and the Revenue Service	241

Preface

I have in the following pages endeavored to resist the temptation to weave a web of pleasant but unreliable fiction round actual occurrences. That which is here set forth has been derived from facts, and in almost every case from manuscript records. It aims at telling the story of an eventful and exciting period according to historical and not imaginative occurrence. There are extant many novels and short stories which have for their heroes the old-time smugglers. But the present volume represents an effort to look at these exploits as they were and not as a novelist likes to think they might have occurred.

Perhaps there is hardly an Englishman who was not thrilled in his boyhood days by Marryat and others when they wrote of the King's Cutters and their foes. It is hoped that the following pages will not merely revive pleasant recollections but arouse a new interest in the adventures of a species of sailing craft that is now, like the brig and the fine old clipper-ship, past and done with.

The reader will note that in the Appendices a considerable amount of interesting data has been collected. This has been rendered possible only with great difficulty, but it is believed that in future years the dimensions and details of a Revenue Cutter's construction, the sizes of her spars, her tonnage, guns, etc., the number of her crew carried, the names and dates of the fleets of cutters employed will have an historical value which cannot easily be assessed in the present age that is still familiar with sailing craft.

In making researches for the preparation of this volume I have to express my deep sense of gratitude to the Honorable Commissioners of the Board of Customs for granting me permission to make use of their valuable records; to Mr. F.S. Parry C.B., Deputy Chairman of the Board for his courtesy in placing a vast amount of data in my hands, and for having elucidated a good many points of difficulty; and, finally, to Mr. Henry Atton, Librarian of the Custom House, for his great assistance in research.

E. KEBLE CHATTERTON.

CHAPTER ONE
Introduction

Outside pure Naval history it would be difficult to find any period so full of incident and contest as this one. It was a time in which the English Preventive Service attempted to deal with the notorious and dangerous bands of smugglers who were a serious menace to the trade and welfare of our nation.

As we shall see from the following pages, their activities covered many decades, and indeed smuggling is not dead even today nor ever will be so long as there are regulations which human ingenuity can occasionally outwit. But the grand, adventurous epoch of the smugglers covers little more than a century and a half, beginning about the year 1700 and ending about 1855 or 1860. Crowded within that space of time is a wealth of adventure, exciting escapes, fierce encounters, clever moves and even more clever counter-moves. There are so many thousands of people involved, and so much money expended, that the story of these smugglers has a right to be ranked second only to those larger battles that occur between two or more nations.

Everyone has, even nowadays, a secret regard for the smugglers of that bygone age. It's an instinct that is based partly on a curious human failing and partly on a keen admiration for men of dash and daring. There is a sympathy, somehow, with a class of men who succeeded not once but hundreds of times in defying the law; who, in spite of all the resources of the Government, were not easily beaten.

In the novels of James, Marryat, and a host of lesser writers the smuggler and the Preventive man have become familiar and standard types. There are very few, surely, who in the days of their youth have not enjoyed the breathless excitement of some story depicting the chasing of

The Fine Art of Smuggling:

a boat loaded with contraband or watched vicariously the landing of tubs of spirits along a pebbly beach on a night when the moon never showed herself. But most of these were fiction and little else. Even Marryat, though he was for some time actually engaged in Revenue duty, is now known to have been inaccurate and loose in some of his stories. Those who have followed afterwards have been scarcely better.

However, there is nothing in the following pages which belongs to fiction. Every effort has been made to set forth only actual historical facts, which are capable of verification, so that what is contained herein represents not what might have happened but what actually *did* take place.

To write a complete history of smuggling would be well-nigh impossible, owing to the fact that many of the records, which today would be invaluable, have long since perished. The burning down of the Customs House by the side of the Thames in 1814 and the lack of appreciation of the value of certain documents by former officials have caused so desirable a history to be impossible to be written. Still, happily, there is even now a vast amount of material in existence, and the present Commissioners of the Board of Customs are using every effort to preserve for posterity a mass of data connected with this service.

Owing to the courtesy of the Commissioners it has been my good fortune to carefully study the documents which are concerned with the old smuggling days, the Revenue cutters, and the Preventive Service generally. It is from these pages and from other sources that I have been able to put forth the story as it is here presented. As such it represents an attempt to afford an authentic picture of an extremely interesting and an exciting period of our national history, to show the conditions of the smuggling industry from the seventeenth to the nineteenth century, and the efforts to put a stop to it.

We shall soon find that this period in its glamour, romance, and adventure contains a good deal of similarity to the great seafaring Elizabethan epoch. The ships were different, but the courage of the English seamen was the same. Nor must we forget that those rough, rude men who ran back and forth across the English Channel in cutters, yawls, luggers, and sometimes open boats—stiffened with a rich ballast of tea, tobacco, and brandy—were some of the finest seamen in the world. Certainly they were the most skillful fore-and-aft sailors and efficient pilots to be found anywhere on the seas which wash the coasts of the United Kingdom. They were sturdy and strong of body, courageous and enterprising of nature, who had "used" the sea all their lives. Consequently the English Government wisely determined that in all cases of an encounter with smugglers the first aim of the Preventive officers should be to capture the smugglers themselves. The reason was so that they could be promptly impressed into the service of the Navy and be put to the good of the nation instead of being to the latter's disadvantage.

As everyone familiar with the sea is aware, the seamanship of the square-rigged vessel and of the fore-and-aft is very different. The latter makes special demands of its own which, for the present, we need not go into. But we may assert with perfect confidence that at its best the handling of the King's cutters and the smuggling craft, the chasing and eluding in all weather, the strategy and tactics of both parties form some of the best chapters in nautical lore. The great risks that were run, the self-confidence and coolness displayed indicated quite clearly that our national seafaring spirit was not yet dead. Today many descendants of these old smugglers remain our foremost fore-and-aft sailors, yet engaged no longer in an illicit trade but in the more peaceful pursuits of line fishing, oyster dredging, trawling during the winter, and often shipping as yachts' hands during the summer.

Even though we are reading fact and not fiction, we will not find the subject lacking in interest. Truth often really is stranger than fiction, and some of the tricks and devices employed by the smuggling communities may well surprise us. We will not attempt to whitewash a class of men who were lawless, reckless, and sometimes even brutal in their efforts. But we will also not hesitate to give the fullest prominence to the great skill and downright cleverness of a singularly virile and unique kind of British manhood. In much the same way as a spectator looks on at a fine sporting contest between two able foes, we shall watch the clashing exploits of the King's men and the smugglers. Sometimes the one side wins, sometimes the other, but nearly always there is a splendidly exciting tussle before either party can claim victory.

No one who has not examined the authentic records of this period can appreciate how powerful the smugglers on sea and land had become. The impudence and independence of some of the former were amazing. We shall give numerous instances in due course, but for now we might take the case of the Revenue cutter which, after giving chase to a smuggling vessel, came up to the latter. Shots were exchanged, but the smuggler turned his swivel guns on the Government craft with such a hot effect that the Revenue captain decided to give up the fight and hurry away as fast as possible. At this point the positions were reversed and the smuggler actually chased the Revenue cutter!

In fact during the year 1777 one of the Customs officials wrote sadly to the Board that there was a large lugger off the coast, that was so well armed that she was "greatly an overmatch" for even two of the Revenue cruisers. It seems almost ludicrous to read a genuine and unquestionable report of a smuggling vessel coming into a bay, finding a Revenue cruiser lying quietly at anchor, and ordering the cruiser, with a fine flow of oaths, immediately to cut his anchor cable and clear out; otherwise the smugglers promised to sink her. The Revenue cutter's commander did not cut his cable, but he did get his anchor up promptly and cleared out just as he was told.

The Fine Art of Smuggling:

It was not until after 1815 that the Government began seriously to make continuous headway in its efforts to cope with the smuggling evil. Consider the times.

Between the years 1652 and 1816 there were years and years of wars by land or by sea. There were the three great Anglo-Dutch wars, the wars with France, with Spain, to say nothing of the trouble with America. They were indeed anxious years that ended only with the Battle of Waterloo, and it was not likely that all this would in any way put a stop to that restlessness which was unmistakable.

Wages were low, the cost of living was high, and the poorer classes of those days had by no means all the privileges possessed today. Add to this the fact that literally for centuries there lived along the south coast of England, especially in the neighborhood of the old Cinque ports, a race of men who were always ready for some piratical or semi-piratical sea exploit. It was in their blood to undertake and long for such enterprises, and all they needed was the opportunity to send them roving the seas as privateers, or running goods illegally from one coast to another. And it is not true that time has altogether eliminated that old spirit.

When a ship today has the misfortune to lose her way in a fog and pile up on rock or sandbank, you read of the numbers of small craft which put out to salvage her cargo. But not all this help comes out of hearts of unfathomable pity. On the contrary, your beachman has an eye to business. He cannot go roving nowadays; time has killed the smuggling in which his ancestors distinguished themselves. But none the less he can legally profit by another vessel's misfortune. As the local families worked in syndicate fashion when they went smuggling, so now they mutually arrange to get the cargo ashore and, incidentally, make a very handsome profit as well.

We need not envy the Government the difficult and trying task that was theirs during the height of the smuggling era. There was quite enough to think about with regard to foreign affairs without wanting the additional worry of these contraband runners. That must be borne in mind whenever one feels inclined to smile at the apparently half-hearted attempts of the authorities to deal with the evil. Neither funds nor seamen, nor ships nor adequate attention could be spared just then to deal with these pests. It was only after the wars had at last ended and the Napoleonic bogey had been settled that this domestic worry could be dealt with in the manner it required.

There were many evils waiting to be remedied, and this lawlessness along the coast of the country was one of the greatest. But it was not a matter that could be adjusted in a hurry. It was not for another forty or fifty years, not, in fact, until various administrative changes and improvements had taken place, that at last the evil was practically stamped out.

As one looks through the existing records one cannot help noticing that there was scarcely a bay or suitable landing-place along the whole

English coast-line that did not become notorious for these smuggling "runs." There is hardly a cliff or piece of high ground that has not been employed for the purpose of giving a signal to the approaching craft as they came on through the night over the dark waters. There are indeed very few villages in proximity to the sea that have not been concerned in these smuggling ventures and taken active interest in the landing of bales and casks. The sympathy of the country-side was with the smuggling fraternity. Magistrates were at times terrorized, juries were too frightened to convict. In short, the evil had grown to such an extent that it was a most difficult problem for any Government to be asked to deal with. The solution required a very efficient service both of craft and men afloat, and an equally able and incorruptible guard on land that could not be turned from its purpose either by fear or bribery. We shall see from the following chapters how these two organizations—by sea and land—worked.

If we exclude fiction, the amount of literature which has been published on smuggling is exceedingly small. Practically the whole of the following pages is the outcome of personal research among original, authentic manuscripts and official documents. Included under this head may be cited the Minutes of the Board of Customs, General Letters of the Board to the Collectors and Controllers of the various Out-ports, Outport Letters to the Board, the transcripts from shorthand notes of Assizes and *Promiscuous Trials of Smugglers*, a large quantity of manuscripts of remarkable incidents connected with smuggling, There were also miscellaneous notes collected on the subject in the Library of the Customs House, instructions issued at different times to Customs officers and commanders of cruisers, General Orders issued to the Coast-Guard, together with a valuable precis (unpublished) of the existing documents in the many Customs Houses along the English coast made in the year 1911 by the Librarian to the Board of Customs on a round of visits to the different ports for that purpose. These researches have been further supplemented by other documents in the British Museum and elsewhere.

This volume, therefore, contains within its pages a very large amount of material hitherto unpublished, In addition to the details gathered together regarding smuggling methods, special attention has been paid to collect all possible information concerning the Revenue sloops and cutters so frequently alluded to in those days as cruisers. I have often heard a desire expressed among those interested in the literature of the sea to learn all about the King's cutters, how they were rigged, manned, victualed, armed, and navigated, what were their conditions of service at sea, and so on. Finally, to obtain accounts of their chasing of smuggling craft, I have relied on the narratives of eye-witnesses of the incidents, the testimony of the commanders and crews themselves, both captors and captives, It is, I believe, the most complete picture of the subject that has ever been attempted.

These cutters were most interesting craft both by themselves and because of the chases and fights in which they were engaged. The King's cutters were also employed in international warfare as in the Preventive

Service. There is an interesting letter, for instance, to be read from Lieutenant Henry Rowed, commanding the Admiralty cutter *Sheerness*, dated September 9, 1803, off Brest, in which her gallant commander sends a notable account to Collingwood concerning the chasing of a French *chasse-maree*. And cutters were also employed in connection with the Walcheren expedition. The hired armed cutter *Stag* was found useful in 1804 as a dispatch vessel.

But the King's cutters in the Revenue work were not always as active as they might be. In one of his novels (*The Three Cutters*) Captain Marryat gives the reader a very plain hint that there was a good deal of slackness prevalent in this section of the service. Referring to the midshipman of the Revenue cutter *Active*, the author speaks of him as a lazy fellow, too inert even to mend his jacket which was out at elbows, and adds, "He has been turned out of half the ships in the service for laziness; but he was born so, and therefore it is not his fault. A Revenue cutter suits him—she is half her time hove-to; and he has no objection to boat-service, as he sits down in the stern-sheets, which is not fatiguing. Creeping for tubs is his delight, as he gets over so little ground."

But Marryat was, of course, intentionally sarcastic here. That this lazy element was not always, and in every ship, prevalent is clear from the facts at hand. It is also equally clear from the repeated admonitions and exhortations of the Board of Customs, by the holding-out of handsome rewards and the threatening of dire penalties, that the Revenue-cutter commanders were periodically negligent in their duties. They were far too fond of coming to a nice snug anchorage for the night or seeking shelter in bad weather, and generally running into harbor with a frequency that was unnecessary. The result was that the cutter, having left her station unguarded, allowed the smugglers to land their kegs with impunity.

But we need not delay our story longer, and may proceed now to consider the subject in greater detail.

CHAPTER TWO
The Earliest Smugglers

It is not our intention to trace the history of the levying of customs through different reigns and in different ages, but it is important to note briefly that the evading of these dues is one of the oldest offenses on record.

The most ancient dues paid to the English sovereigns would seem to have been those which were levied on the exportation and importation of merchandise across the sea. As a result, nowadays when we speak of smuggling we tend to think only of those acts concerned with imports; but the word applies equally to unlawful exporting. Before it is possible for any crime to be committed there must the opportunity to carry it out. Throughout the history of our nation—or at least from the thirteenth century on—that portion of England, the counties of Kent and Sussex, which is adjacent to the Continent, has always been both the most tempted and the most inclined towards this offense. While there are many other localities which were made notorious by generations of smugglers, these two between them have been responsible for more smuggling activity than all the rest put together.

What I would like to emphasize is the fact that, although smuggling rose to unheard-of importance as a national danger during the eighteenth and nineteenth centuries, it was not a practice which suddenly rose into prominence during that period. Human nature is much the same under various kings and at various times; and under similar circumstances men and women perform similar actions. Confronted with the temptation to cheat the Crown of its dues, you will find persons in the time of George V repeating the very crimes of Edward I The difference is primarily in the nature of the articles and the manner in which they were smuggled. Today it might be cigars—centuries ago it was wool.

Although the golden age (if we may use the term) of smuggling has long since passed, I am not convinced that if the occasion arose to carry on this trade as it was conducted during the eighteenth and the first half of the nineteenth centuries, that there would be very many who would do it. To some extent the modern improvements in living, in education, and increased respect for lofty ideals would modify this tendency; and long years have awakened so keen a regard for the benefits of law and order that I don't believe the practice would break out immediately on a large scale. When we speak of smuggling it is perhaps more correct to speak of it as a disease which has not been exterminated from the system, but is, as it were, a microbe that is kept well under control and not allowed to spread.

Everyone who is familiar with English history is aware of the important position which was occupied by the wool trade. Because of the immense value to the nation of the fleece, it was necessary that this commodity should be kept in the country and not sent abroad. If in the present day most of our iron and coal were to be dispatched abroad regardless of what was required by our manufacturers it would not be long before the country would begin to suffer serious loss. So it was, in the thirteenth century, with the wool.

As a check to this a tax was levied on that wool which was exported out of the country, and during the reign of Edward III attempts were made to prevent the Continent from receiving our chief product. But the temptation was too great, the rewards were too alluring for the practice to be stopped.

The fleece was carried across from England, made into cloth, and in this state sent back to us. Even in the fourteenth century the town of Middleburgh was the headquarters of this clandestine trade. I won't bore you with the details of the steps that were taken to stop this trade by the English kings. It is enough to state that practically all the ports of Sussex and Kent were busily engaged in the illegal business. Neither the penalties of death, nor the fixing of the price of wool, nor the regulating of the rate of duty worked in the long-run. Licenses to export this article were continually evaded, creeks and quiet bays were the scenes where the fleece was shipped to France and the Low Countries. Sometimes the price of wool fell, sometimes it rose; sometimes the Crown received a greater amount of duty, at other times the royal purse suffered greatly. In the time of Elizabeth the encouragement of foreign weavers to make their homes in England was likely to do much to keep the wool in the country, especially as there began to be increased wealth in our land, and families began to spend more money on personal comforts.

Even in the time of Charles I proclamations were issued against exporting wool, yet it still went on. In the time of Charles II men readily

King's Cutters vs Smugglers -1700-1855

"risked their necks for 12d. a day."[1] The greatest part of the wool was sent from Romney Marsh, where, after nightfall, it was put on board French shallops with ten or twenty men to guard it, all well armed. And other parts of Sussex as well as Kent and even Essex were engaged in similar exportations.

But it is from the time of Charles II that the first serious steps were taken to cope with smuggling, and from here we take our starting-point.

Prior to his time the Customs, as a subsidy of the king, were prone to much variability. In the time of James I, for instance, they had been granted to the sovereign for life, and he had the power to alter the rates as he chose when pressed for money. When Charles I came to the throne the Commons, instead of voting those rights for the sovereign's life, granted them for one year only. At a later date in the reign of that unhappy king the grant was made only for a couple of months. These dues were known as tonnage and poundage, the former being a duty of 1s. 6d. to 3s. levied on every ton of wine and liquor exported and imported. Poundage was a similar tax of 6d. to 1s. on every pound of dry goods.

It was not until after the Restoration that the custom duties were more firmly established, a subsidy being "granted to the king of tonnage and poundage and other sums of money payable upon merchandise exported and imported." Nominally the customs were employed for defraying the cost of "guarding and defending the seas against all persons intending the disturbance of his subjects in the intercourse of trade, and the invading of this realm." And so, also, there was inaugurated a more systematic and efficient method of preventing export smuggling. So far as one can find any existing records of this early Preventive system, the chronological order would seem to be as follows:

The first mention of any kind of marine service that I can trace is found in a manuscript of 1674, which shows the establishment of the Custom House organization in that year for England and Wales. From this it is clear that there was a beginning of the system which was later to develop into the Revenue cutters. When we recollect how extremely interested Charles II was in everything related to the sea and to sloop-rigged craft especially, it seems natural to believe that he inspired, or at least encouraged, the formation of a small fleet of Custom House sailing craft.

Later I will discuss this matter at greater length. For now, suffice it to say that Charles was the monarch who brought the first yacht into England, presented to him by the Dutch; and from this was born the sport of yachting and the building of English yachts. He was very much concerned with the rigging of sloops, and loved to sail in such craft, and his yacht was also most probably the first vessel of that rig which had ever been employed by English sailors. He was also something of a naval ar-

---

[1] *Smuggling in Sussex* by William Durrant Cooper, F.S.A., in Vol. X of the Sussex Archæological Collection, to which I am indebted.

chitect, the founder of the Greenwich Royal Observatory and the Nautical Almanac, and under his rule a fresh impulse was given to navigation and shipbuilding generally.

At any rate, by the year 1674 there were among the smaller sailing craft of England a number of sloops and smacks employed for fishing and coasting work. As a kind of marine police, the Custom House authorities determined to hire some of these to keep a watch on the "owlers," as the wool-smugglers were termed—so called, no doubt, because they had to pursue their calling always by night. Whatever efforts had been adopted prior to his reign probably had consisted for the most part, if not entirely, of a land police. But under this second Charles the very sensible and obvious idea of utilizing a number of sailing craft was started.

In the above referenced manuscript volume the first reference is to "Peter Knight, Master of ye smack for ye wages of him self and five men and boy, and to bear all charges except wear and tear... £59." "For extraordinary wear and tear," he was to be paid £59. His vessel was the *Margate* smack. In the same volume there is also a reference to the "*Graves End* smack," and to "Thomas Symonds for wages and dyett [diet] for himself, master and six men... £56, 5s. 0d." And for the "wear and tear to be disposed as ye Commrs. direct... £14, 15s. 0d." There was yet a third vessel stationed a few miles away, the "*Quinborrough* smack," and a reference to "Nicholas Badcock for hire of ye smack, two men, and to bear all charges... £23."

These vessels were not known as Revenue cutters at this time, but as Custom House smacks. They were hired by the Commissioners of the Customs from private individuals to prevent the owlers from smuggling the wool from Kent, Essex, and Sussex. But it would seem that these smacks, even if they modified a little the activities of the owlers, did not succeed in bringing about many convictions. Romney Marsh still sent its contribution across to France and Holland, much as it had done for generations.

But in 1698 the attack on the men of Kent and Sussex was strengthened by legislation. It was enacted that "for the better preventing the exportation of wool and correspondence with France... the Lord High Admiral of England, or Commissioners for executing the office of Lord High Admiral for the time being, shall from time to time direct and appoint one ship of the Fifth Rate, and two ships of the Sixth Rate, and four armed sloops constantly to cruise off the North Foreland to the Isle of Wight, with orders for taking and seizing all ships, vessels, or boats which shall export any wool or carry or bring any prohibited goods or any suspected persons." It was due to William III's Government also that no person living within fifteen miles of the sea in those counties should buy any wool before he entered into a bond, with sureties, that all the wool he might buy should be sold by him to no persons within fifteen miles of the sea, and all growers of wool within ten miles of the sea in those counties were obliged within three days of shearing to account for the number of fleeces, and where they were lodged.

Instructions were duly issued to captains of sloops, and a scheme drafted for surrounding the whole of the coast with sloops, the crews consisting of master, mate, and mariners. But from an entry in the Excise and Treasury Reports of 1685, it is clear that a careful regard even at that date was being had for the import smuggling as well. The reference belongs to September 24, and shows that a "boarding" boat was desired for going alongside vessels in the Downs, and preventing the running in of brandies along the coast in that vicinity. The charge for building such a boat is to be £25. In another manuscript touching on the Customs, there is under date of June 1695 an interesting reference to "a Deale yoghall to be built," and that "such a boat will be here of very good use." She is to be "fitt to go into ye roads for boarding men or other ocations when ye sloops may be at sea."

So much, then, for the moment as to the guarding by sea against the smugglers. Let us now turn to look into the means adopted by land.

The wool-owners of Romney Marsh were still hard at their game, and the horses still came down to the beach ladened with the packs ready to be shipped. If any one were sent with warrants to arrest the delinquents, they were attacked, beaten, and forced to flee, followed by armed gangs on horseback. But it was evident that the Crown was determined not to let the matter rest, for a number of surveyors were appointed for nineteen counties and 299 riding officers as well. They made few seizures, and obtained still fewer convictions, but did it at great expense to the State.

In 1703 it was believed that the owling trade—or export smuggling—especially in Romney Marsh, was broken if not dead, although import smuggling was on the increase, especially as regards silks, lace, and such "fine" goods. At that time for the two hundred miles of coastline between the Isle of Sheppey and Emsworth—practically the whole of the Kentish and Sussex shore—fifty officers were being employed at a salary of £60 per annum, with an allowance to each of another £30 annually for a servant and horse to assist them during the night. And there was authority also for the employment of dragoons to aid the riding officers, especially in the neighborhood of Romney Marsh; but there was a number of "weak and superannuated" men among the latter, who did not exactly make for an efficient service.

We need not say much more about the wool exportation. In spite of all the efforts of the Custom House smacks and the assistance of his Majesty's ships of war, in spite of further legislation, it still continued. It went on merrily until the end of the eighteenth century, by which time import smuggling had long since eclipsed its importance.

It was the wars with France during the time of William and Mary that increased and rendered more easy the smuggling into England of silk and lace. And by the same means there used to be smuggled also a good deal of Jacobite correspondence. As Kent and Sussex had been famous for their export smuggling, so these counties were again to distinguish themselves by illicit importation. From then until the middle of the eighteenth century this newer form of smuggling rose gradually to wondrous heights. And yet it was by no means new. In the time of Edward III steps had to be taken to prevent the importation of base coin into the realm, and in succeeding reigns the king had been cheated many a time of that which ought to have come to him through the duties of goods entering the country.

It was impossible instantly to put down a practice which had been pursued by so many families for so many hundreds of years. But, even so, the existing force was not equal to coping with the increase. As a consequence the daring of the smugglers knew no bounds—the more they succeeded the more they ventured. A small gang of ten would blossom into several hundred, there would be no lack of arms nor clubs, and adequate arrangements would be made for cellar-storage of the goods when they were brought into the country. Consequently violence became more frequent than ever—bloodshed and all sorts of crimes occurred.

In the year 1723 several commissions or deputations were issued by the Chancellor of the Exchequer to captains of his Majesty's sloops to make seizures, and the following year the Treasury authorized the construction of seven sloops for service off the coast of Scotland. The smugglers had in fact become so desperate, the English Channel was so thoroughly infested with them, and the Revenue service so incapable of dealing with them, that the Admiralty had to enter the picture. They ordered the captains and commanders of His Majesty's ships to assist the Revenue officers all they could in order to prevent the smuggling trade; and they were to look out and seize all vessels employed in illegally exporting wool. The Admiralty had been informed by the Commissioners of Customs that the Revenue officers frequently met with insults from French smuggling luggers manned by armed crews, who carried on a brisk smuggling trade by force and even dared the Revenue men to come aboard them.

But as the Revenue service afloat was assisted now by the Navy, so the Revenue land guard was also aided by the Military. In 1713 arrangements had been made that dragoons should co-operate with the riding officers in their operations against the owlers, and there are plenty of skirmishes recorded showing that the dragoons were actually so employed. Originally these soldiers were employed under the direction of the riding officers. As can well be expected, however, there was a good deal of jealousy and friction caused in the rewards for seizures. After the year 1822 this military assistance was not utilized to any great extent, although legally Army officers could still be called upon to render assistance against smuggling. In passing, one might mention that this co-operation afloat between the Customs men and the Navy was equally noticeable for a certain amount of ill-feeling, as we shall mention on a later page.

Before the first quarter of the eighteenth century was over, smuggling between England and the Continent was proceeding at a brisk pace, and by the middle of that century it had well-nigh reached its climax for fearlessness.

We have already alluded to hired smacks and sloops being used towards the end of the seventeenth century. The sloop rig, as I have shown in another volume,[1] had probably been introduced into England from Holland soon after the accession of Charles II. But from that date its merits of handiness were so obvious that for yachts, for fishing craft, for the carrying of passengers and cargo up and down the Thames and along the coast as well as across to Ireland and the Continent, the rig was adopted very readily in place of the lug-sails.

The smack was also a sloop-rigged vessel. We need not enter here into a discussion of the comparative merits of sloops, cutters and smacks. It is enough say that fishermen, coasters, and so on readily took to this improvement. It was quickly realized that a vessel of say 100 tons, sloop-rigged, with her one mast, mainsail, and two headsails and square topsail could be handled with fewer men (and was therefore less expense) than a lugger of similar size. It was also more suitable for maneuvering in narrow channels, and for entering and leaving small harbors. Thus most naturally the larger smuggling craft were sloops or cutters until well on into the nineteenth century; and it was equally natural that the Revenue Service also availed themselves of this rig first by hiring smacks, and, later, by building them for themselves.

These sloops, whether hired or owned, were given each a particular station to guard, and that plan was followed by the Revenue cruisers for many years. Among the Exeter documents of the Customs Department is an interesting document dated July 10, 1703. In it the Board of Customs informs the collector at the port of Dartmouth of the vessels appointed by the Commissioners to cruise against owlers, the district comprised extending from Pembroke in the west to the Downs in the east. The following is the list of these vessels with their respective cruising territories:

NAME OF CRUISER	TERRITORY
Rye	Pembroke to Lundy Island
Discovery	Milford to Swansea
Dolphin	Milford to Exmouth
Hastings	Milford to Exmouth
Woolwich	Downs to Falmouth
Swan	Downs to Falmouth
Fly	Off Folkestone
Dispatch	Off Folkestone

This fairly well covered the region to which goods were likely to be run from the Continent as well as that from which the owlers were wont to export their wool. From an entry among the documents preserved in the Custom House at Newcastle, dated September 1729, we can see that the northeast coast was guarded thus:

---

[1] *Fore and Aft: The Story of the Fore-and-Aft Rig.* London, 1911.

The Fine Art of Smuggling:

NAME OF CRUISER	TERRITORY
Cruiser	Flamborough Head to Newcastle
Deal Castle	Newcastle to Leith
Spy	Firth of Forth to Newcastle

And about this time the *Deal Castle* had succeeded in capturing four French smuggling craft and brought them into Shields.

To the other side of England the Isle of Man, which was a veritable contraband depot, used to send quantities of dutiable goods, Liverpool being the favorite destination. But it smuggling was a more difficult matter to deal with here than in many other ports.

On October 9, 1713, the Collector at Liverpool writes to the Board of Customs that he thinks a sloop would be of little service for that port. Some time ago they had one, which was not a success "by reason of ye dangerousness and difficulty of the harbor and ye many shoals of sand, which often shift in bad weather." The Manxmen were a thoroughly lawless, desperate species of smugglers. They stopped at nothing, and were especially irate towards all Revenue and public officials, recognizing no authority other than physical force, although they had a certain respect for the Duke of Atholl, the owner of the Isle of Man.

Among the letters to Southampton there is a record dated June 14, 1729, which shows that a number of his Majesty's sloops were appointed by the Admiralty to cruise off the coasts of the kingdom to prevent the exporting of wool and the running of goods by the import-smugglers. For instance, the Admiralty sloop *Swift* was appointed to cruise between Portland, Poole, and Jack-in-the-Basket off the entrance to Lymington Harbor, Hants, her commander being a Captain Cockayne. Similarly the sloop *Success* (Captain Thomas Smith, commander) was to cruise between Portland and Spithead, and the Rye (Captain John Edwards) between the Isle of Wight and Beachy Head to the eastward. It was part of the duty of the Revenue officers at Southampton to see that these three ships constantly cruised on their station, and if their commanders were found negligent of this duty the matter was to be reported to the Board of Customs.

The Revenue craft were apparently themselves not above suspicion. In November of 1729 the Southampton officers of the Customs reported to headquarters that the *Swift*, every time she went across to Guernsey in connection with her duties of prevention, used to bring back quantities of wine, brandy, and other dutiable goods under the pretense that they were the ship's stores. The intention, however, was nothing less than that which dominated the actions of the smugglers themselves—the very class against which the *Swift* was employed. Captain Cockayne's men used to find it no very difficult matter to run these goods ashore clandestinely under the very eyes of the unsuspecting Customs officers.

The Commissioners of the Customs soon sent down strict instructions that the *Swift* was to be rummaged every time she arrived at Southampton from Guernsey. We shall have reason presently to refer more especially to the Channel Isles again, but it may suffice for the present to state that they were in the south the counterpart of the Isle of Man in the north. They were a depot from which the import smugglers fetched their goods across to England.

In addition to the Naval sloops just mentioned, there were two other cutters belonging to the Southampton station that were Revenue and not Admiralty-owned craft. These vessels were respectively the *Calshot* and the *Hurst*, and it is worth noting that at the time we are thinking of (1729) these vessels are referred to generally as "yatchs" or "yachts." It was not quite seventy years since the first yacht—that presented to Charles II, named the *Mary*—had arrived in England, and it was only in 1720 that the first yacht club had been established, not in England, but in Cork. If we may judge from contemporary paintings of yachts we can visualize the *Hurst* and *Calshot* as being very tubby, bluff-bowed craft with ample beam. But what would especially strike us in these modern days would be the exceptionally long bowsprit, the forward end of which was raised considerably above the water than its after end, both jib and foresail each working on a stay.

The commander of the *Calshot* yacht was a Captain Mears, and there is an entry in the Southampton documents to the effect that he was paid the sum of £2, 12s. 6d. for piloting his vessel from Southampton to Guernsey and back in connection with the Preventive duties. This trip took him five days, his pay being half a guinea a day. It is clear from a record of the following year that Mears was employed by special arrangement. On July 18, 1730, the Board of Customs decided that it was necessary that Captain John Mears, commander of the *Calshot* yacht at Southampton, should now be placed on the same footing as the other commanders of the Revenue sloops and smacks in regard to the matter of wear and tear. Henceforth the sum of 30s. per ton was to be allowed him instead of £47 per annum.

Both the yacht and her boats were to be kept in good order and reasonable repair, loss by violence of the sea or other unavoidable accidents excepted. The commander was also to fit the sloop and her boats with all manner of necessaries and materials, so that the Crown was to be at no charge on that account in the future. Every quarter the Comptroller and Collector of the port were to certify to the Board as to whether the yacht and boats were in good repair.

It would appear that these two vessels were not actually owned by the Customs but hired from Captain Mears. Less than a month before the above order the Surveyor-General of the Customs for Hampshire represented to the Board that it would be necessary to allow the commander of the *Hurst* half-a-dozen muskets, two pairs of pistols, and half-a-dozen swords or cutlasses. These were accordingly ordered to be sent, together with two swivel guns, from Weymouth "by the first coast vessel bound to" Southampton. There was certainly need for a strict vigilance to be kept in that neighborhood, for there was a good deal of smuggling then being

The Fine Art of Smuggling:

carried on along the Hampshire shore in the vicinity of Hurst Castle and Beaulieu.

In another chapter we shall go into the important matter touching the flags that were worn by the vessels employed in looking after smuggling. In passing, however, we may call attention to a letter which the Board sent to Southampton at this time referring to the proclamation of December 18, 1702, by which no ships whatsoever were allowed to wear a pendant excepting those engaged in the service of the Royal Navy. The sloops employed in the several public offices (as, for instance, the Customs and the Excise) should wear Jacks, whereon was to be described the seal used in the respective offices. Captain John Mears, senior, of the *Calshot*, and Captain John Mears, junior, of the *Hurst*, were to be informed that they must deliver up their pendants to the Customs' office at Southampton and for the future forbear wearing a pendant. Instead thereof they are to wear a Jack and ensign with the seal of office therein, "but the mark in the ensign is to be twice as large as that in the Jack; and if the captain should hereafter find that the not wearing a pendant will be any obstruction or hindrance to the service," the Board of Customs is to be informed.[1]

We have now seen something of the sloops and cutters on the south, the west, and the northeast coasts. Let us take a glance at the district to the south of Flamborough during this same period.

From the Hull letter book we find that in September of 1733 the Admiralty appointed Captain Burrish of the *Blandford* and Sir Roger Butler of the *Bonetta* to cruise between Flamborough and Newcastle; but Captain Oates of the *Fly* and Captain Rycant of the *Tryal* were to cruise between Flamborough and Yarmouth. There is also a reference to the Revenue sloop *Humber* employed in this neighborhood on Preventive work.

She was a somewhat expensive craft to keep up, as she was frequently needing repairs and renewals. First, she was to have a new cable which was to cost £20, 14s. 3-1/2d.; and it is a striking reminder of those days of hemp and sail that this bill was paid to the "ropemakers." A few months later she had to undergo repairs which amounted to £31, 10s. 6-1/4d., and less than six months afterwards she had to be given a new anchor which cost £18, 8s. 9d. Three years later she was given a new suit of sails which came to £25, 17s. 1d. but her old suit was sold for the sum of eight guineas. And finally, in 1744, as she had begun to cost so much for repairing, the Board determined to sell her.

Notwithstanding that the south coast, by reason of its proximity to the Continent and the Channel Isles, was a convenient and popular ob-

---

[1] *Southampton Letters*, November 6, 1730. But in 1719, the Customs Commissioners had, *inter alia*, agreed to provide Captain Mears with "a suit of colours" for the *Calshot*. This provision was, therefore, now cancelled in the year 1730.

jective for the smugglers running their goods from France and Holland, yet the Yorkshire coast was by no means neglected. From Dunkirk and especially Flushing goods poured into the county. There was a small sloop, for instance, belonging to Bridlington, which was accustomed to sail across the North Sea to one of the ports in Zealand. There a cargo was taken aboard consisting of the usual dutiable articles such as tea, tobacco, and gin. The return voyage was then made and the goods landed clandestinely at some convenient spot between the Spurn Lighthouse and Bridlington.

Similarly, farther south than the Humber smuggling by illegal importation went on extensively in the early eighteenth century. Sometimes a Dutch vessel would arrive in Grimsby Roads and succeed in quietly running her goods to the shore. In the autumn of 1734 the master of the Dutch schuyt The *Good Luck of Camphire*, alias *The Brotherly Love*, had succeeded in running as many as 166 half-ankers[1] of brandy and 50 lbs. of tea on the coast near Great Yarmouth, the skipper's name being Francis Coffee. He was a notorious smuggler. But on this occasion both he and his vessel were captured.

Still, matters were not always satisfactory on board the Revenue sloops and smacks. At this time, whenever there was an encounter with the smugglers afloat the latter were so violent and desperate that the captors went about their work with their lives in their hands. Furthermore, it was not altogether a pleasing business to have to fire at fellow countrymen, many of whom they had known since boyhood. There was not the space on these sloops and cutters, nor the deck room to be found on the men-of-war; and to on these comparatively small vessels was to be continually cooped up. They ships were usually near the shore but the men were able to have shore-leave all too rarely. Added to this a considerable portion of the crews of these Revenue craft was composed of men who had spent years of their lives as smugglers themselves.

Consequently it was not altogether surprising that mutinies and refusals to obey their commander's orders were a frequent occurrence. After a time it was decided that those members of the crew that had to be dismissed were to be handed over to the commander of the next man-of-war that should come along, and be pressed into the service of the Navy. Needless to say, this was not always a welcome gift to the Naval commander compelled to receive a handful of recalcitrant men aboard his ship.

Then, again, when at last a handful of smugglers had been captured it was the duty of the Revenue officers to prosecute them before the magistrate at their own expense. This was regarded as an unfair hardship, and in 1736 the system was modified by the Treasury allowing an officer a third of whatever amount was recovered, the prosecution to be carried on at the King's expense.

---

[1] A half-anker held 3-1/4 gallons.

The Fine Art of Smuggling:

At the same time it was undeniable that some commanders of these sloops and cutters were not quite as active on their station as they might be. There was too ready an excuse to run in from the sea and too great an inclination to spend valuable time in port.

They were accordingly now ordered not to lay up for the purpose of giving the ship's bottom a scrub, or for a refit, without previously giving the Collector and Comptroller of the port ten days notice. This was not to occur unless the cruiser really needed such attention; but if it was essential then to prevent the station remaining unguarded some other smack or vessel was to be sent out to take her place for the time being. For the smugglers were kept so well informed of the movements of the Revenue ships that a contraband cargo of goods would soon be found approaching the shore during the night when the watch had been relaxed.

But from an early date—at any rate as far back as 1694—the East India ships were also notorious for smuggling into the country a considerable amount of goods that ought to have paid duty. We shall present instances below of East Indiamen, homeward bound, being boarded as they come up Channel, or while waiting in the Downs and putting some of their cargo on board smuggling cutters and Deal boats, which was subsequently quietly and secretly brought into the country.

Silks were especially popular among the smugglers on those ships. In those days, too, the more wealthy passengers coming home via East Indiamen used to leave the ship at Spithead, or would then be put ashore at Portsmouth. This allowed them to proceed by coach to London, thus shortened their sea journey. But notwithstanding their ample means, many of these travelers were found trying to land dutiable articles.

In short, rich and poor, high and low, there was no class that did not try to engage in smuggling either directly or indirectly. Even if the party never ventured on the sea, he might be a very active aider and abettor in meeting the boat as it brought the casks ashore, or keeping a look-out for the Preventive men, giving the latter false information, thus throwing them on the wrong scent. Or again, even if he did not act the part of signaler by showing warning lights from the cliff, he could loan his cellars, his horses, or his financial support. In fact there were many apparently respectable citizens who, by keeping in the background, were never suspected of having any interest in these nefarious practices, whereas they were in fact the instigators and the capitalists of many a successful run. And as such they were without doubt morally responsible for the deaths by murder which occurred in those incidents, when violence was used after the Revenue men had come on to the scene.

But as to morality, was there ever a period when the national character was so slack and corrupt as in the eighteenth century?

CHAPTER THREE
The Growth of Smuggling

About the middle of the eighteenth century the smuggling of tea into the country had reached such an extent that the revenue which ought to have been expected from this source was sinking instead of rising. In fact it had gotten to the point where, of all the tea that was consumed in this country, not one half had paid duty and the rest was smuggled.

The bands of smugglers were well financed, were themselves hardy sailors and skillful pilots. They had some of the best designed and best built cutters and luggers of that time. They were able to purchase from an almost inexhaustible market, and to make a quick passage to the English shores. Arriving there they could rely on both moral and physical support; for their friends were well mounted, well armed, and exceedingly numerous. Ordinarily the cargo could be rapidly unshipped, and either hidden or run into the country with dispatch.

Not once, but times without number the smuggling cutters had evaded the Revenue cruisers at sea, showing them a clean pair of heels. With equal frequency the Preventive men on land had been outwitted, bribed, or overpowered. And in as much as the duties on the smuggled articles were high, had they passed through the Customs, so, when smuggled, they could always fetch a big price, and the share for the smugglers themselves was by no means inconsiderable.

But it is always the case that, when large profits are made by lawless, reckless people, these proceeds are as quickly dissipated in extravagance. It is sad to think that so many of these seafaring men, who possessed so much grit and pluck, actually died paupers. As one reads through the pitiful petitions, written on odd scraps of paper in the most illiterate of hands begging for clemency on behalf of a convicted smuggler, one can see all too clearly that on the whole it was not the actual workers but the middle-men who, as is usually the case, made the profits.

A life of such uncertainty and excitement, an existence full of so many hairbreadth escapes did not fit them for the peaceful life of either the fisherman or the farmer. With them money went as easily as it had come, and taking into account the hardness of the life, the risks that were undertaken, the possibility of losing their lives, or of being transported after conviction, it cannot be said that these men were any too well paid. Carelessness of danger led to recklessness; recklessness led to a life that was dissolute and thriftless. And in spite of the fact that these tear-stained appeals were usually signed by all the respectable inhabitants of the seaside village—the rector, the local shipbuilder, Lloyds' shipping agent, the chief landowners and so forth—many a wife and family had to starve or become chargeable to the Union. In the meantime the bread-winner was spending his time in prison, serving as an impressed sailor on board one of his Majesty's ships; or, if he had been found physically unfit for such service, condemned to seven or more years of transportation.

But by the year 1745 smuggling had reached such a pitch that something had to be done. The country was in such a state of alarm and the honest traders made such bitter complaints of the disastrous effect which these illicit practices were having on their prosperity that, on the 6th of February in that year, a Parliamentary Committee was formed "to inquire into the causes of the most infamous practice of smuggling and consider the most effectual methods to prevent the said practice." It was clear that in spite of all that had been done by the Customs and Excise, by the Admiralty and the military, they had not succeeded in obtaining the desired effect.

During the course of this inquiry a great deal of interesting evidence came out from expert witnesses, some of whom had not long since been the greatest smugglers in existence, but had come forward and received the pardon of the State. We may summarize the testimony obtained by this Committee as follows.

The smugglers, after sailing away from England, used to purchase the tea abroad sometimes with money but at other times with wool. Either way that was a serious matter if, as was the case, the transactions were carried on to any large extent. The country simply could not afford to be denuded either of its valuable wool—since that crippled the wool manufacturers—or of the coin of the realm, which made for bankruptcy. But this was not all. England was at war with her neighbors, and the French only too gladly admitted the smuggling vessels into her ports, since these lawless and unpatriotic men were able to give information of the state of affairs in England.

There was in the Isle of Man at this time no levying of Customs or other duties, so that between that island and France there was kept up a constant trade especially in teas, other East India goods and brandies.

These were afterwards conveyed clandestinely to English ports, especially to Liverpool, as we have already noted, and also to Glasgow, Dumfries, as well as to Ireland. In the days when there were sloops at Liverpool doing duty for the Crown they used to set forth and do their best to stop this running, "but as it is a very dangerous station, a seizure is scarce heard of."

Illustrating the sheer magnitude of the smuggling at that time it was reported officially from Yarmouth that on July 11 fifty smugglers had run a cargo of tea and brandy at Benacre in Suffolk, and only a fortnight later a band of sixty smugglers landed another contraband cargo at the same place, while a gang of forty got another cargo safely ashore at Kesland Haven. A week later a still larger band, this time consisting of seventy men, passed through Benacre Street with a large quantity of goods, a cart and four horses. The smugglers at Kesland Haven had been able to bring inland their cargo of tea and brandy by means of fifty horses. In one month alone—and this at the depth of the winter when cross-channel passages could not be expected to be too safe for small sailing craft—nine smuggling cutters had sailed from the port of Rye to Guernsey. It was estimated that during the last half of the year there had been run on to the coast of Suffolk 1835 horse-loads of tea as well as certain other goods, and 1689 horse-loads of wet and dry goods, to say nothing of a large quantity of other articles that should have paid duty. These were conveyed away up country by means of wagons and other vehicles, guarded by a formidable band of smugglers and sympathizers well armed.

Notwithstanding that the Revenue officers were in some cases aware of what was going on, yet they positively dared not attempt any seizures. And in those instances where they had undertaken the risk they had been frequently beaten and left cruelly wounded with bleeding heads and broken limbs.

One reliable witness testified that it was estimated that at this time about 4,000,000 lbs. of tea were consumed in this kingdom, yet only about 800,000 lbs. of this had ever paid duty, so that there was considerably over 3,000,000 lbs. of tea smuggled in. On just this one item the loss to the Crown must have been something enormous. Multiply this by the long years during which the smuggling went on, add also the duties which ought to have been paid on tobacco and spirits, even if you omit to include the amount which should have accrued from lace and other commodities, and you may begin to realize the seriousness of the smuggling as viewed by the Revenue authorities.

It was noted that a great deal of this contraband stuff was fetched over from Flushing and from Middleburgh, a few miles farther up on the canal. The big merchant sailing ships brought the tea from the East to Holland, France, Sweden, and Denmark. But the Dutch, the French, the Swedes, and the Danes were not great tea drinkers, and certainly used it in nothing like the quantities which were consumed in England. But it was profitable to them to purchase this East Indian product and to sell it again to the smugglers who would run across from England. It should be added, however, that the species of tea in question were of the cheaper qualities. It was also frankly admitted in evidence that many of the civil magistrates, whose duty it was to grant warrants for the arrest of these delinquents, were intimidated by the smugglers, while the officers of the Customs and Excise were terrorized.

At this period of the smuggling era, that is to say prior to the middle of the eighteenth century, most of the smuggled tea was brought over to the south coast of England in Folkestone cutters of a size ranging from fifty to forty tons burthen. These vessels usually came within about three or four miles of the shore, when they were met by the smaller boats of the locality and the goods unladened. Indeed the trade was so successful that as many as twenty or thirty cargoes were run in a week, and Flushing became so important a base that not merely did the natives subsidize or purchase Folkestone craft, but ship-builders actually migrated from that English port to Flushing and pursued their calling in Dutch territory.

As to the profits that the smugglers themselves made on the transactions, the rates of payment varied at a later date, but about the years 1728 and 1729 the tea-dealers paid the men eight shillings a pound for the commodity. True, the Revenue cutters and the land guard made seizures, but those losses, admitted a witness, were a mere trifle to the smugglers. In fact he affirmed that some of the tea-dealers hadn't suffered a seizure in six or seven years. We can therefore readily believe that, on the whole, the financiers netted a very handsome profit. Indeed, there are still standing plenty of fine mansions in different parts of our country which are generally supposed to have been erected from the proceeds of this form of activity.

There was a kind of local intelligence network in most of the smuggling centers on the south coast. So loyal and so watchful were these networks that the inhabitants of the coast-line managed to let their confreres know exactly when the Custom House sloops had sailed out of port or when they hauled up for repairs and refit. As a consequence the smuggling craft commonly escaped capture.

These people were animated by a natural hatred of all Government officials in general, especially of all those whose duty it was to collect taxes, dues, and any kind of tolls. They disliked the men of the Customs and Excise most of all, and, further, being allied by sympathy and blood relationship to many of the smugglers themselves, it was almost impossible for the representatives of the Crown to make any steady progress in limiting smuggling activity.

We all know that when a number of even average law-abiding people get together, that crowd somehow tends towards becoming a mob. Each person, so to speak, forfeits his own individuality, that becomes merged into the personality and character of the mob, which all the time is being impelled to break out into something unlawful of a greater or lessor degree. Whenever you have stood among crowds you must have noted this for yourself. It gets restive at the least opposition with which it is confronted, it boos and jeers with the smallest incitement; and, finally, realizing the full strength of its unity, breaks out into some rash violence and rushes madly on, heedless of the results. Many murders have been committed in this way by men who ordinarily and in their individual capacity would shrink from such crimes. But having become merely one of the limbs, as it were, of the crowd they have moved with the latter and obeyed its impulses.

It was much the same when many of the dwellers of the countryside—many of the fishermen, laborers, and farm-hands—found themselves assembled on the report of a pistol shot or the cry of angry voices coming up from the beach below. Something was happening, someone was in trouble, and the darkness of the night or the gloom of the fog added a halo of mystery round the occasion. Men and women came out from their cottages, someone got hit, and then a general fray began. Clubs and pistols and cutlasses were busy, men were bellowing forth oaths, women shrieking, and the galloping of horses heard rapidly approaching. Amid such excitements we can readily understand that a good many acts of violence and deep injury occurred which afterwards, when the heat of the event had vaporized, were regretted.

At the same time we cannot help but feel some sort of sympathy with a crew who, after a long and exciting passage through bad weather all the way across the Channel, after perhaps a breathless race against the Government cruisers, had finally succeeded in landing their tubs on the shore only to be pounced on immediately by the riding officers and a posse of dragoons. It must have been heart-breaking that all their carefully laid plans, all their hardships and trials would end in disaster. Realizing this and that their craft as well as their persons would be seized, it was natural that they would fight like the most desperate of men. And, at the same time, those their relatives on shore who largely depended on them for their bread and butter would rush to their aid with a spirit and an impetuosity that could only end in one way. The pity of it all was that so much fine daring and enthusiasm were not being employed for a better cause and for more worthy results.

But the smugglers found that, contrary to what one would expect, their greatest risk was not when landing the goods, but when bringing them across from the Continent. A seizure on land was, at any rate during the first half of the eighteenth century, comparatively rare if they had been able to get away from the initial sloops and cutters. For the bodyguard of armed men on horseback who promptly met and escorted the contraband into the country were frequently successful. And when once the tea has arrived inland it was easily sold to people who bought it not in small quantities but took as much as 1000 lbs. at a time.

In addition, there were a number of men called "duffers," who used to walk inland wearing coats in which a hundred-weight of tea was concealed between two layers of cloth stitched together. They were accordingly said to "quilt" so much of this commodity. These duffers, having set forth on their walk, would eventually arrive in London and dispose of the tea to hawkers who, in turn, carried it about the town and sold it to the consumers, who, even if they had possessed any scruples, could not possibly know that the leaves had been smuggled in without paying the Crown's levy.

But it was not merely by exercising the strictest vigilance, nor entirely by resort to trickery and violence, or to threats and intimidation, that the smugglers managed to keep out of the hands of justice. They advanced one step further still, for there was a man named Norton whom they employed as their agent to defend them against prosecutions.

This Norton at one time had actually been in the employ of the Crown as clerk of the late Solicitor to the Customs. And it was generally believed that Norton by some means—most probably by offering tempting bribes—obtained news from the clerks of the Customs' solicitor when a smuggler was likely to be arrested and a warrant was about to be issued. Norton would then give the smuggler an immediate warning and the man was able to make himself scarce. It was quite an easy operation. In those days when there was no telegraph and no steamboat service across the Channel, all the "wanted" man had to do was instantly to board his cutter, set sail, and hurry across to France or Holland. When he got there he was sure of a welcome, and could employ himself in arranging for cargoes to be run into England perhaps in the very vessel which had brought him across. There were plenty of his compatriots resident in Flushing, so he need not feel homesick, and when at last the incident had blown over he could find his way back to Kent or Sussex.

It was reckoned that about this time there were at least 20,000 people in England employed in smuggling, and in some parts (as, for instance, the village of Hawkhurst, about which we shall have more to say presently) gangs of large numbers could be got together in a very short time. In Hawkhurst alone 500 smugglers could be collected within an hour. Folkestone, however, ran Hawkhurst fairly close with a similar notoriety. Such gangs, well armed as they were, went about with impunity. Even though they were well known, no one dared to stop them.

We mentioned just now that the danger to the State of this import smuggling was not merely that goods were brought into the country without payment being made to the Customs, but that in as much as the contraband goods were purchased abroad partly by wool and partly by actual coin England was being robbed both ways. As the wool exportation declined and the import smuggling rose, so the amount of gold that passed out of the country seriously increased. At least £1,000,000 sterling were carried out of the kingdom each year to purchase these goods, and of this amount somewhere about £800,000 were paid for tea alone. At a later date the price of tea often went up, but the dealer still made a profit of 40s. on every 100 lbs.

We alluded just now also to the dangers of seizure, and it is worth remarking that these were recognized by the smugglers as being greater in one district than in another. For instance, it was much more difficult to run goods into the counties of Kent and Sussex than into Suffolk, owing to the fleet at sea and the troops on the coast. And as to the amount of support which could be relied on, it was an admitted fact that there was not one person in ten in the country but would give the smugglers assistance, and even lend them horses and carts. For this assistance the supporters were well paid.

There was one witness before the Commission who stated that he knew of about sixty English cutters of from thirty to forty tons burthen each, and five or six vessels of the same burthen belonging to merchants at Flushing which were employed in constantly running goods across to England. Several of those who gave evidence confessed that they had for years been actively engaged in smuggling, but had taken advantage of the Act of Indemnity.

One reason alleged for smuggling tea was that the East India Company did not sufficiently supply the dealers with the low-priced kinds, whereas the Dutch did. And it was further contended that if the price of tea were lessened sixpence per lb. it would put a stop to smuggling of the commodity. At this date, although other articles such as spirits and tobacco were brought in, there was far more tea run than anything else.

At the same time the smugglers liked to include a quantity of brandy casks among their cargo for the reason that they were heavy and made very good ballast. And as to the ships themselves, it was agreed that those of the smugglers were the best sailing fore-and-afters that were built in those days, and could easily out-sail both the King's ships and the Custom House sloops.

Finally, it was shown that in spite of the large and tempting rewards that were offered for the apprehension of smugglers, no one would come forward to give information. The reason was that, even if they wanted to, they dared not.

In addition the call of smuggling was apparently a fascinating one. While there were those who had willingly embraced the pardon granted them by the Act of Indemnity and forsaken this illegal trade, there were many others who had returned to their former practices.

After accumulating this evidence, the Committee issued their first report on March 24, 1745, and said that the high duties charged on tea and other commodities had certainly been one cause of smuggling. They also added that government selling of seized boats and vessels was certainly another potent reason, for these craft were frequently bought back by the smugglers. They therefore recommended that all captured craft should be burned.

Furthermore, the Commission condemned the custom of allowing penalties to be compounded so easily. As an instance of this we might call attention to three smugglers belonging to the county of Hampshire. There is a reference to them in the Southampton Letters under date of April 28, 1730, from which it appears that Matthew Barton, John Gibort, and William Moadon of Fordingbridge were under prosecution for running goods ashore. They subsequently offered to compound for the said offense on the following terms: Barton to pay the sum of £35, Gibort to pay £25, and Moadon £15. But before allowing the matter to be settled straight away the Collector and Comptroller at Southampton were ordered to look carefully into the affair and to inquire what these men were generally esteemed to be worth.

CHAPTER FOUR
The Smuggler's Methods

It was not until June of 1746 that the Committee issued their second report, and the evidence contained in it is even more interesting to us than any of the previous ones.

It began with the Solicitor to the Commissioners showing how biased juries frequently were towards prisoners brought up on charges of smuggling, and how they declined to bring in a verdict against them even with the clearest of evidence. Another official (the Surveyor of the Searchers in the Port of London) stated that several times he had received information that there had been a run of goods in a certain locality and had even received information as to the road along which they would be brought. To intercept them, however, he had to travel by night and carefully avoid all the beaten paths. Indeed, if people whom they might meet on the road noticed a Custom House officer and any soldiers together, their design would immediately be suspected and warning would promptly be sent to the smugglers, who would hide their goods. He added, also, that he remembered on one occasion that a couple of vessels landed as much tea as could be loaded on the backs of two hundred horses on the Isle of Thanet.

But it was when the ex-smugglers came to give their evidence that the real secrets of the trade were revealed. Robert Hanning, had been involved with the smugglers for years, and was their principal dealer in Dunkirk. Some idea of the colossal size of the business which he carried on may be gathered from his admission that he had sold over £40,000 per year of teas, brandies, and wines to be run into England. And let us not forget that this probably represented the value of the goods when they were put on board. What they actually realized after they were smuggled into the English market must have been considerably greater.

The Fine Art of Smuggling:

Hanning was followed by a certain Captain Joseph Cockburn, who had a very instructive story to tell, which must have amazed even the Commissioners.

This gallant skipper was now commanding one of his Majesty's sloops, but prior to that he had been engaged in privateering, and before that had commanded several vessels employed in smuggling. From childhood he had been involved in smuggling, and his apprenticeship had been served to a smuggler at Rochester, who was nominally a fisherman. Consequently, with the knowledge gained first as a smuggler and subsequently as a pursuer of smugglers, there was not much, if anything at all, that could have missed his attention. He proved himself a veritable encyclopedia of smuggling information, and even the following brief summary will show that his experience was something exceptional.

First of all, he cited the case of five cutters which he knew were constantly employed in running tea and brandy from Boulogne into Kent and Sussex. They imported at least six tons of tea and two thousand half-ankers of brandy every week. He estimated that the six tons of tea would be purchased abroad for £1920. The two thousand half-ankers of brandy, even if they cost but ten shillings apiece, would represent the sum of £1000; so altogether there was a total of nearly £3000 being carried out of the country every week by these five cutters alone. But he also knew of five other cutters which were constantly employed in fetching brandy and tea from Middleburgh and Flushing, and he reckoned that these ten cutters in the aggregate smuggled into the United Kingdom each year goods to the value of £303,680. Possibly there was no living person who possessed so perfect and exact a knowledge of the smuggling trade, so we can have little reason to doubt for a moment the accuracy of his figures.

He moved on to describe the methods employed by these men, he divided them into two classes. First, there were those adopted by the cutters and smacks that did little other than smuggle; and, second, there were the British ships that primarily carried on a legitimate trade to foreign parts.

As to the first group, the practice of these cutters and smacks was to put to sea from their home port—London, Dover, Rye, Folkestone, or wherever it might be—having on board a small number of hands, their professed object being to fish. Having stood some distance away from the land, they would be met during the night by a number of smaller craft, and under cover of darkness would take on board from the latter large crews, much merchandise, and a considerable amount of money. The smaller craft rowed or sailed back to the beach before daylight, and the bigger craft, now well supplied with men, money, and merchandise, stood on their course for some Dutch or French port. There they purchased such goods as they required, disposed of those which they had brought, and again set sail for home. The vessel was again met at a convenient distance from the English shore by smaller boats if a favorable signal had been flashed from the land; and, using the darkness of the night, once more both the cargo and the extra men were put into the boats, after which the latter ran the stuff ashore in casks already slung and in bales, while the smack headed for her harbor whence she had set out. Because she had the same small crew as before, no suspicions were aroused, and it was presumed she had been out fishing.

But additional to these comparatively large vessels there were smaller craft—open boats, yawls, and little sloops—which in fine weather ran across from the south coast of England to Boulogne, Guernsey, and from the west of England to the Isle of Man. They also loaded up with as much cargo as they could carry, and, since they were able to be beached, the process of discharging their contents as soon as they returned was much simpler. These smaller craft also were in the habit of running out well clear of the land and meeting Dutch vessels, from which they would purchase similar kinds of goods and run them in by the usual methods. In these lesser craft were frequently carried a great many stones, anchors, and heavy weights by means of which the half-ankers of brandy could be sunk near the shore and afterwards taken up as required. The exact way in which this was done we shall discuss fully in a later chapter.

Some of the cobbles, "hovelings," and small fishing craft that were accustomed to run out to big sailing merchantmen under pretense of shipping pilots to take them into the next port, were actually engaged in smuggling all sorts of goods out of these ships. Captain Cockburn suggested that it was because the Dutchmen brought such large quantities of fish into Billingsgate that the English fishermen found their work unprofitable, and were accordingly driven to devote themselves to smuggling. From evidence in other documents it would certainly seem that Cockburn was telling the truth and that the fishing industry was not a very good livelihood at that time.

Then, secondly, there was the smuggling that was carried on by the trading sailing ships from abroad. Great quantities of goods were being run into the country by colliers—they were usually brig-rigged—by corn-ships, packet-boats from the Continent and other vessels trading with Holland. At least, one thousand five hundred vessels were engaged in this trade, and, added Cockburn, he "scarcely ever knew one of them return without some prohibited or high duty goods."

The smuggling from these vessels was done in various ways. There were the pilot-boats and fishing craft which frequently met them near the coast, as already explained. Another way was for the merchantmen to put into harbors, roadsteads, and rivers, where they lay at anchor under pretense of waiting for orders. Another method still, that was as simple as it was successful, consisted of landing their goods at outports on such holidays as the King's birthday, etc., when the Revenue officers were absent. Cockburn admitted that he had done this himself and had run great quantities of brandies, teas, and Spanish licorice even as much as nearly a ton of the latter at a time.

But besides these two classes there was a third. The whole of the coasting trade in those days was of course done in sailing ships; and in as

The Fine Art of Smuggling:

much as there were no railways for carrying merchandise there was a good deal more encouragement for the sailing ship owner than there is today. The methods of smuggling adopted by these coasters was a little more complicated, and this was done by such means as fraudulently obtaining permits, by cockets clandestinely obtained, by false entry of one sort of goods for another, and by corrupting the Customs' officers. To prove his case the captain gave the following examples, all of which he had himself employed since the year 1738!

With regard to obtaining fraudulent permits, he said that he had gone to Dunkirk, taken aboard 2040 gallons of French brandy and cleared for North Bergen in Norway. Of course he had no intention whatever of steering for that port, but in case he met any of the Custom House sloops as he approached the English coast, it would be convenient to show this clearance and so prevent his brandy being seized. From Dunkirk, then, he sailed across the North Sea and ran up the river Humber. There, by previous arrangement, one of those keels which are so well known in the neighborhood of the Humber and Trent met him. The keel had been sent from York down the Ouse with permits to cover the brandy. The keel was cleared by a merchant at York, who obtained permits for conveying to Gainsborough a quantity of French brandy equal to that which Cockburn had on board his ship, though in fact the keel, notwithstanding that she obtained these permits, set forth with no brandy in her at all.

It was the point where the Ouse crosses the Trent at right angles that had been arranged as the trysting-place, and there the keel took on board from Cockburn the brandy which had come from Dunkirk. Cockburn himself nailed the permits on to the heads of the casks, which in due course were taken by the keel, when the flood tide made again, to Gainsborough some distance up the Trent. Arrived there the casks were properly taken into stock and entered in the Custom House books as if the brandy had been actually brought down from York and had previously paid duty. On this one venture the garrulous skipper admitted that he cleared a profit by the brandy of 250 per cent., which was a remarkably handsome reward for so short a voyage as from Dunkirk.

Port wines, he said, were purchasable at Dunkirk because they had been taken from English merchantmen by privateers. Since there was little or no market for such wines in Spain, they were brought into Dunkirk where there was no shortage of smugglers eager to buy them.

He proceeded also to explain another method of cheating the customs. Large quantities of very inferior British brandy were taken on board a ship and clearance was obtained for some other English port, but instead of proceeding to the latter the vessel would run across to Dunkirk or Holland, where she would unload the cheap brandy, and in its place take on board some high-priced French brandy equal in quantity to the British commodity which had been put ashore at the French port. After this, with now a much more valuable cargo, the vessel would put to sea again and make for that British port for which originally she had cleared.

And as to the practice of bribery, he himself had several times bought permits from the Excise officers to cover smuggled brandy and tea. On one occasion he had paid an officer fifty guineas for a permit to cover a certain quantity of tea and brandy about to be run into the country.

Next came Captain Ebenezer Hartley, who had also formerly commanded a ship that was engaged in smuggling. He had known of large quantities of muslins and silks brought into the country on board East Indiamen. These goods were smuggled by throwing them through the port-holes at night into boats waiting below, alongside the ship, or while the Custom officer was being entertained on board with food and drink. Sometimes, he said, this was even done under the very eyes of the Revenue officer, who took no notice of it. He recalled an incident in an earlier part of his life when he had sailed from England to Holland, where he had filled up with twenty-six casks of oil. After that his orders were to cross the North Sea and meet a certain vessel which would await him off Aldborough. This last-mentioned craft would give Hartley's vessel the signal by lowering her jib three times.

A more tragic story was related by George Bridges, a tidesman of the Port of London. He showed that it did not always "pay" to be diligent in one's duty. He quoted the case of a Captain Mercer, in the employ of the Custom House, who actually made a seizure now and then, but "was broke for doing his duty." When Mercer then came into Cork on the occasion in question, the mob set upon him so that he was compelled to escape into the sheriff's house. The mob then surrounded the house in their thousands until the sheriff interceded with them. They were wild with fury and threatened to pull the house down, until the sheriff gave them his oath that Captain Mercer should never again be guilty of seizing the wool which the smugglers had tried to export. But the mob afterwards went to Passage and took hold of a Custom House officer named May. They brought him from his house, cut out his tongue and cut off his ears, one of which the witness said he remembered seeing nailed on to the Cork Exchange. They dragged the man with a rope round his neck, gave him several blows, hurled him into the river, where the poor fellow finally died of his wounds. Although handsome rewards were offered for the discovery of the offenders, no one ever came forward.

One could quote similar instances of the vehemence of the smugglers from other sources. For instance, on February 2, 1748, the Collector of the Port of Penzance wrote to the Board to give them some idea of the people with whom he had to work. "The insolence," he said, "of some of the smuglers [sic] and wreckers in this neighborhood is run to such a heighth, that tho our officers have from time to time secured severall Hogsheads, it has been by force taken from them [again], 'and the officers forced to save their lives.'" Writing again on the 14th December, the same correspondent added that "the smugglers never behaved with more insolence than at present, or was it ever known to be carried on with

The Fine Art of Smuggling:

more audaciousness," mentioning also that the previous night the snow[1] *Squirrel* of North Yarmouth had driven ashore loaded with a cargo of brandy. The country-folk had immediately boarded her, stripped the master of everything valuable, and then carried off all the brandy they could lay their hands on, and, in their haste, had set fire to the rest of the cargo, so that at the time of writing the whole ship was in flames. He mentioned also a couple of months later the difficulty he had of securing the arrests of smugglers, for even when he had obtained warrants for the apprehension of eight most notorious men, the constables excused themselves from doing their duty in serving the warrants, and pretended that the eight men had left the area.

Anyone who cares to examine the Treasury Books and Papers for this period will find similar cases. In July of 1743 some smugglers had seized the Custom House boat at Dover and coolly employed her for their own purposes in running tea. The Custom officers deemed matters to be in such a state that they begged that a man-of-war might be stationed on that coast to prevent smuggling.

Similarly in January of 1743, during a skirmish near Arundel between the preventive men assisted by some dragoons against a band of smugglers, the latter had wounded three of the soldiers and carried off an officer and two other dragoons on board the smugglers' cutter. This was no unique occurrence. Sometimes the contraband runners, when infuriated, captured the would-be captors, hurried them out to sea, and then, having bound the unfortunate victims with a bit of spare rope and having tied a piece of ballast to their live bodies, they would be hurled overboard into the sea. The soldier or preventive man would never be seen or heard of again unless his lifeless body were cast upon the beach.

At Folkestone, about this time, three men were carried off by the smugglers while trying to effect an arrest, and the supervisor at Colchester had been also carried off, but afterwards he had been released on promising not to mention the smugglers' names. It was bad enough, therefore, for the Revenue men when they had the assistance of the dragoons, but it was infinitely worse when they had to contend alone. There is an almost pathetic petition from the Folkestone riding-officers sent on New Year's Day 1744-45, begging for military assistance against the smugglers. Although there were soldiers stationed at Dover, they were unobtainable, since they refused to march more than five miles.

And it was just as bad, if not worse, about this time in the Isle of Man, for the latter's inhabitants consisted almost exclusively of smugglers and their families, some of whom had long since been outlawed

---

[1] A snow was a vessel with three masts resembling the main and foremast of a ship with a third and small mast just abaft the mainmast, carrying a sail nearly similar to a ship's mizzen. The foot of this mast was fixed in a block of wood or step but on deck. The head was attached to the afterpart of the maintop. The sail was called a trysail, hence the mast was called a trysail-mast. (Moore's *Midshipman's Vocabulary*, 1805.)

King's Cutters vs Smugglers -1700-1855

from England and Ireland. So rich and prosperous had these Manxmen become by means of smuggling that they were recognized with a degree of importance that was almost ludicrous.

The two deemsters (or deputy-governors) of the island even countenanced and protected the men, who would often assemble together to scheme and drink to the damnation of His Britannic Majesty. Unhindered in their work, and able to obtain all the cargo they required from France and the Channel Isles, they became exceedingly independent and wealthy. At Douglas they had built themselves a good quay for the shelter of their ships and for convenience in landing their cargoes, the only drawback being that the harbor dried out at low water.

It happened that on the 26th of June 1750, that Captain Dow, commanding H.M. cruiser *Sincerity*[1] was, according to the orders received from the Board of Customs, on duty in Douglas Roads. A notorious Irish smuggling wherry came in from Ireland and ran under the *Sincerity's* stern, while the smugglers "with opprobrious, treasonable, and abusive language abused His Majesty King George and all that belonged to or served under him." This, of course, was too much for any naval officer to endure, and Captain Dow immediately caused the ship to come alongside. After being rummaged, she was found to have concealed in a jar of buttermilk twenty-five English guineas tied up in a bag. There were also papers on board that proved that this money was to be expended in the purchase of brandies and tea, etc., and that, having obtained these articles, she was then to return to Ireland. The English captain therefore promptly seized both money and papers.

On the same day that this incident occurred a Dutch dogger[2] also came into Douglas Roads loaded with prohibited goods from Holland. As soon as he had noticed her come to anchor, Dow sent his boat to board her with his mate and six men, and to see if she had the prohibited goods which he suspected were on board. If she had, then she was to be seized. At the same time Dow had requested Mr. Sidebotham, his Majesty's officer in the Isle of Man, to cast off the *Sincerity's* headfast and sternfasts from the shore. Immediately a riotous and angry mob formed. Fearing that the cruiser might get under weigh and seize the Dutch dogger, then refused to allow Sidebotham to let go the ropes. Armed with bludgeons, muskets, swords, and stones they rushed down on to the quay, and did all they could to force the cruiser on shore by aiming showers of stones at the cruiser's men and restraining Sidebotham in his endeavor to help the *Sincerity*. They even carried the latter away by force, and beat and bruised him in the most brutal manner.

---

[1] It was the frequent custom at this time to speak of sloops as cruisers.

[2] A dogger was a two-masted Dutch fishing-vessel usually employed in the North Sea off the Dogger Bank. She had two masts, and was very similar to a ketch in rig, but somewhat beamy and bluff-bowed.

The Fine Art of Smuggling:

Captain Dow, realizing that the intention of the mob was to get the *Sincerity* stranded, determined to cut his cable and exhorted them in his Majesty's name to disperse. The mob paid not the slightest attention except to send more showers of stones on to the cruiser's decks. Seeing from afar what was happening, the mate and six men who had been sent to board the dogger now returned to the *Sincerity*. Whereupon the dogger, perceiving her chance, promptly got under way. As the crowd on

Dow sent his mate and ten men on board her.

shore still continued to pelt his ship with stones and had already wounded two of his crew, the cruiser's commander fired amongst them. For a time, at least, this dispersed them, and so Dow was able to get his vessel clear. He immediately proceeded to follow the Dutch dogger, and chased her until she decided to run herself on to the sands at Ramsey to the north of the island. Determined not to be beaten, Dow now sent his mate and ten men on board her, seized her, and marked her in several places with the sign of a broad arrow to denote her capture.

But when the mate came to open the hatches several of the islanders who had been secreted on board, with the assistance of two boat-loads of armed men who had rowed off from the shore, seized the mate and his men, and threatened that if they resisted they would kill them. Being completely overpowered, the eleven naval men were compelled to yield and be carried ashore, where they were shut up in cellars and finally carried down to Castletown Castle.

Meanwhile, the smugglers set to work on the dogger's cargo and landed it safely. A few days later six of the eleven were released, but the other five were detained until Captain Dow should refund the twenty-five guineas he had seized from the Irish wherry. In order to give him a fright they also sent word that the five men should be tried before one of their Courts of Judicature on the following Thursday, were he to fail to send the money. As the captain declined to accede to their demands, the five prisoners were on July 5 brought up and remanded until a month later. Finding it was impossible to obtain their release the commander of the *Sincerity* weighed anchor and ran back to Ramsey to take in the six released men, and then, sailing away to Whitehaven, arrived at that place on the 10th of July.

We need not say more. The story is sufficient to indicate the utter state of lawlessness which prevailed there. Peopled by outlaws and by the scum of France, Holland, Ireland, Scotland, and England, they were a pretty tough proposition. Their violence was rivaled only by their impudence; and fleets of wherries[1] would sail in company into Ireland and Scotland loaded with cargoes of cheap brandy, which had been brought from Holland for that purpose.

As a means of checking these Manx smugglers it was suggested that the English Government should employ a number of tenders in this area, since they drew less water than the sloops-of-war and so would be more useful for a locality that was not well supplied with deep harbors. Moreover, these tenders would be well able to take the ground in the harbors which dried out. Such craft were of about 160 tons, mounted twelve to fourteen carriage guns, and were manned by a captain, second officer, two mates, two quartermasters, a gunner, a boatswain, carpenter, surgeon, and forty seamen.

From the southeast corner of England came reports not much better. Just before the close of the year 1743 the Surveyor at Margate and his men were out on duty along the coast one night when five of them came upon a gang of about twenty-five smugglers. An encounter quickly ensued, and as the latter were well armed they were, by their superior numbers, able to give the officers a severe beating, especially in the case of one unfortunate "whose head is in such a miserable condition that the Surveyor thought proper to put him under the care of a surgeon." Both this Surveyor and the one at Ramsgate asserted that the smugglers were accustomed to travel in such powerful gangs, and at the same time were so well armed, that it was impossible to cope with them, there being seldom less than thirty in a gang "who bid defiance to all the officers when they met them."

On the 7th April 1746, the Collector and Controller of the Customs at Sandwich wrote to the Board:

---

[1] These, of course, were not the light rowing-boats of the kind that were in use on the Thames and elsewhere. The term wherry was applied to various decked fishing-vessels belonging to England, Ireland, and the Isle of Man.

The Fine Art of Smuggling:

"We further beg leave to acquaint your Honors that yesterday about four o'clock in the afternoon a large gang of near 100 smuglers [sic] with several led horses went thro' this town into the island of Thanet, where we hear they landed their goods, notwithstanding that we took all possible care to prevent them.

"*P.S.* This moment we have advice that there is a gang of 200 smugglers more at St. Peter's in the Isle of Thanet."

Seven months later in that year, at nine o'clock one November morning, a gang of 150 smugglers managed to land some valuable cargo from a couple of cutters on to the Sandwich flats. Several Revenue officers were dispatched into the country for the purpose of meeting with some of the stragglers. The officers came into collision with a party of these men and promptly seized two horse-loads of goods consisting of five bags of tea and eight half-ankers of wine. But they were only allowed to retain this seizure for half-an-hour, in as much as the smugglers presently overpowered the Revenue men and wrested back their booty. The preventive men were also considerably knocked about, and one of them had his thumb badly dislocated. The officers declared that they knew none of the people, the latter being well supplied not with firearms but with great clubs.

A fortnight later, just a few miles farther along the coast, a gang of 150 smugglers succeeded in landing their goods at Reculvers near Birchington; and ten days later still another gang of the same size was able to land their goods near Kingsgate, between the North Foreland and Margate.

But it cannot be supposed that the Revenue officers were not aware of the approach of these incidents. The fact was that they were a little lacking in courage. Indeed, they were candid enough to admit that they dared not venture near these ruffians "without the utmost hazard of their lives." But the riding-officers were not solely to blame, for where were the Custom House sloops? How was it they were always absent at these critical times? Indeed, the Collector and Controller informed the Commissioners that not one of these sloops had been seen cruising between Sandwich and Reculvers for months.

This complaint about the cruisers was made in March 1747, and in that same month another gang, two hundred strong, appeared on the coast, but this time, after a smart encounter, the officers secured and placed in the King's warehouse a ton of tea as well as other goods, and three horses. A day or two later a gang of smugglers threatened to rescue these goods back again. The property formed a miscellaneous collection and consisted of fifty pieces of cambric, three bags of coffee, some Flemish linen, tea, clothes, pistols, a blunderbuss, and two musquetoons. To prevent the smugglers carrying out their intention, however, a strong guard was formed by an amalgamation of all the officers from Sandwich, Ramsgate, and Broadstairs, who proceeded to Margate. In addition to these, it was arranged that Commodore Mitchell should send ashore from the Downs as many men as he could spare.

This united front was successful, and for once the smugglers were overmatched. And but for a piece of bad luck, or sheer carelessness, a couple of years later a smart capture might well have been brought about.

It was one day in August when the officers had received information that a gang of twenty men and horses had appeared near Reculvers to receive goods from a cutter that was seen to be hovering near the coast. The smugglers on shore were acute enough to locate the officers, and by some means evidently signaled to the cutter, for the latter now put to sea again and the gang cleared off. Although for some time after this incident both officers and dragoons patrolled the coast in the neighborhood no one was ever fortunate enough to gather information either as to the cutter or the people who had vanished into the country with such rapidity.

And yet in spite of the numerous sympathizers which these illicit importers possessed, there were some individuals who were as much against them as any officer of the Customs. In the neighborhood of Plymouth legitimate trade had suffered a great deal owing to these practices. The mayor, aldermen, and merchants of Saltash were at last compelled to send a message to the Lords of the Treasury complaining that in the rivers adjacent to that place there were several creeks and inlets which were being used by the smugglers for landing their goods. This was especially the case up the river Tamar, and all this had been and still was "to the great prejudice of the fair traders and merchants."

They pointed out that a great deal of it consisted of clandestine running from ships in the Sound, Hamoaze, and other anchorages around there. Large quantities of French linings, wines, and brandies were being run ashore with impunity and speedily sold in the adjacent towns or conveyed some distance into Devonshire. The mayor therefore begged the Treasury for three additional Custom officers consisting of an inspector of roads and two tide-waiters to be established at Saltash, but the Treasury could not see their way to grant such a request.

But in other parts of the country the roads were kept carefully watched to prevent goods being brought inland. The coaches which ran from Dover to London with passengers who had come across from the Continent were frequently stopped on the highway by the riding-officers and the passengers searched. Harsh as this procedure may seem to us today, it was made necessary by the fact that a good many professional contraband carriers were wont to travel back and forth between England and abroad. Some years later, for example, when the Dover coach was stopped at "The Half-Way House," a foreigner, who was traveling by this conveyance and had been able to evade the Customs search at Dover, was found to be carrying two gold snuff-boxes set with diamonds, four lockets also set with diamonds, eighteen opals, three sapphires, eight amethysts, six emeralds, two topazes, and one thousand two hundred torquoises—all of which were liable to duty.

And thus the illegal practices continued all round the coast. From Devonshire it was reported that smuggling was on the increase—this was

The Fine Art of Smuggling:

in the autumn of 1759—and that large gangs armed with loaded clubs openly made runs of goods on the shore, the favorite locale being Torbay, though previously the neighborhood of Lyme had been the usual aim of these men who had sailed as a rule from Guernsey. All that the Collector could suggest was that an "impress smack" should be sent to that district, as he promised that the notorious offenders would make excellent seamen.

There was an interesting incident also off the northeast coast of England, where matters were still about as bad as ever. We referred some pages back to the capture of a Dutch dogger off the Isle of Man; we shall now see another of these craft seized in the North Sea.

Captain Bowen of the sloop *Prince of Wales*, hearing that the dogger *Young Daniel* was running brandy on the coast near to Newcastle, put to sea in search of her. He came up with a number of those cobbles—open boats—which are peculiar to the northeast coastline, though at one time they were used as far south as Great Yarmouth. The cobbles which he was able to intercept had just been employed in transferring the contraband from the dogger to the shore. Bowen captured one of these small craft with a dozen casks aboard. Another was forced ashore and secured by the land officers. Meanwhile, the Dutchman stood out to sea so that he might be able to draw off the spirits from large casks into smaller ones, which were the better fitted for running ashore.

It was found afterwards that he had large numbers of these lesser casks, and during that evening she put about and crept stealthily in towards the shore until she approached within about a mile of the mouth of the Tees. Her intention was to run the rest of her cargo under cover of darkness, and her skipper had arranged for large numbers of men to be on that coast ready to receive and carry off these casks. But Bowen was determined to head her off.

An exciting chase followed, during which—to quote an official report of the time—the dogger did her best "to eat the sloop out of the wind," that is to say sailed as close to the wind as she could travel in the hope of causing her adversary to drop to leeward. For seven hours this chase continued, but after that duration the *Prince of Wales* captured the *Young Daniel* eight leagues from the shore.

This is interesting because, as the chase began when the dogger was a mile from the mouth of the river, the vessels must have traveled about 23 statutory miles in the time, which works out at less than 3-1/2 miles an hour. Not very fast, you may suggest, for a Revenue cutter or for the Dutchman either. But we have no details as to the weather, which is usually bad off that part of the coast in February (the month when this incident occurred), and we must remember that the doggers were too bluff of build to possess speed, and the time had not yet arrived when those much faster Revenue cutters with finer lines and less ample beam were to come into use.

CHAPTER FIVE
The Hawkhurst Gang

We come now to consider the desperate character of a band of men who rendered themselves for all time notorious both by acts of unbridled violence and consummate cruelty.

But before we proceed to relate the details of these incidents as fully as our limited space will allow, it is necessary to remind ourselves once again of the great, solid mass of sympathy, both active and passive, that was always at the back of the smugglers. Without this, such daring runs by night could never have occurred. If it were not for the assistance which was whole-heartedly given by the people on shore, the seafaring men would never have dared to take such enormous risks of life and goods.

Not merely did the villagers come down to the shore to help to bring the goods inland, not only did they lend their horses and carts, but they would tacitly allow the smugglers to hide casks of spirits in wells, haystacks, cellars, and other places. In Cornwall, for instance, fifty-five tubs of spirits were found concealed in a well, over the top of which a haystack had been built. This was near Falmouth, one of the most notorious of the smuggling localities. And there is actual record of at least one instance where the natives charged a rent of a shilling a tub for stowing away the smuggled goods. In another county a cavern had most ingeniously been hollowed out under a pond big enough to hold a hundred casks, the entrance being covered over with planks carefully strewed with mould. So clever and original was this idea that it was not discovered for many years.

But the most notorious, the most formidable, and certainly the most abominably cruel gang of smugglers was the Hawkhurst contingent. The "Hawkhurst Gang," as they were known, were a terror to whatever law-

The Fine Art of Smuggling:

abiding citizens existed in the counties of Kent and Sussex. They feared neither Custom officers nor soldiery, they respected neither God nor man, and in the course of attaining their aims they stopped at no atrocity nor brooked any interference from anyone.

By the year 1747 smugglers had become so daring and committed such terrible crimes that the only course left open for decent people was to band together in mutual protection. The inhabitants of one locality joined together under the title of the "Goudhurst Band of Militia," their leader being a man named Sturt, a native of Goudhurst, who had recently obtained his discharge from the Army. But this union became known to the smugglers, who waylaid one of the militia, and by means of torture the whole of the defenders' plans were revealed. After a while he was released and sent back to inform the militia that the smugglers on a certain day would attack the town, murder all its inhabitants, and then burn the place to the ground.

The day arrived and both forces were prepared. Sturt had gathered his band, collected fire-arms, cast balls, made cartridges, and arranged entrenchments, when, headed by one Thomas Kingsmill, the Hawkhurst gang appeared in order to make the attack. But after a smart engagement in which three were killed and many wounded, the smugglers were driven off, whilst others were captured and subsequently executed.

Kingsmill escaped for a time, and became the leader of the famous attack on the Poole Custom House in October 1747.

Another of the gang was named Perin and belonged to Chichester. Perin was really a carpenter by trade, but after being afflicted with a stroke of the palsy, he became attached to the smugglers, and used to sail with them to France to purchase goods that were to be smuggled, such as brandy, tea, and rum.

In September of 1747 Perin went across the Channel in a cutter called *The Three Brothers*, loaded up with the above commodities, and was approaching the English coast when he was met with a rebuff. For Captain William Johnson, who held a deputation from the Customs to seize prohibited goods, got wind of Perin's exploit, and on the 22nd of this month, whilst cruising in the *Poole* Revenue cutter, sighted *The Three Brothers* to the eastward of Poole. Whereupon the smuggler began to flee, and, running before the wind, fled to the N.N.W. From five in the afternoon until eleven at night the Revenue cutter, with every stitch of canvas set, chased her, and after firing several shots caused her to heave-to. Johnson then boarded her, and found that the tea was in canvas and oil-skin bags, but Perin and the crew of six had escaped in *The Three Brothers* boat. However, Johnson captured the cutter with her cargo and took the same into Poole. The two tons of tea, thirty-nine casks of brandy and rum, together with a small bag of coffee, were conveyed ashore and locked up safely in the Poole Custom House. Such was the introduction to the drama that should follow.

Enraged at their bad luck, the smugglers took counsel together. They assembled in Charlton Forest, and Perin suggested that they should go in a body and, well-armed, break open the Poole Custom House. So the next day they met at Rowland's Castle with swords and firearms, and were presently joined by Kingsmill and the Hawkhurst gang. They secreted themselves in a wood until night had fallen, and eventually reached Poole

Ye Smugglers breaking open ye King's Custom House at Poole

at eleven o'clock at night. Two of their members were sent ahead to reconnoitre, and reported that a sloop-of-war lay opposite to the quay, so that her guns could be pointed against the doors of the Custom House; but afterwards it was found that, owing to the ebb-tide, the guns of the sloop could not be made to bear on that spot. The band, numbering about thirty, therefore rode down to spot, and while Perin and one other man looked after their horses, the rest proceeded to the Custom House, forced open the door with hatchets and other implements, rescued the tea, fastening packages of the latter on to their horses, with the exception only of five lbs. The next morning they passed through Fordingbridge in Hampshire, where hundreds of the inhabitants stood and watched the cavalcade. Now among the latter was a man named Daniel Chater, a shoemaker by trade. He was known to Diamond, one of the gang then passing, for they had both worked together once at harvest time. Recognizing each other, Diamond extended his arm, shook hands, and threw him a bag of tea, for the booty had been divided up so that each man carried five bags of 27 lbs.

After the Poole officers discovered what had happened to their Custom House, there was a tremendous fuss, and eventually the King's proclamation promised a reward for the apprehension of the men concerned in the deed. Nothing happened for months after, but at last Diamond was

The Fine Art of Smuggling:

arrested on suspicion and lodged in Chichester Jail. We can well imagine the amount of village gossip to which this would give rise. Chater was heard to remark that he knew Diamond and saw him go by with the gang the very day after the Custom House had been broken open. When the Collector of Customs at Southampton learned this, he got into communication with the man, and before long Chater and Mr. William Galley were

Mr. Galley and Mr. Chater put by ye Smugglers on one Horse near Rowland Castle

Key: *A. Steele who was Admitted a Kings Evidence* **B.** *Little Harry.* **C.** *Iackson* **D.** *Carter* **E.** *Downer.* **F.** *Richards.* **1.** *Mr. Galley.* **2.** *Mr.*

sent with a letter to Major Battin, a Justice of the Peace for Sussex. Galley was also a Custom House officer stationed at Southampton. The object of this mission was that Chater's evidence should be taken down, so that he might prove the identity of Diamond.

On Sunday February 14, then, these two men set out for Chichester. On the way they stopped at the White Hart Inn, Rowland's Castle, for refreshment. But the landlady suspecting that they were going to hurt the smugglers, with the intuition of a woman and the sympathy of a mother decided to send for two men named Jackson and Carter. For this Mrs. Paine, a widow, had two sons herself, who though nominally blacksmiths were in fact smugglers.

Jackson and Carter came in, to whom the widow explained her suspicions, and these two men were presently followed by others of the gang. Before very long they had got into conversation with Galley and Chater, and plied them with drink, so that they completely gave away the nature of their mission, and after being fuddled were put to bed intoxicated. After a while, they were aroused by Jackson brutally digging his spurs on their foreheads and then thrashing them with a horse-whip. They were then taken out of the inn, both put on to the same horse, with their legs tied together below the horse's belly. They were next whipped as they went along, over the face, eyes, and shoulder, until the poor victims were unable to bear it any longer, and at last fell together, with their hands tied underneath the horse, heads downwards. In this position the horse

Galley and Chater falling off their Horse at Woodash drags their Heads on the Ground, while the Horse kicks them as he goes; the Smugglers still continuing their brutish Usage.

struck the head of one or the other with his feet at every step. Afterwards the blackguardly tormentors sat the two men upright again, whipped them, and once more the men fell down, with heels in air. They were utterly weak, and suffering from their blows.

We need not enlarge upon the details, some of which are too outrageous to repeat. After a while they thought Galley was dead, and laid him across another horse, with a smuggler each side to prevent him falling. They then stopped at the Red Lion, at Rake, called the landlord, drank pretty freely, and then taking a candle and spade dug a hole in a sand-pit where they buried him. But at a later date, when the body was exhumed, it was seen that the poor man had covered his eyes with his hands, so there can be little doubt but that Galley was buried alive.

As for Chater, they delayed his death. Throughout Monday they remained drinking at the Red Lion, discussing what to do with him, Chater being meanwhile kept secured by the leg with an iron chain, three yards long, in a turf-house. At dead of night they agreed to go home separately so that the neighbors might not be suspicious of their absence. On Wednesday morning they again repaired to the Red Lion, after having left Chater in the charge of two of their number. Then, having discussed what should be done with Chater, someone suggested that a gun should be loaded with two or three bullets, and after having tied a long string to the trigger, each member of the gang should take hold of the string together, and so become equally guilty of the poor man's death. But this

The Fine Art of Smuggling:

Chater Chained in the Turff House at Old Mills. Cobby is kicking him & Tapner is cutting him across the Eyes & Nose, while he is saying the Lords Prayer. Several of the other smugglers are standing by.

idea was unwelcomed, as it was thought it would put Chater too quickly out of his sufferings. Meanwhile, Chater was visited at various times, to receive kicks and severe blows, and to be sworn at in the vilest and most scurrilous language.

One of the gang now came up to him, and uttering an oath, brandishing aloft a large clasp-knife, exclaimed: "Down on your knees and go to prayers, for with this knife I will be your butcher." Terrified at the menace, and expecting momentarily to die, Chater knelt down on the turf and began to say the Lord's Prayer. One of the villains got behind and kicked him, and after Chater had asked what they had done to Galley, the man who was confronting him drew his knife across the poor man's face, cut his nose through, and almost cut both his eyes out. And, a moment later, gashed him terribly across the forehead. They then proceeded to conduct him to a well. It was now the dead of night, and the well was about thirty feet deep, but without water, being surrounded with pales at the top to prevent cattle from falling in. They compelled him to get over, and not through these pales, and a rope was placed round his neck, the other end being made fast to the paling. They then pushed him into the well, but as the rope was short they then untied him, and threw him head foremost into the former, and, finally, to stop his groanings, hurled down rails and gate-posts and large stones.

Chater hanging at the Well in LADY HOLT Park, the Bloody Villains Standing by.

The Bloody Smugglers flinging down Stones after they had flung his Dead Body into the Well.

I have omitted the oaths and some of the worst features of the incident, but the above outline is more than adequate to suggest the barbarism of a lot of men bent on lawlessness and revenge. Drunk with their own success, the gang now went about with even greater desperation. Everybody stood in terror of them; Custom officers were so frightened

The Fine Art of Smuggling:

that they hardly dared to perform their duties, and the magistrates themselves were equally frightened to convict smugglers. Consequently the contraband gangs automatically increased to great numbers.

But, finally, a reward of £500 was offered by the Commissioners of Customs for the arrest of every one of the culprits, and as a result several were arrested, tried, convicted, and executed. The murderers were tried at a special assize for smugglers held at Chichester, before three judges, and the seven men were sentenced to death.

William Jackson died in prison a few hours after sentence. He had been very ill before, but the shock of being sentenced to death, and to be hung afterwards in chains and in ignominy, rapidly hastened his death, and relieved the executioner of at least one portion of his duty. He had been one of the worst smugglers in his time, and was even a thief among thieves, for he would even steal his confederates' goods. Between the sentence and the hour for execution a man came into the prison to measure the seven culprits for the irons in which their bodies were subsequently to be hung by chains. And this distressed the men more than anything else, most of all Jackson, who presently succumbed as stated.

Mills, senior, had gradually been drawn into the smuggling business, though previously he had been quite a respectable man. After giving up actual smuggling, he still allowed his house to be used as a store-place for the contraband goods. His son, Richard, also one of the seven, had been concerned in smuggling for years, and was a daring fellow. John Cobby, the third of the culprits, was of a weaker temperament, and had been brought under the influence of the smugglers. Benjamin Tapner was especially penitent, and "hoped all young people would take warning by his untimely fate, and keep good company, for it was bad company had been his ruin." William Carter complained that it was Jackson who had drawn him away from his honest employment to go smuggling, but John Hammond was of a more obdurate nature, and had always hated the King's officers.

According to the testimony of the Rev. John Smyth, who visited them in jail, all the prisoners received the Holy Communion at ten o'clock, the morning after being sentenced to death. All the prisoners except the two Mills admitted that they deserved the sentence, but all the surviving six acknowledged that they forgave everybody.

On January 19, 1749, they were executed. The two Mills were not hung in chains, but having neither friend nor relation to take them away their bodies were thrown into a hole near the gallows, into which also was placed Jackson's body. Carter's body was hung in chains on the Portsmouth Road, near Rake; that of Tapner on Rook's Hill, near Chichester; those of Cobby and Hammond on the sea coast near Selsey Bill; so that from a great distance they could be observed across the sea by the ships as they went by east and west.

Later on, John, the brother of Richard Mills, and one of the gang, was also arrested. When the above three judges were traveling down to

Chichester for the trial of the seven men, John had intended waylaying their lordships on Hind Heath, but his companions had refused to support him. But soon after his father's and brother's execution he met with a man named Richard Hawkins, whom he accused of having stolen two bags of tea. Hawkins denied it, and was brutally and unmercifully thrashed to death in the Dog and Partridge Inn at Slindon Common, his body being afterwards carried a dozen miles, thrown into a pond, with stones attached, and then sunk. John Mills was convicted and hanged at East Grinstead, and afterwards remained hanging in chains on Slindon Common. Other members of the gang were also arrested, tried at the same assizes as highwaymen, and then executed.

* * * * *

Later on, two of the smugglers who had given evidence against the men that were hanged at Chichester, gave information also, which led to the arrest of Kingsmill, Perin, and two others who had been concerned in breaking open the Poole Custom House. Kingsmill, Perin, and one other were hanged at Tyburn in April of 1749; the other man, however, was pardoned.

Thus at length this dreaded Hawkhurst Gang was broken up.

CHAPTER SIX
The Revenue Cruisers

We drew attention some time back to the assistance occasionally rendered by soldiers when the Riding officers were about to arrest smugglers. Early in the year 1740, or about the close of 1739, Thomas Carswell, one of the Revenue officers stationed at Rye, was murdered, and a corporal and three dragoons whom he had taken to his assistance were badly wounded, and a large quantity of tea that had been seized was rescued. It was after this incident that Revenue officers of this port—perhaps the most notorious of all the southeast smuggling territory—were ordered that in future when they went forth to make seizures they were to have with them an adequate military force, and to this end they were to make previous arrangements with the commanding-officer of the forces in that district.

But in spite of the seizures which the officers on land from time to time effected, and notwithstanding the shortcomings of the Custom House cruisers in regard to speed, and the frequent negligence of their commanders, they continued to be the principal and the most important of all the machinery set in motion against the smugglers.

We have seen this service in working order as far back as the year 1674, at any rate, when the fleet consisted of only hired vessels. We have also seen that they were employed in sufficient numbers all round the coast, and that the Customs authorities, not content merely to hire such vessels, also presently obtained some of their own. It is possible that the smacks were used for such service even before the date 1674—perhaps very soon after Charles came to the throne—but there are no existing records of this to make the matter certain.

The Fine Art of Smuggling:

The Revenue preventive work, in so far as the cruisers were employed, was carried on by a mixed control, and embraced six separate and distinct types:

1. There were the English Custom House smacks, cutters, and sloops, some of which were hired vessels: others were actually owned by the English Customs Board.

2. There were the English Excise cruisers, which were controlled by the English Excise Board. They appeared to be very similar to the craft in the first class.

3. There were the Scottish Customs cruisers, under the control of the Scottish Customs Board. The official at the head of these was known as the Agent for Yachts.

4. There were the Scottish Excise cruisers, controlled by the Scottish Excise Board.

5. There were the Irish Revenue cruisers, controlled by the Irish Customs and Excise.

6. And lastly, there were these vessels of the Royal Navy which were employed to assist the Revenue, such vessels consisting of ships of the fifth-rate, sixth-rate, and especially the armed sloops.

In the present volume it has been necessary, owing to the limits of our space, to restrict our consideration of cruisers chiefly to the most important of these, viz. those of the English Custom House and those of the Royal Navy.

Under such a mixed rule it was obvious that many difficulties arose, and that the clashing of interests was not infrequent. For instance, between the English Custom House cruisers and the English Excise cruisers there was about as much friendship as there exists usually between a dog and a cat. Similarly between the former and the Naval cruisers there was considerable jealousy, and every display of that pompous, bombastic exhibition of character which was such a feature of the life of the eighteenth century, and the first years of the next.

Although the Revenue cruisers were employed primarily and ordinarily for the purpose of protecting the revenue, yet from time to time they were mobilized for coast defense. On different occasions during the eighteenth century they were lent to the Admiralty, and well supplied with men and arms in readiness for actual warfare. After the third quarter of the eighteenth century these Revenue cruisers seem to have been built in greater numbers and with some improvement as to design, which, seeing that they had so frequently been left well astern by the smuggling cutters, was more than necessary.

In November of 1780, the Board of Customs issued an interesting letter that shows how closely these cruisers approximated vessels of war, even when they were not under the jurisdiction of the Admiralty. This letter was sent to the Collector and Controller at the different English

Customs ports, and began by referring to the fact that many applications had been made to the Board asking permission to take out Letters of Marque.

It will be remembered that this was a time when wars seemed to go on interminably, and there had been only a few brief intervals of peace ever since the Anglo-Dutch wars began. The Commissioners replied that they had no objection to the commanders of the cruisers providing themselves with Letters of Marque, if done at the latter's own expense "during present hostilities." But the Board declined to bear any part of the expense for any damages that might be sustained in an engagement where no seizure had been made and brought into port for a breach of the Revenue laws, so long as a commander should continue to hold these Letters of Marque. It was, in fact, a basis of no cure, no pay. Each commander was, further, strictly enjoined not to quit his station and duty as a Revenue officer "under pretense of looking for captures, it being our resolution to recall the permission hereby granted, as soon as it shall be discovered in any instance to be prejudicial to our service."

But this war-like and semi-war-like service was entirely subservient to their ordinary work. It is evident from the correspondence of the Customs Board of this same year, 1780, that their minds were very uneasy. The smugglers, far from showing any slackening, had become more active than ever. These men had, to quote the words of the Commissioners, considerably increased the size and force of their vessels; they had also added to their number of both men and guns. They had become so violent and outrageous, they had acquired so much audacity as to "carry on their illicit designs in sight of the Revenue cruisers," and "whenever they have appeared within a certain distance have actually fired into and threatened to sink them."

In such cases as these, it was reported to the Board, the mariners on board these cruisers have frequently refused to bear down and repel their attacks, explaining their conduct by saying that no provision was made for their support in case they received injury during these encounters. To meet such objections as these the Board resolved to allow the sum of £10 per annum to every mariner employed on board their cruisers who should lose a hand or foot, or receive any greater injury by firearms "or other offensive weapons of the smugglers while in the actual execution of their duty so as to disable them from further service; and we have also resolved to pay the surgeons' bills for such of the mariners as may receive slighter wounds." But it was stipulated that no allowance was to be paid unless certificates were produced from the commanders of these cruisers.

And before we go any further with the progress of these cutters, let us afford actual instances of the kind of treatment which had led the Board to make this allowance to its men.

Three years before the above resolution, that is to say on April 24, 1777, Captain Mitchell was cruising in command of the Revenue cutter *Swallow* in the North Sea. Off Robin Hood's Bay he fell in with a smuggling cutter commanded by a notorious contraband skipper who was known as "Smoker," or "Smoaker." Mitchell was evidently in sufficient awe of him to give him a wide berth, for the cruiser's commander in his official report actually recorded that "Smoker" "waved us to keep off!" However, a few days later, the *Swallow*, when off the Spurn, fell in with another famous smuggler. This was the schooner *Kent*, of about two hundred tons, skippered by a man known as "Stoney." Again this gallant Revenue captain sent in his report to the effect that "as their guns were in readiness, and at the same time waving us to go to the Northward, we were, by reason of their superior force, obliged to sheer off, but did our best endeavors to spoil his Market. There [sic] being a large fleet of colliers with him."

But that was not to be their last meeting, for on May 2, when off Whitby, the *Swallow* again fell in with the *Kent*, but (wrote Mitchell) the smuggler "would not let us come near him." The following day the two ships again saw each other, and also on May 13, when off Runswick Bay. On the latter occasion the *Kent* "fired a gun for us, as we imagined, to keep farther from him." The same afternoon the *Swallow* chased a large lugsail boat, with fourteen hands in her, and supposed to belong to the *Kent*. But the *Swallow* was about as timid as her name, for, according to her commander, she was "obliged to stand out to sea, finding that by the force they had in their boat, and a number of people on shore, we had no chance of attacking them with our boat, as they let us know they were armed, by giving us a volley of small arms." None the less the *Swallow* had also fourteen men as her complement, so one would have thought that this chicken-hearted commander would at least have made an effort to try conclusions.

No doubt, the *Kent* was a pretty tough customer, and both skipper and his crew likewise. But there was something wanting in Captain Mitchell. For consider another of the latter's exploits.

It was the last week of September of that same year, and the scene had again the Yorkshire coast for its background. During the evening they saw what they rightly believed to be a smuggling cutter. They got as far as hailing her, but, as it was very dark, and the *Swallow* did not know the force of the cutter, Mitchell "thought it most prudent to leave her," and so came to anchor in Saltburn Bay. But the smuggler was not done with this enterprising gentleman; so the next day the smuggler came into the bay, stood down under full sail, and came charging down on the poor *Swallow*, striking her on the quarter, the smuggler swearing terrible oaths that if Mitchell did not promptly cut his cable—it was the days of hemp, still—and hurry out of that anchorage, he would sink him.

What happened, you ask? Of course the *Swallow* ought to have been under way, and should never have been lying there. She was acting contrary to the orders of the Board. But what must we think of a captain who calmly awaits the on-coming of a smuggler's attack? Why, as soon as the *Swallow* saw him approaching, did he not up anchor, hoist sails, and go to meet him with his crew at their stations, and guns all shotted? But

Came charging down... striking her on the quarter.

even after this gross insult to himself, his ship, and his flag, was the commander of a Revenue sloop to obey?

Yes—it is shameful to have to record it—Mitchell did obey. True, he didn't cut his cable, but he soon tripped his anchor and cleared out as ordered. The poor *Swallow* had been damaged both as to her tail and her wings, for the smugglers had injured the stern, taken a piece out of the boom, and carried away the topping-lift. But evidently in those days the Revenue service attracted into its folds men of the type of Mitchell.

Take the case of Captain Whitehead of the Revenue cruiser *Eagle*. Spying a smuggling vessel, he gave chase, and eventually came up with her, also off Saltburn. Whitehead hailed her, but the smuggler's skipper replied—one cannot resist a smile—"with a horrid expression," and called his men to arms. The smuggler then fired a volley with muskets, wounding one of the *Eagle*'s crew. Presently they also fired their swivel-guns, "on which Captain Whitehead thought it prudent to get away from her as fast as he could, the greatest part of his people having quitted the deck."

The smuggler continued to fire at the retreating cruiser, and chased

The Fine Art of Smuggling:

the *Eagle* for the next hour. The cutter turned out to be that which Mitchell had encountered on April 24, 1777, and her skipper was our friend "Smoker" again.

This smuggling craft was described as a stout cutter of 130 tons, and a crew of upwards of forty men. She carried fourteen carriage guns, four three-pounders, as well as a great number of swivels. "Smoker's" real name was David Browning, and he was recognized by the *Eagle*'s crew from his voice, which was familiar to several of them. During that affray the Revenue cruiser received about twenty shot in her sails, about a dozen in her boat, and half as many in her fore-and main-mast. She also had her mizzen halyards shot away. From these details it would seem that she was dandy-rigged, that is to say, she had a mizzen or jigger in addition to her cutter rig, and on this jigger would be set a small lugsail as was the old custom.

Following Mitchell's meeting with the *Kent*, we have a record belonging to July of that same year—1777. This time a different result was to come about. For instead of acting single-handed, the sloops *Prince of Wales* and the *Royal George*—both being employed by the Scottish Excise Board, aided by H.M.S. *Pelican* and *Arethusa*—four of them—at last managed to capture this schooner. She was found to be armed with sixteen four-pounders and twenty swivel-guns, and also had a large stock of gunpowder, blunderbusses, and muskets. "Stoney" was taken out of her, and he was said to be an outlaw whose real name was George Fagg. The guns and ammunition were taken ashore and put in the King's warehouse at Hull, and the crew of thirty-nine were placed on board the *Arethusa*. Among these prisoners were those who had murdered a dragoon the previous year, while the latter was assisting a Custom officer at Whitby. The arrest of these men was all the more interesting for a reward of £100 for their capture had been long outstanding.

The capture of the *Kent* had been effected as follows. The two Excise cruisers were off St. Abb's Head on July 8. Hearing that the *Kent* had been seen off Flamborough Head they sailed south, and off Filey fell in with her. On being hailed, the smuggler beat to quarters, shouting to the cruisers. "Fire, you ——, and be —— to you." The battle at once commenced and continued smartly for an hour, when the *Pelican* came up to give assistance to the two cruisers. The *Kent*, big as she was, now used sweeps—it was reminiscent of the days of Elizabethan galleasses—and drew away. However the *Pelican* (a frigate) overhauled her, and the *Arethusa* which had also come up gave valuable aid as well. The two naval captains allowed the cruisers to seize the *Kent*, and to take her into Hull, but the prisoners were put on board the *Arethusa* as stated. The *Kent*'s master and four of the men had been killed.

It should be added that the day before this incident the *Pelican* had also chased the *Kent* out of Bridlington Bay, so the smuggler must have come further north in the meanwhile, thus meeting the two Scottish cruisers bound south. The hatches of the *Kent* were found to be unbattened, and her cargo in great disorder. The latter consisted of 1974 half-ankers, and a large amount of tea packed in oilskin-bags to the number of 554.

This schooner had been built at that other famous home of smugglers, Folkestone. She was specially rigged for fast sailing, her mainmast being 77 feet long, and her main-boom 57 feet. It was found that her sails were much damaged by shot. Her mainmast was shot through in two places, and her main-boom rendered quite unserviceable. Ship and tackle were appraised at £1405, 16s., so with the addition of her cargo she represented a fair prize.

But "Smoker" was still at large even though "Stoney" was a prisoner.

It was in April of 1777, when Captain Mitchell had fallen in with him off Robin Hood's Bay. A month later the Collector of Hull wrote up to the Board to say that a large lugger had been seen off Whitby, and well armed. She was described as "greatly an overmatch" for any of the Revenue cruisers, "or even for a joint attack of two of them"; and that as long as she and the armed cutter commanded by Browning, alias "Smoker," continued so daringly to "insult" the coasts, there was little prospect of success.

For the previous six months the Revenue cruisers had not been able to make any seizures, because these smuggling craft not only brought over vast quantities themselves, but protected the smaller ones from the attempts of the Revenue cruisers.

A year later we find that Mitchell was every bit as slack as before. This is made quite clear from a letter which the Collector of Hull was compelled on November 12 (1778) to write. In this epistle he informs Mitchell that either he or his mate, one of them, must remain on board the *Swallow* at night, when lying in the Humber. For it appeared that two days earlier both were ashore. The mariner who had the midnight watch on board the cruiser saw a vessel, supposed to be a privateer, come right up the Humber into Hull Roads, sail around the naval tender there lying, then sail round the *Swallow*, and finally down the river again. Although there were twelve or fourteen men on the supposed privateer's deck, yet the *Swallow*'s watchman did not even hail her, Mitchell and his mate being ashore all the while.

Such incidents as the above show that there undoubtedly was cause for the complaints of the Customs Board that the commanders of their cruisers were not doing all that might have been done towards suppressing the evil at hand. On the other hand, it was equally true that the delinquents with whom these commanders had to contest were of a particularly virulent and villainous type. Thus, between the negligence of the one side, and the enterprise of the other, his Majesty's revenue had to suffer very considerably.

No better instance of the potency of this lawlessness could be afforded than by an event which happened in the summer of 1777. Everyone knows, of course, that those were the days when men had to be impressed into the service of the Navy. Thus when any of these hardy

The Fine Art of Smuggling:

smugglers were captured, they were valuable acquisitions to the Service, and far more useful than many of the disease-stricken crews which so often had to be shipped to make up a man-of-war's complement. In the year we are speaking of a number of smugglers who had been captured on the North Sea were put on board H.M. tender *Lively* by Captain O'Hara of the Impress service, the intention being to convey these men to one of his Majesty's ships at the Nore. The tender got under way and was proceeding to her destination when the smuggler-prisoners mutinied, overpowered the *Lively's* crew, and carried the *Lively* into Flushing.

And similar examples of the impudence and violence of other North Sea smugglers could also be quoted. On the 7th of May 1778, Captain Bland, of the *Mermaid* Revenue cruiser, was off Huntcliff Fort, when he sighted a smuggling shallop.[1] Bland promptly bore down, and as he approached hailed her. But the shallop answered by firing a broadside. The Revenue cruiser now prepared to engage her, whereupon the shallop hoisted an English pennant, which was evidently a signal for assistance, for a large armed cutter promptly appeared and came to the shallop's rescue. Seeing that he was overmatched, Bland, therefore, sheered off.

During the same month Captain Whitehead, of the *Eagle*, to whom we have already referred, reported that he seldom went for a cruise without being fired on, and he mentioned that sometimes these smuggling vessels carried musket-proof breast-works—a kind of early armor-plating.

The principal rendezvous of the smuggling craft in the North Sea was Robin Hood's Bay. Whenever the cruisers used to approach that bight the smugglers would sail out, fire upon them, and drive them along the coast. Before firing, the smugglers always hoisted English colors, and on one occasion a smuggling craft had the temerity to run alongside a Revenue cruiser, hail her, and in a derisive manner ordered the commander to send his boat aboard.

We spoke just now of the superior sailing qualities which these smuggling craft frequently possessed over the Revenue cruisers, and on one occasion, in the North Sea, the master of a smuggling shallop, when being pursued, impudently lowered his lugsail—that would be his mizzen—to show that the cruiser could not come up and catch him.

And lest that dishonorable incident previously mentioned, of a cruiser being ordered out of Saltburn Bay, may be thought a mere isolated event, let us hasten to add that the cruiser *Mermaid* was lying at anchor off Dunstanburgh Castle, on the Northumbrian coast, when Edward Browning came alongside her in an armed shallop named the *Porcupine*, belonging to Sandwich. He insisted on the Mermaid getting up her anchor and leaving that region: "otherwise he would do him a mischief." Indeed, were these facts not shown unmistakably by actual eye-witnesses to be the very reverse of fiction, one might indeed feel doubtful

---

[1] A "shallop" is a large boat with two masts, and usually rigged like a schooner.

as to accepting them. But it is unlikely that cruiser-commanders would go out of their way to record incidents which injured their reputation, had these events never in fact occurred.

Some idea of the degree of success which smuggling vessels attained during this eighteenth century may be gathered from the achievements of a cutter which was at work on the south coast. Her name was the *Swift*, and she belonged to Bridport.

She was of 100 tons burthen, carried no fewer than 16 guns and a crew of fifty. During the year 1783 she had made several runs near Torbay, and on each occasion had been able to land about 2000 casks of spirits, as well as 4 or 5 tons of tea. Afterwards the whole of this valuable cargo had been run inland by about 200 men, in defiance of the Revenue officers.

Then there was the *Ranger*, a bigger craft still, of 250 tons. She carried an enormous crew for her size—nearly 100—and mounted 22 guns. She had been built at Cawsand, that village which in smuggling days attained so much notoriety, and stands at the end of a delightful bay facing the western end of Plymouth Breakwater. This vessel had a successful time in landing cargoes to the east of Torbay without paying the lawful duty. And there were many fishing-boats of from 18 to 25 tons, belonging to Torbay, which were at this time accustomed to run across the Channel, load up with the usual contraband, and then hover about outside the limits of the land. When they were convinced that the coast was clear of any cruisers they would run into the bay and land, sink or raft their cargoes, according to circumstances.

And now, leaving for the present actual skirmishes and chases in which the Revenue cruisers were concerned, let us look a little more closely into their organization.

From the report by the Commissioners appointed to examine the Public Accounts of the kingdom, and issued in 1787, it is shown that the Custom House cruisers were of two classes: (1) Those which were owned by the Board, and (2) Those which were hired by contract. As to this latter class there was a further subdivision into two other classes; for one section of these vessels was furnished by the Crown, no charge being made for the hire. But her outfit, her future repairs, in addition to the wages and victualing of the crew, and all other expenses, were paid out of the produce of the seizures which these cruisers effected. After this, if anything remained beyond these deductions, the residue was to be divided between the Crown and the contractor.

Very often, of course, when a fine haul was made of a £1000 worth of cargo, there was quite a nice little sum for both parties to the contract, and a few other, smaller, seizures during the year would make the business quite a profitable undertaking. But when the amount of seizures was not sufficient to defray the expenses the deficiency was supplied by the contractor and Crown in equal proportions. That, then, was one of these two subdivisions of contracted cruisers.

The Fine Art of Smuggling:

But in the second of these the contractor provided the vessel, for which he was paid the sum of 4s. 6d. a ton per lunar month. It may seem at first that this was poor remuneration, especially when one recollects that today, when the Government hires liners from the great steamship companies, the rate of payment is £1 per ton per month. In the case of even a 10,000-ton liner there is thus a very good payment for about thirty days. But in the case of a cutter of 100 tons or less, in the eighteenth century, 4s. 6d. per ton may seem very small in comparison.

However, we must bear in mind that, although for this money the contractor was to find the outfit of the vessel and be responsible for all repairs needed, yet the aforesaid contractor might make a good deal more in a lucky year. It was done on the following basis.

From the produce of the seizures made by this subdivision of cruisers all remaining charges additional to those mentioned above were paid, but the surplus was divided between the Crown and contractor. Thus the latter stood to gain a large sum if only a moderate number of seizures had been made, and there was, by this method, every incentive for the hired cruisers to use their best endeavors to effect captures. Still, if there was a deficiency instead of a surplus, this was also shared by both contracting parties.

In the year 1784 there were, reckoning all classes, 44 cruisers employed, and 1041 men as crews. Of these cruisers the Commander, the Chief Mate and Second Mate, and, in certain vessels, the Deputed Mariners, were all officers of the Customs. In the case of the first class of cruisers—those which were on the establishment—these officers were appointed by the Board pursuant to warrants from the Treasury. In the case of the second—those which were hired by contract—the officers were appointed by the Customs Board. The captain of the cruiser was paid £50 per annum, the chief mate either £35 or £30, and the crew were each paid £15. But, as we shall see later on, the rate of pay was considerably increased some years afterwards. The victualing allowance was at the rate of 9d. per diem for each man on board, and an allowance of 1s. each was made by the lunar month for fire and candle. This last-mentioned allowance was also modified in the course of time. Some idea as to the seriousness, from a financial point of view, of this cruiser fleet may be gathered from the statement that these 44 vessels cost the Government for a year's service the sum of £44,355, 16s. 1d.

The largest of these forty-four cruisers was the *Repulse*, 210 tons. She carried 33 men and was stationed at Colchester. Her cost for this year (1784) was £1552, 16s. 8d. She was not one of the hired vessels, but on the establishment. Next in size came the *Tartar*, 194 tons, with 31 men, her station being Dover. She was on the establishment, and her annual cost was £1304, 6s. 2-1/2d. Of the same tonnage was the *Speedwell*, which cruised between Weymouth and Cowes. There was also the *Rose*, 190 tons, with 30 men, stationed at Southampton, being on the establishment likewise. Next to her in size came the *Diligence*, 175 tons, with 32 men. She cruised between Poole and Weymouth. She was one of the hired vessels, and was in 1784 removed from Weymouth to have her headquarters at Cowes. The smallest of all the cruisers at this time was the *Nimble*, 41 tons and a crew of 30. She also was a hired craft. Her station was at Deal, and her annual cost was £1064, 9s. 9d. for the year mentioned.

But though there was less expenditure needed at the outset, these contract ships were not altogether satisfactory. More specifically, it was the ship's method that was unsatisfactory more so than the cruisers themselves. For if we have any knowledge at all of human nature, and especially of the dishonest character which so frequently manifested itself in the eighteenth century, we can readily imagine the following. That the contractor, unless he was a scrupulously honorable man, would succumb to the temptation to economize too strictly with regard to keeping the ship in the best condition of repair; or he might gain a little by giving her an sufficient crew, thus saving both wages and victuals. For the Crown allowed a certain number of men, and paid for the complement which they were supposed to carry.

Therefore, since this arrangement was marked by serious drawbacks, the contract system was discontinued, and at the beginning of 1788 fifteen contracts were ended, and five other cruisers' contracts were not renewed when they expired in that year. All the cruisers in the employment of the Customs Service were now placed on the establishment, and the practice of paying the charges and expenses out of the King's share of the condemned goods was rescinded.

In the year 1797 the number of Customs cruisers was 37, the commanders being appointed by the Treasury; and it may be not without interest to mention the names, tonnage, and guns of some of those which were on the books for that year.

There was the *Vigilant*, which was described as a yacht, 53 tons, 6 guns, and 13 men; the *Vigilant* cutter, 82 tons, 8 guns. During the winter season she cruised with ten additional hands off the coasts of Essex, Kent, and Sussex. There was another, the *Diligence*, given as of 152 tons; the *Swallow*, 153 tons and 10 guns; the *Lively*, 113 tons, 12 guns, and 30 men. The *Swift*, 52 tons and 8 men, used to cruise between the Downs and the Long Sand (to the North of the North Foreland at the mouth of the Thames). Some of the old names under the former dual system are seen to be commemorated in the *Nimble* (41 tons, 2 guns, 15 men). Her station was Deal, and she used to cruise between the Forelands. The *Tartar* of this period was of 100 tons, had 10 guns and 23 men. But the *Greyhound*, probably one of the fastest cruisers, was of 200 tons, mounted 16 guns, and carried 43 men. Her cruising ground was between Beachy Head and the Start, and her station at Weymouth. A much smaller craft was the cruiser *Busy* (46 tons and 11 men). Her cruising was in a much smaller area—around Plymouth Sound and Cawsand Bay.

Owing to the fact that commanders had a tendency to run into port too often for real or imaginary repairs, the Commissioners decided that

The Fine Art of Smuggling:

in the future, when a cruiser put in, she was to inform the Collector and Controller of that port by means of her commander. He had to give his reasons for coming in to both, and to estimate the length of time he was likely to remain in port, before his being able to sail again.

With regard to the prize-money which these cruisers were able to make; before the year 1790 there had been a diversity of practice in the method of sharing. In allotting rewards to officers for seizing vessels which afterwards had been taken into the Revenue Service, it had formerly been the practice to deduct the whole of the charges out of the officers' moiety of the appraised value. But from April 14, 1790, "for the encouragement of the seizing officers," the charge was deducted from the total appraised value, and the seizing officers were to be paid a moiety of the net produce, if any. It had also been the custom to allow the commanders of Admiralty cruisers permission to use seized vessels as tenders. But from May 6, 1790, this practice was also discontinued by the Board, who ordered that in case any such vessels were so employed at the different ports, the commanders were to deliver them up "with their tackle, apparel, and furniture," to the Collector and Controller of Customs.

We referred some time back to the fact that these Revenue cruisers at times were mobilized for war, and also that to them were granted Letters of Marque. In this connection there is to be noted an interesting warrant, under the King's sign-manual, dated June 11, 1795, which reads:

> Whereas the Commissioners of our Treasury have represented unto us that the cutters in the service of our Revenues of Customs have captured several Ships and Vessels belonging to the enemy, and have recommended it unto us to issue our warrant to grant the proceeds of the Prizes that have been or shall be taken by the cutters in the service of our Customs, granted to the cutters capturing such prizes respectively, and the expenses of the proceedings, in regard thereto, among officers and crews of the vessels in the search of our Customs, who made the said captures, together with the head-money, in all cases where head-money is or may be due by law...

> Our will and pleasure is that the proceeds of all such Prizes as have been or shall be taken from the enemy in the course of the present war, by the cutters in the service of our Revenue of Customs, after deducting all expenses of the Letters of Marque granted to the cutters capturing such Prizes respectively, and the expenses of the proceedings in regard thereto, together with the head-money in all cases where head-money is or may be due by law, shall be distributed in the manner following; that is to say:

The Commander	14/32 ds.
Mate	7/32 ds.

Deputed Mariner, or deputed
mariners if more than one   3/32 ds., exclusive of
their shares as Mariners.
Other Mariners   8/32 ds.

If there is no deputed Mariner:
- The Commander   1/2
- The Mate   1/4
- Mariners   1/4

It may be mentioned, in passing, that a "deputed" mariner was one who held a deputation from the Customs Board. Another warrant, similar to the above, and to the same effect, was issued on July 4, of that memorable year 1805.

In July of 1797, the Customs Commissioners drew attention to the third article of the "Instructions for the Commanders and Mates of the Cruisers employed in the service of this Revenue," reminding them that the commanders, mariners, and mates were in no case to be allowed to participate in the officers' shares of seizures made by the crews of the cruisers unless the first-mentioned had been actually present at the time when the seizure was made, or could afford satisfactory proof that they were necessarily absent on some duty. Therefore the Board now directed that, whenever the crews of the cruisers made a seizure, a list of the officers who were not actually on board or in the boats of the cruisers at that time was to be transmitted to the Board with the account of the seizure.

Then follows the other instruction which has already been alluded to. In order that the station of the aforesaid cruisers may never be left unguarded by their coming into port for provisions, or to be cleaned and refitted, or for any other necessary purpose, the commanders were instructed to arrange with each other "that nothing but absolute necessity shall occasion their being in Port at one and the same time."

It will be recognized that the object of this was, if possible, to keep the officers of the cruisers on board their vessels, and at sea, instead of forever running into port. For it would seem that by more than one of these gentlemen the work of cruising on behalf of the Revenue Service was regarded too much in the light of a pleasant, extended yachting trip—with an occasional chase and seizure of a smuggling craft to break the monotony of their existence and to swell their purses. But such a pleasant life was not that contemplated by the Customs authorities.

CHAPTER SEVEN
Cutters and Sloops

We have spoken in the preceding chapters of the revenue cruisers sometimes as cutters and sometimes as sloops. For the reason that will soon become apparent let us now endeavor to straighten out any confusion which may have arisen in the mind of the reader.

Practically speaking, sloops and cutters in those days were one and the same, with only very minor differences. In a valuable French nautical volume published in 1783, after explaining that the cutter came to the French from England, the definition goes on to state that in her rigging and sail-plan she resembles a sloop, except that the former has her mast longer, and inclined further aft, and has greater sail-area. The cutter also has but little freeboard, and in order to carry her large sail-area she draws more water. This authority then goes on to mention that such craft as these cutters are employed by the smugglers of the English Channel, "and being able to carry a good deal of sail they can easily escape from the guard-ships. The English Government, for the same reason, maintain a good many of these craft so as to stop these smugglers."

Our English authority, Falconer, described the cutter as having one mast and a straight-running bowsprit that could be run inboard on deck. But for this, and the fact that the cutter's sail-area was larger, these craft were much the same as sloops. Falconer also states that a sloop differs from a cutter by having a fixed steeving bowsprit and a jib-stay. Moore, who was also a contemporary, makes similar definitions in almost identical language. The real difference, then, was that the cutter could run her bowsprit inboard, but the sloop could not.

Now, in the year 1785, a very interesting matter occupied the attention of the Board of Customs in this regard. It seems that in an important trial concerning a certain vessel the defense was set up that this vessel had changed her character by so altering her "boltsprit" that it became fixed and could not be run inboard. It was found that all which her owners had done was to pass an iron bolt through the bits and heel of the bowsprit, clenching it. The defendant insisted that thus he had rendered it a complete standing "boltsprit," and not a running one; and that, therefore, by such alteration, his vessel became transformed from a cutter to a sloop.

According to the definitions which we have just brought forward, one would have thought that this was a good defense. However, the Crown thought otherwise, and contended that the alteration was a mere evasion of the Act in question, and that the vessel remained a cutter because such fastening could be removed at pleasure, and then the "boltsprit" would run in and out as it did before the alteration. The jury also took this view, and the cutter, which thought herself a sloop, was condemned.

The Revenue officers and commanders of Admiralty sloops were accordingly warned to make a note of this. For a number of years the matter was evidently left at that. But in 1822 the Attorney and Solicitor-General, after a difficult case had been raised, gave the legal distinction as follows, the matter having arisen in connection with the licensing of a craft: "A cutter may have a standing bowsprit of a certain length without a license, but the distinction between a sloop and a cutter should not be looked for in the rigging but in the build and form of the hull, and, therefore, when a carvel-built vessel corresponds as to her hull with the usual form of a sloop, she will not merely, by having a running bowsprit, become a cutter within the meaning of the Act of the 24 Geo. III cap. 47, and consequently will not be liable to forfeiture for want of a license." From this it will be seen that whereas Falconer and other nautical authorities relied on the fixing of the bowsprit to determine the difference, the legal authorities relied on a difference in hull. The point is one of great interest, and I believe the matter has never been raised before by any modern nautical writer.[1]

As to what a Revenue cutter looked like, the illustrations which have been here reproduced will afford the reader a very good idea. And these can be supplemented by the following description which Marryat gives in *The Three Cutters*. It should be mentioned that the period of which he is speaking is that which we have been contemplating, the end of the eighteenth century.

"She is a cutter," he writes, "and you may know that she belongs to the Preventive Service by the number of gigs and galleys which she has hoisted up all round her. She looks like a vessel that was about to sail with a cargo of boats: two on deck, one astern, one on each side of her. You observe that she is painted black, and all her boats are white. She is not such an elegant vessel as the yacht, and she is much more lumbered

---

[1] See also Appendix I

up... Let us go on board. You observe the guns are iron, and painted black, and her bulwarks are painted red; it is not a very becoming color, but then it lasts a long while, and the dockyard is not very generous on the score of paint—or lieutenants of the navy troubled with much spare cash. She has plenty of men, and fine men they are; all dressed in red flannel shirts and blue trousers; some of them have not taken off their canvas or tarpaulin petticoats, which are very useful to them, as they are in the boats night and day, and in all weathers. But we will at once go down into the cabin, where we shall find the lieutenant who commands her, a master's mate, and a midshipman. They have each their tumbler before them, and are drinking gin-toddy, hot, with sugar—capital gin, too, 'bove proof; it is from that small anker standing under the table. It was one that they forgot to return to the Custom House when they made their last seizure."

In 1786, by the 26 Geo. III c. 40, section 27, it was made lawful for any commander of any of his Majesty's vessels of war, or any officer by them authorized, to make seizures without a deputation or commission from the Commissioners of the Customs. Those were curious times when we recollect that apart altogether from the men-of-war of varying kinds, there were large numbers of armed smuggler-cutters, Custom-House cutters with letters of marque, privateers, and even Algerine corsairs from the Mediterranean, in the English Channel. It is today only a hundred and fifty years ago since one of these Algerine craft was wrecked near Penzance in the early autumn.

We mentioned just now the Act of George III which required craft to be licensed. This was another of the various means employed for the prevention of smuggling, and since the passing of this Act those luggers and cutters which engaged in the running of goods endeavored to evade the Act's penalties by possessing themselves of foreign colors and foreign ship's papers. Now, as a fact, by far the greater part of such craft belonged to Deal, Folkestone, and other south-coast ports of England. Their masters were also from the same localities, and very few of them could speak Dutch or French. But for the purpose of evading the English law they got themselves made burghers of Ostend, and notwithstanding that their crews were for the most part English they designated their craft as foreign.

During the year 1785 it happened that two of these pseudo-foreign smuggling craft were chased by an English frigate. Owing to the fact that the frigate had no pilot on board, one of these vessels escaped, but the other, after a chase lasting five hours, realized that she would soon be overhauled. Her master, therefore, threw overboard his cargo as the frigate fast approached, and in company with a number of his crew took to his large boat. The lugger, after no fewer than twenty shots had been fired at her, hove-to. On taking possession of the lugger and examining her papers it appeared that her master's name was the very English-sounding Thomas March, and yet he described himself as a burgher of Ostend, the vessel being owned by a merchant. The master's excuse was that he was a pilot-boat cruising with a number of pilots on board, and for this reason it was decided to give him the benefit of the doubt and not detain him. But the frigate's captain had noticed that before the lugger had hove-to during the evening a part of the cargo had been thrown overboard. The following morning, therefore, he proceeded on board a Revenue cutter, "went into the track where the cargo was thrown overboard," and was able to find just what he had expected, for he located and drew out of the sea no fewer than 700 half-ankers of foreign spirits.

This precedent opened up an important question; for if a neutral vessel, or indeed any craft similarly circumstanced as the above, were to anchor off the English coast it was hardly possible to detect her in running goods, as it seldom took more than an hour to land a whole cargo, owing to the great assistance which was given from the people on the shore. For, as it was officially pointed out, as soon as one of these vessels was sighted, 300 people could usually be relied on with 200 or more carts and wagons to render the necessary service. Therefore the commanders of the cutters sought legal advice as to how they should act on meeting with luggers and cutters without Admiralty passes on the English coast but more or less protected with foreign papers and sailing under foreign colors.

The matter was referred to the Attorney-General, who gave his opinion that vessels were forfeitable only in the event of their being the property in whole or part of his Majesty's subjects; but where the crew of such a vessel appeared all to be English subjects, or at any rate the greatest part of them, it was his opinion that there was a sufficient reason for seizing the vessel if she was near the English coast. She was then to be brought into port so that, if she could, she might prove that she belonged wholly to foreigners. "A British subject," continued the opinion, "being made a burgher of Ostend does not thereby cease to be a subject. Vessels hovering within four leagues of the British coast, with an illicit cargo, as that of this vessel appears to have been, are forfeited whether they are the property of Britons or foreigners."

It was not once but on various occasions that the Customs Board expressed themselves as dissatisfied with the amount of success which their cruisers had attained in respect of the work allotted to them.

At the beginning of the year 1782 they referred to "the enormous increase of smuggling, the outrages with which it is carried on, the mischiefs it occasions to the country, the discouragement it creates to all fair traders, and the prodigious loss the Revenue sustains by it." The Board went on to state that "diligent and vigorous exertions by the cruising vessels employed in the service of the Customs certainly might very much lessen it." The Commissioners expressed themselves as dissatisfied with the lack of success, and ordered that the officers of the Waterguard were especially to see that the commander and mate of every Revenue vessel or boat bringing in a seizure were actually on board when such seizure was made.

A few days later—the date is January 16, 1788—the Board, received information that great quantities of tobacco and spirits were about to be smuggled in from France, Flanders, Guernsey, and Alderney. They warned the Preventive officers of the various ports, and directed the commanders of the Admiralty cruisers, which happened to be stationed near the ports, to be especially vigilant to intercept "these attempts of the illicit dealers, so that the Revenue may not be defrauded in those articles to the alarming degree it has hitherto been." The officers were bluntly told that if they were to exert themselves in guarding the coast night and day such fraudulent practices could not be carried on in the shameful manner they now were. "And though the Riding officers may not always have it in their power to seize the goods from a considerable body of smugglers, yet if such officers were to keep a watchful eye on their motions, and were to communicate early information thereof to the Waterguard, they may thereby render essential service to the Revenue."

When the soldiers assisted the Revenue officers in making seizures on shore it was frequently the case that the military had difficulty in recovering from the Revenue men that share of prize-money which was their due. The Collector of each port was therefore directed in future to retain in his hands out of the officers' shares of seizures so much as appeared to be due to the soldiers, and the names of the latter who had rendered assistance were to be inserted in the account of the seizures sent up to headquarters. But the jealousy of the military's aid somehow never altogether died out, and ten years after the above order there was still delay in rendering to the army men their due share of the seizures.

The commanders of the Revenue cruisers were told to keep an especial watch on the homeward-bound East Indiamen to prevent "the illicit practices that are continually attempted to be committed from them." Therefore these cruisers were not only to watch these big ships through the limits of their own station, but also to keep as near them when under sail as possible, provided this can be done with safety and propriety. But when the East Indiamen come to anchor the cruisers are also to anchor near them, and compel all boats and vessels coming from them to bring-to in order to be examined. They are "then to proceed to rummage such boats and vessels. And if any goods are found therein they are to be seized, together with the boats in which they are found." The importance of this very plain instruction is explained by the further statement that "some of the commanders of the cruisers in the service of the Revenue endeavor to shun these ships, and thereby avoid attending them through their station."

On Christmas Eve of 1784 the Customs Commissioners sent word to all the ports saying that they suspected that there were a good many vessels and boats employed in smuggling which were thus liable to forfeiture. Therefore, within forty-eight hours from the receipt of this information sent by letter, a close and vigorous search was to be made by the most active and trusty officers at each port into every bay, river, creek, and inlet within the district of each port, as well as all along the coast, so

The Fine Art of Smuggling:

as to discover and seize such illegal vessels and boats. And if there were any boats quartered within the neighborhood of each port, timely notice of the day and hour of the intended search was to be sent by the Collector and Controller in confidence to the commanding officer only, that he might hold his soldiers in readiness.

Yet, again the Board exhorted the Revenue officers "to exert yourselves to the utmost of your power... and as it is very probable that the places where such boats and vessels are kept may be known to the officers who have long resided at your port, you are to acquaint such officers that if they value their characters or employments, or have any regard to the solemn oath they took at their admission, we expect they will, on this occasion, give the fullest and most ample information of all such places, and will cheerfully afford every other aid and assistance in their power, to the end that the said vessels and boats may be discovered and seized.

"And to prevent them from being launched into the water, and carried off by the smugglers after seizure, you are to cause one of the streaks (i.e., strakes) or planks to be ripped off near the keel, taking care at the same time to do as little other injury to each boat as possible."

We now come to witness the reappearance of an old friend of whom we last made mention in the North Sea. The year we are now to consider is 1788, and the 15th of July. On that day H.M. cutter *Kite* was sailing from Beachy Head to the westward. She passed to the southward of the Isle of Wight without sighting it, as the weather was thick. Later in the day it cleared as they got near to the Dorsetshire coast, and about 7:30 P.M., when they were between Peveril Point (near Swanage) and St. Alban's Head, and it was clearer and still not night, the ship's surgeon discovered a vessel some distance away on the weather bow.

The weather had now cleared so much that the house on the top of St. Alban's Head was quite visible. The surgeon called the attention of a midshipman on board to the strange vessel. The midshipman, whose name was Cornelius Quinton, took a bearing, and found that the stranger bore W.S.W. from the cutter, and was steering E.S.E. He also took a bearing of Peveril Point, which bore N.1/2W., and judged the smuggler to be about 9 miles from Peveril Point.

About 8 o'clock the cutter began to give chase, and this continued until 11 P.M., the course being now S.E. After a time the lugger hauled up a point, so that she was heading S.E. by S., the wind being moderate S.W. During the chase the lugger did her best to get away from the cutter, and set her main topsail. The cutter at the time was reefed, but when she saw the lugger's topsail going up she shook out her reefs and set her gaff topsail. It was some little time before the *Kite* had made up her mind that she was a smuggler, for at first she was thought to be one of the few Revenue luggers which were employed in the service. About 11 o'clock, then, the *Kite* was fast overhauling her, notwithstanding that the lugger, by luffing up that extra point, came more on the wind and so increased her pace. It was at first a cloudy night—and perhaps that may have made the *Kite's* skipper a little nervous, for he could hardly need to be reefed in a moderate breeze—but presently the sky cleared.

As the *Kite* approached she hoisted her signals and fired a musket shot.[1] But in spite of these signals, which every seafaring man of that time knew very well meant that the pursued vessel was to heave-to, the lugger still held on and took no notice. After that the *Kite* continued to fire several times from her swivel guns. Later still, as the *Kite* came closer, the latter hailed her and requested her to lower her sails, informing her at the same time that she was a King's cutter.

Still the lugger paid no heed, so the cutter now fired at her with muskets. It was only after this that the lugger, seeing her chance of escape was gone, gave up, lowered sail, wore round, and came under the Kite's stern. The cutter hoisted out a boat, the midshipman already mentioned was sent aboard the lugger, and the latter's master was brought to the *Kite*, when whom should they find to be their prisoner but David Browning, better known as "Smoker," of North Sea fame? When the *Kite's* captain asked for his papers "Smoker" replied that he had no papers but a bill of sale. He was afterwards heard to remark that if he had understood the log line he would not have been so near the land as he was, and admitted he had been bound for Flushing, having doubtless just landed a cargo on the beach.

The lugger was found to be decked and clinker-built with a running bowsprit on which she set a jib. Six carriage guns were also found on board, mounted on her deck. Four of these guns were observed to be loaded, three with powder and one with shot, and they were 4-pounders. After the capture was made the two vessels lay for a time hove-to on the heaving sea under the star-specked sky. The lugger was then put in charge of the midshipman and a prize crew from the cutter, the prisoners being of course taken on board the *Kite*. Both lugger and cutter then let draw their sails, and set a course N.E. for the Isle of Wight until 2 A.M. As it then came on thick the vessels hove-to until daylight, when sail was made again, the lugger being sent on ahead to sound, so as to see how near they were approaching the Isle of Wight.

Later on they found themselves in 12 fathoms and judged themselves to be near the Owers. Eventually, having steered about N.N.E. and sighted Chichester Church in the distance, they went about and stood south, the wind having veered to W.N.W., and at 3:30 P.M. let go anchor in Spithead. Browning in due time appeared in Court, and a verdict was given for the King, so that at last this celebrated smuggler had been caught after many an exciting chase.

---

[1] As there is a good deal of confusion existing concerning the signals of the old Revenue cutters, it is worth noting that although it was night these signals were displayed. I make this statement on the unimpeachable sworn evidence of the *Kite's* crew, so the matter cannot be questioned.

The Fine Art of Smuggling:

It was not many years after this incident that a 70-ton cutter named the *Charming Molly* arrived at Portsmouth. A Customs officer went on board her and found a man named May, who produced the key of the spirit-room, saying he was master of the ship. In the spirit-room the Customs officer found a hogshead of gin containing 62 gallons. May was anxious to show that this was quite legitimate, as there were sixteen men aboard and the contents of this cask were for their use.

The Customs officer now inquired if there was any more liquor on the ship, and May replied in the negative, at first. The officer then said he would search the cabin, whereupon May added that there was a small cask which he had picked up at sea and had kept for the crew's use. This cask was found in May's own state-room, and contained about three gallons of brandy, though it was capable of holding another gallon and no doubt had recently done so. However, May now said that that was the entire lot, and there was not a drop of anything else on board.

Yet again the officer was not to be put off, and found in the state-room on the larboard side a place that was locked. May then explained that this locker belonged to a man named Sheriff, who was at present ashore, and had the key with him. However May volunteered, if the officer saw fit, to open it, but at the same time assured him there was no liquor therein. The officer insisted on having it broken open, when there were discovered two new liquor cases containing each twelve bottles of brandy, making in all eight gallons, and two stone bottles of brandy containing five gallons. Even now May assured the officer that he had no more in the ship, but after a further search the officer found twelve dozen bottles of wine in a locked locker in the cabin.

We need not follow this case any further, but as a fine example of deliberate lying it is hard to beat. Throughout the exciting career of a smuggler, when chased or captured, in running goods by night or stealing out to get clear of the land before the sun came up, this one quality of coolness in action or in verbal evasion ever characterized him. He was so frequently and continuously face to face with a threatening episode that he became used to the condition.

CHAPTER EIGHT
Preventive Organization

We have already frequently referred to the Riding officers who were attached to practically all the chief ports of England. For the reasons already given the southeast coast had especially to be well provided in this respect. And, because of the proximity to the Isle of Man, the Solway Firth had also to be protected efficiently by these officers, additional, of course, to the aid rendered by the cruisers. Wales, however, seems to have been left practically unprotected. In the year 1809 there was inaugurated what was known as the Preventive Waterguard in order to supplement the endeavors of the cruisers and Riding officers. Under this arrangement the coast of England and Wales was divided into three districts, each of which was under an Inspecting Commander, the Revenue cruisers being now included in the Preventive Waterguard.

The three districts with the three Inspecting Commanders were as follows:

District 1.—Land's End to the Port of Carlisle inclusive. Inspecting Commander, Captain John Hopkins.

District 2.—North Foreland to Land's End. Inspecting Commander, Captain William Blake.

District 3.—North Foreland to the Port of Berwick inclusive. Inspecting Commander, Captain John Sayers, "whose duty it is constantly to watch, inspect, and report to us [the Customs Board] upon the conduct of the Commanders of Cruisers and the Sitters of Preventive Boats along the district."

It was because they required a more effective control and inspection of the officers employed in preventing and detecting smuggling that this new organization was made. Certain stations were also allotted to the commanders of the cruisers, within each district—two to each station—and the stations and limits were also appointed for Preventive boats. The "sitters" of the Preventive boats were those who sat in the stern of these open, rowed craft and acted in command of them.

The Collector and Controller were also addressed in the following terms, which showed that the Board were still doing their utmost to rid the service of the inefficiency and negligence to which we have had occasion to draw attention. "You are to observe," wrote the Commissioners, "that one material object of the duty imposed upon the Inspecting Commanders is to see that the cruisers are constantly and regularly on their stations, unless prevented by some necessary and unavoidable cause, and with their proper complements of men and boats, and if they are off their station or in port personally to examine into the occasion of their being so, and that they are absent from their station no longer than is essentially requisite."

At the end of every year the Inspecting Commanders were to lay before the Board of Customs the conduct of the several officers within their district and the state in which smuggling then was, and "whether on the progress or decline, in what articles, and at what places carried on." For the Board was determined "to probe the conduct of the Preventive officers and punish them" for any laxity and negligence, for which faults alone they would be dismissed. And in order that the vigilance and faithful duty in the commanders and officers on board the cruisers "may not be deprived of fair and due reward" their rate of pay was now increased, together with some addition made to the allowance for victualing, "and also to provide for the certainty of an annual emolument to a fixed amount in respect to the commanders and mates, by the following regulations:"

INSPECTING CRUISERS

Commander, each per annum, £200 to be made up to £500 net.
1st Mates, each per annum, £75 to be made up to £150 net.
2nd Mates, each per annum, £50 to be made up to £75 net.

But these increases were conditional on their salaries, shares of seizures and penalties, and all other emoluments of that description not having amounted to the salaries now offered. The deputed mariners were to have £3 or £5 each, per lunar month. Mariners who had no deputation were to have £3 a month, boys on the cruisers £10 per annum. As to victualing, the commanders and mates were to have 3s. each per diem, mariners 1s. 6d. each per diem. Fire and candle for each person were to be allowed for at the rate of 1s. 6d. per lunar month.

Under each Inspecting Commander were to be two tenders in each district, and the mates who were acting as commanders of these were to have their existing £75 a year raised to £150 net in case their salaries, shares of seizures, and other emoluments of that description should not amount to these sums. Deputed mariners, mariners, boys, victualing, fire, and candle were all to be paid for just as in the case of the inspecting cruisers above mentioned. This was to date from October 10, 1809. A few months later a similar improvement was made in the salaries of cruisers in general, for from the 5th of January 1810, commanders of these were to have their £100 per annum raised to £250 net—the above conditions "in case their salaries, shares of seizures, etc." did not make up this amount being also here prevalent—whilst first mates were to be raised from £60 to £100 net. If second mates were carried they were to have £50 per annum, deputed mariners £5 per annum and £2, 10s. per lunar month. Mariners were to have £2, 10s. per lunar month each, boys £10 per annum. Victualing, fire, and candle to be as already stated.

The early years of the nineteenth century showed that the evil of the previous hundred years was far from dead. The Collector at Plymouth, writing to the Board three days before Christmas of 1804, reported that there was a good deal of smuggling done, but that the worst places in his neighborhood were two. Firstly, there was that district which is embraced by Bigbury, the Yealm, and Cawsand. In that locality the smuggling was done in vessels of from 25 to 70 tons. But in summer time the trade was also carried on by open spritsail boats of from eight to ten tons. These craft used to run across from Guernsey loaded with spirits in small casks. Up the river Yealm (just to the east of Plymouth Sound) and at Cawsand Bay the goods were wont to be run by being rafted together at some distance from the shore and afterwards "crept" up (i.e. by means of metal creepers or grapnels). The local smugglers would go out in their boats at low water during the night when the weather and the absence of the cruisers permitted and bring to land their booty. It appeared that 17,000 small casks of spirits were annually smuggled into Cawsand and the Yealm.

Secondly, the district to the west of Plymouth embracing Polperro and Mevagissey. The smuggling craft which brought goods to this locality were fast sailers of from 80 to 100 tons. But the goods which came into the general district of Plymouth were not carried far inland. Those whose work it was to carry the goods after being landed were known as "porters," and were so accustomed to this heavy work that they could carry a cask of spirits six miles across the country at a good rate. When it is remembered that these casks were made necessarily strong of stout wood, that they contained each from 5 to 7-3/4 gallons, making a total weight of from 70 to 100 lbs. at least, we can realize something of the rude physical strength possessed by these men.

During this same year the Collector at Dartmouth also reported that smuggling had increased a good deal recently in the counties of Devon and Cornwall. The cutters and luggers from Guernsey carried their cargoes consisting of from 400 to 800 ankers of spirits each, with a few casks of port and sherry for the wealthier classes, who winked at the illicit trade, and some small bales of tobacco. During the summer the goods were landed on the north side of Cornwall, between Land's End and Hartland Point, and thence distributed by coasters to Wales and the

The Fine Art of Smuggling:

ports of the Bristol Channel, or carried inland on the backs of twenty or thirty horses, protected by a strong guard. But in the winter the goods were landed on the shores of the Bristol Channel, the farmers coming down with horses and carts to fetch the goods, which were subsequently lodged in barns and caves. Clovelly, Bideford, Combe Martin, and Porlock were especially notorious in this connection.

These goods were also regularly conveyed across Exmoor into Somersetshire, and other goods found a way into Barnstable. Coasters on a voyage from one part of England to another frequently broke their voyages and ran over to Guernsey to get contraband. The Island of Lundy was a favorite smuggling depot in the eighteenth century. From Ireland a good deal of salt was smuggled into Devonshire and Cornwall, the high duties making the venture a very profitable one—specially large cargoes of this commodity being landed near to Hartland Point. And this Dartmouth Collector made the usual complaint that the Revenue cruisers of that period were easily outsailed by the smugglers.

The reader will recollect those regrettable incidents on the North Sea belonging to the eighteenth century, when we had to chronicle the names of Captains Mitchell and Whitehead in that connection. Unhappily there were occasional repetitions of these in the early part of the nineteenth century on the south coast.

It happened that on the 19th of March in the year 1807 the *Swan* Revenue cutter, a vessel of considerable size (for she had a burthen of 154 tons, a crew of twenty-three men, and was armed with twelve 4-pounders, two 9-pounders, and a chest of small arms) was cruising in the English Channel and found herself off Swanage. It should be added that at that time there was a kind of volunteer Preventive Guard at various places along the coast, which was known as the "Sea Fencibles." The Swanage "Fencibles" informed Mr. Comben, the cruiser's commander, that there were three luggers hovering off the coast, and these volunteers offered a number of their men to reinforce the Swan's crew so that the luggers might be captured. To this Comben replied with a damper to the volunteers' enthusiasm: "If I was to take them on board and fall in with the enemy we could not do anything with them."

So the *Swan* sailed away from Swanage Bay to the eastward and at midnight made the Needles. It now fell calm, but the luggers hove in sight and approached by means of their sweeps. As they came on, the cutter, instead of preparing to receive them in the only way they deserved, did nothing. But one of the *Swan's* crew, whose name, Edward Bartlett, deserves to be remembered for doing his duty, asked Comben if he should fetch the grape and canister from below. Comben merely replied: "There is more in the cabin than we shall want. It will be of no use; it is all over with us." Such was the attitude of one who had signed into a service for the prevention of smuggling. Instead of taking any definite action he waited despairingly for the enemy to come on. He then issued no orders to his crew to prepare to engage; he just did nothing and remained inactive under the white cliffs.

But if their commander was a coward, at any rate his crew were determined to make a contest of it. They had actually to urge him to fight, but the luggers were right close on to the cutter before Comben had given the word. After that for three-quarters of an hour the crew fought the ship, and were at their respective quarters when Comben actually turned to the luggers and shouted to them: "Leave off firing; I have struck." During the engagement he had shown great signs of fear and never encouraged his crew to fight.

Seeing that they were led by a coward, the *Swan's* crew also took fright and thought it best to flee. They therefore jumped into the cutter's boats and rowed ashore, leaving their valiant commander to look after the *Swan* as best he might. She was of course immediately captured by the luggers, and as for Comben, he was taken prisoner, carried to France, detained there, and did not return to England for seven years. When an investigation was made into his conduct by the Surveyors-General of the Customs, his defense was that "his men had deserted him." As for the latter, they reached the shore safely and were again employed in the Preventive Service.

It is quite clear that the Customs Board sometimes lent their cutters to the Admiralty; and there is a letter dated October 10, 1809, from the Admiralty, in which permission is given for the cutters in the service of that Revenue to be released from their station at Flushing under the command of Rear-Admiral Sir Richard Strachan. There is also a Customs House minute of July 7, 1806, to the effect that the *Swan* and *Hound* Revenue cutters might be placed under the orders of Lord Keith in the room of the *Stag* and *Swallow*, for use at Cowes and Shoreham, where these cruisers were to be stationed.

It was in this same year that the Board again emphasized the importance of the Revenue Service being supported by the Navy and Army, and that to this end the most effective encouragement should be held out to both branches, so that they might co-operate vigorously in the suppression of smuggling. They further expressed themselves of the opinion that "nothing will more effectually tend to encourage them to exert themselves than the certainty of receiving a speedy reward." And yet, again, were the Revenue officers enjoined "to be particularly careful to secure the men employed in smuggling vessels whenever it may be possible to effect it, as their lordships have the strongest reasons for believing that the apprehension of being detained and impressed into his Majesty's service will have a great effect in deterring the persons engaged in these illegal pursuits from continuing their pernicious habits."

It was also part of the duty of the Customs officers to attend to the Quarantine, and the Customs Board resolved "that it is fit to direct a distinguishing flag to be used on board all boats employed in the Quarantine service." At Sandgate Creek, Portsmouth, Falmouth, Bristol, Milford, Hull, Liverpool and Plymouth, by the advice of the Surveyor for Sloops, a flag was deposited in the Custom House at every port of the kingdom, and it was resolved that in the above ports there should be two, except

The Fine Art of Smuggling:

Plymouth, which should have three. Cruisers were also employed in the Quarantine Service.

We have already seen something of the conditions of service and the pay of the cruisers' crews. He who was responsible for the upkeep and supervision of these cruisers was known as the Surveyor for Sloops.

For some time the Customs Board had been deliberating as to the adoption of some regulations for ascertaining the qualifications of those who desired to be commanders and mates of the cruisers. That some improvement was essential must already have been made clear to the reader from the type of men who sometimes were placed in such positions of responsibility. The following regulations were therefore adopted in the year 1807, "which appear to the Commissioners highly necessary for the safe conduct of the Service, as also for the safety of the vessels and crews committed to their charge." They resolved accordingly:

> That all persons who shall be hereafter nominated to the situation of Commander or Mate of a Cruiser in the service of this Revenue, do attend the Surveyor of Sloops, etc. in London for the purpose of being examined on the several points submitted in the report of the said Surveyor, as essential for the qualification of officers of that description, namely, whether he understand navigation, is competent to lay off and ascertain courses and distances on the charts, can work a day's work and find the time of high and low water in any port of great Britain, and understand the use of a quadrant.

It was also further resolved:

> That no person be admitted to either of those situations who shall not be certified by the said Surveyors to be fully qualified in the particulars above referred to, which certificate is to be laid before the Board for their consideration, whether in case such person does not possess a competent knowledge of the coast on which he is to be stationed, or is not sufficiently acquainted with the sailing and management of cutters and luggers tho' generally qualified, it may not be fit to direct him to repair on board some cruiser, whose station is contiguous to that to which he is nominated, and cruise in such vessel for the space of one month, or until the commander thereof shall certify that he is thoroughly acquainted with that part of the coast, and also be fully competent to take charge of a cutter, or lugger, as the case may be, such a certificate to be referred to the Surveyor for Sloops, etc. for his report previous to such commander's or mate's commission being ordered to be made out." And the commanders of the cutters who shall be ordered to instruct such persons are to be acquainted that they are at liberty to crave the extra expense they shall incur for victualing such persons for the Board's consideration.

And the Surveyor for Sloops, etc. is to report more particularly the nature and objects of enquiry as to the qualification of persons nominated Sitters of Boats and by what officers in the outports those enquiries are made and the qualification of such persons certified: for the Commissioners' further consideration, as to any additional regulations in respect of persons so nominated.

It was, no doubt, because of such incidents as those which we have seen occurring in the Channel and North Sea that the Commissioners tightened up the regulations in the above manner. That these incidents were not confined to any particular locality let us show by the two following examples.

The first had reference to William Horn, the Deputed Mariner and Acting Mate of the Revenue cutter *Greyhound*, whose station was at Weymouth. On the 5th of March 1806 he was in charge of the cutter whilst on a cruise to the westward. Off Portland the cutter fell in with a French lugger, which was a privateer. Horn gave chase, gradually overhauled her, and even came up with her. For a time he also engaged her, but because he subsequently gave up the fight, bore up and quitted her, allowing the privateer to escape, he was deemed guilty by the Customs Board of not having used his utmost endeavors to effect a capture, and was ordered to be superseded.

The second incident was of a slightly more complicated nature, and occurred on October 20, 1805, about midnight. The two men implicated were a Captain Riches, who was in command of the Revenue cutter *Hunter*, and his mate Oliver.

This vessel, whose station was Great Yarmouth, was on the night mentioned cruising in the North Sea. Presently the cutter sighted what turned out to be the Danish merchant ship, *The Three Sisters*, Fredric Carlssens master, from Copenhagen bound for St. Thomas and St. Croix. Oliver got into the cutter's boat and boarded the Dane. He also demanded from the latter and took from him four cases of foreign Geneva, which was part of *The Three Sisters'* cargo. In spite of Carlssen's opposition, Oliver put these into his boat and rowed off with them to the *Hunter*. Riches was obviously party to this transaction, and was accused "that contrary to the solemn oath taken at his admission into office, he did not only neglect to report to the Collector and Controller of Yarmouth or to the Board the misconduct of his Mate, in unlawfully taking from the said ship the four cases of Geneva in question, but did take out of them for his own use, and by so doing did connive at and sanction the aforesaid unproper conduct of his Mate." It was also brought against Riches that he had not entered any account of this incident into his ship's journal, or made any record of the mate boarding the Dane.

In the end Riches was adjudged by the Board guilty of not giving information regarding his mate's conduct and of receiving one case of Geneva for his own use, but he was acquitted of connivance for want of evidence. He was found guilty also of not having entered the incident in his journal. Oliver was acquitted of having boarded the Danish ship for want of proof, but found guilty of having failed to keep a complete journal of his proceedings. But a further charge was made that Riches caused a case of foreign spirits, which had been taken out of the Danish ship, to be brought ashore from the cutter and taken to his home at Yarmouth without paying the duty thereon. Oliver was also accused of a similar crime with regard to two cases. Riches was acquitted for want of proof of having caused the gin to be taken to his house, but found guilty of having received it, knowing the duty had not been paid. Oliver was also found guilty, and both were accordingly dismissed.

And there was the case of a man named Thomas Rouse, who was accused of having been privy to the landing of a number of large casks of spirits and other goods from a brig then lying off the Watch-house at Folkestone. This was on the night of May 20 and the early hours of May 21, 1806. He was further accused of being either in collusion with the smugglers in that transaction or criminally negligent in not preventing the same. It was still further brought against him that he had not stopped and detained the master of the brig after going on board, although the master was actually pointed out to him by a boat's crew belonging to the *Nimble* Revenue cutter. Rouse was found guilty of the criminal negligence and ordered to be dismissed. And, in addition, the chief boatmen, five boatmen, and two riding-officers of the Preventive Service at that port were also dismissed for failing to do their utmost to prevent this smuggling, which had, in fact, been done collusively.

Those were certainly anxious times for the Customs Commissioners, and we cannot but feel for them in their difficulties. On the one hand, they had to wrestle with an evil that was national in its importance, while on the other they had a service that was anything but incorruptible, and required the utmost vigilance to cause it to be instant in its elementary duties.

One of the reforms recommended towards the end of 1809 had reference to the supply of stores and the building and repairing of Custom House boats in London. The object aimed at was to obtain a more complete check on the quantities and quality of the stores required for cruisers and Preventive boats. And the example of the outports was accordingly adopted that, when articles were required for these craft that were of any value, the Collector and Controller of the particular port first sent estimates to the Board, and permission was not allowed until the Surveyor of Sloops had certified that the estimates were reasonable. Nor were the bills paid until both the commander and mate of the cruiser, or else the Tide Surveyor or the Sitter of the Boat, as the case might be, had certified that the work was properly carried out. And the same rule applied to the supply of cordage and to the carrying out of repairs.

As one looks through the old records of the Custom House one finds that a Revenue officer who was incapable of yielding to bribery, who was incorruptible and vigilant in his duty, possessed both courage and initiative, and was favored with even moderate luck, could certainly rely on a fair income from his activities.

In the year we are speaking of, for instance, Thomas Story, one of the Revenue officers petitioned to be paid his share of the penalty recovered from William Lambert and William Taylor for smuggling, and he was accordingly awarded the sum of £162, 2s. It was at this time also that the salaries of the Collectors, Controllers, and Landing Surveyors of the outports were increased so that the Collectors were to receive not less than £150 per annum, the Controller not less than £120, and the Landing Surveyor not less than £100. And in addition to this, of course, there were their shares in any seizures that might be made.

Sometimes, however, the Revenue officers suffered not from negligence but from excess of zeal, as, for instance, on that occasion when they saw a rowing-boat containing a couple of seafaring men approach and land on the beach at Eastbourne. The Revenue officials were quite certain that these were a couple of smugglers and seized their boat. But it was subsequently discovered that they were just two Portuguese sailors who had escaped from Dieppe and rowed all the way across the Channel. The Admiralty interfered in the matter and requested the release of the boat, which was presently made. But two other Revenue officers, named respectively Tahourdin and Savery, in August of 1809 had much better luck when they were able to make a seizure that was highly profitable.

We have already referred to the considerable exportation which went on from this country in specie and the national danger which this represented. In the present instance these two officials were able to seize a large quantity of coin consisting of guineas, half guineas, and seven shilling pieces, which were being illegally transported out of the kingdom. When this amount came to be reckoned up it totaled the sum of £10,812, 14s. 6d., so that their share must have run into very high figures.

CHAPTER NINE
Cutters' Equipment

In an earlier chapter we quoted a passage from Marryat which showed that the mariners of a Revenue cutter were dressed in red flannel shirts and blue trousers, and also wore canvas or tarpaulin petticoats. The reason for the latter was appreciated by smuggler and Preventive men alike, and if you have ever noticed the Thames River Police dodging about in their small craft you will have noticed that at any rate the steersman has in cold weather some sort of apron wrapped round his legs. But in the period of which we are now speaking the attached apron or petticoat was very useful for keeping the body warm in all weather, especially when the sitter of the Preventive boat had to be rowed out perhaps in the teeth of a biting wind, for several miles at night. And the smugglers found their task of landing tubs through the surf a wet job, so they were equally glad of this additional protection.[1]

The period to which Marryat referred was the end of the eighteenth century. As to the uniform of the Revenue officers we have the following evidence. Among the General Letters of the Customs Board was one dated June 26, 1804, from which it is seen that the commanders of the cruisers petitioned the Board for an alteration in their uniform and also

---

[1] The use of the petticoat as a seaman's article of attire dates back to the time of Chaucer:

        A Shipman was ther, woning fer by weste:
        For aught I woot, he was of Dertemouthe.
        He rood up-on a rouncy, as he couthe,
        In a gowne of falding to the knee.
        ("Falding" was a coarse cloth.)

that of the mates, this alteration to be made at the expense of the officers. The commanders suggested for their own dress:

A silver epaulette, the button-holes worked or bound with silver twist or lace, side-arms, and cocked hats with cockades, and the buttons set on the coat three and three, the breeches and waistcoats as usual:

For the undress, the same as at present.

For the mates, the addition of lapels, the buttons set on two and two, and cocked hats with cockades.

The Board consented to these alterations with the exception of the epaulettes, "the adoption of which we do not approve, lest the same should interfere with His Majesty's Naval Service."

Now in reading this, it is important to bear in mind that between the Revenue and Navy there was a great deal of jealousy.[1] It went so far, at least on one occasion, as to cause a Naval officer to go on board a Revenue cutter and haul the latter's flag down. The reason these epaulettes were disallowed may be explained by the fact that it was only nine years before the above date that epaulettes had become uniform in the Navy, for notwithstanding that epaulettes had been worn by officers since 1780, yet they were not uniform until 1795, although they were already uniform in the French and Spanish navies.[2]

Since, therefore, these adornments had been so recently introduced into the Navy, it was natural that, with so much jealousy existing, this feature should not be introduced into the Revenue service. Just what "the undress, the same as at present" was I have not been able to discover, but in the Royal Navy of that time the undress uniform for a captain of three years' post consisted of a blue coat, which was white-lined, with blue lapels and cuffs, a fall-down collar, gold-laced button-holes, square at both ends, arranged regularly on the lapels. For a captain under three years the uniform was the same, except that the nine buttons were arranged on the lapels in threes. For master or commander it was the same, except that the button-holes were arranged by twos.[3]

It was in January 1807 that the Customs Board took into consideration the appointment of several Revenue cruisers and the expediency of one general system for manning them according to the tonnage and construction of the vessel, and the service and station on which she was to be employed. They therefore distinctly classed the different cruisers according to their tonnage, description, and number of men originally allowed and since added, whether furnished with letters of marque or not. And believing that it would be beneficial to the service that the complement of men should be fixed at the highest number then allotted to cutters in

---

[1] See Appendix VIII

[2] See Captain Robinson's, *The British Fleet*, p. 503.

[3] Ibid., p. 502.

each respective class, they accordingly instructed the commanders of the different cruisers to increase their respective complements "with all practicable dispatch."

We now come to an important but uncertain point. By a letter dated July 17, 1807, Revenue officers were reminded that they were by law bound to hoist the Revenue colors and fire a gun as a signal "before they in any case fire on any smuggling vessel or boat."

"We direct you to convene the officers of the Waterguard belonging to your port," write the Commissioners to the Collector and Controller at each station, "including the officers and crew of the cruiser stationed there, and strictly to enjoin them whether on board cruisers or boats in no instance to fire on any smuggling vessel or boat, either by night (whether it be dark or light), or by day, without first hoisting the colors and firing a gun as a signal, as directed by law, and to take care that on any boat being sent out armed either from the shore or from a cruiser, in pursuit of seizures or any other purpose, such boat be furnished with a proper flag."

Two years later, on April 11, 1809, it was decided that cruisers could legally wear a pendant "conformable to the King's Proclamation of the 1st January 1801," when requiring a vessel that was liable to seizure or examination to heave-to, or when chasing such a vessel, but "at no other time." It is important to bear in mind that the flags of chase were special emblems, and quite different from the ceremonial flags borne on the Customs buildings, hulks, and vessels not actually used in the chasing of smugglers.

In addition to my own independent research on this subject I am indebted for being allowed to make use of some manuscript notes collected by Mr. Atton, Librarian of the Custom House. In spite of the unfortunate gaps which exist in the historical chain, the following is the only possible attempt at a connected story of the Custom House flag's evolution.

We have already explained that from the year 1674 to 1815 the Revenue Preventive work was under a mixed control. We have also seen that in the year 1730 the Board of Customs called attention to the Proclamation of December 18, 1702, that no ships were to wear a pendant except those of the Royal Navy, but that the sloops employed in the several public offices might wear Jacks with the seal of the respective office.

From a report made by the Harwich Customs in 1726 it is clear that the King's colors were at that date hoisted when a Revenue cruiser chased a suspect. But as to what the "King's Colors" were no one today knows. Among the regulations issued to the Revenue cruisers in 1816 the commanders were informed that they were not to wear the colors used in the Royal Navy, but to wear the same pendants and ensigns as were provided by the Revenue Board.

By 24 George III cap. 47, certain signals of chase were prescribed. Thus, if the cruiser were a Naval vessel she was to hoist "the proper pendant and ensign of H.M. ships." If a Custom House vessel she was to

The Fine Art of Smuggling:

hoist a blue Customs ensign and pendant "with the marks now used." If an Excise vessel, a blue ensign and pendant "with the marks now used." After this had been done, and a gun fired (shotted or unshotted) as a warning signal, she might fire if the smuggler failed to heave-to. And this regulation by the Customs Consolidation Act of 1876 is still in force, and might today be made use of in the case of an obstinate North Sea cooper.

What one would like to know is what were the marks in use from 1784 to 1815. Mr. Atton believes that these marks were as follows:

> At the masthead: a blue pendant with the Union in canton and the Customs badge of office (a castellated structure with portcullis over the entrance, and two barred windows and two portholes, one barred and one open, the latter doubtless to signify that through which the goods might enter) in the fly.
>
> At the gaff: a blue ensign similarly marked.

The English Excise, the Scottish Customs, Scottish Excise, and the Irish Revenue signals of chase were blue pendants and ensigns similarly flown, but as to the badges of office one cannot be certain. The matter of English Customs flags has been obscured by the quotation in Marryat's *The King's Own*, where a smuggler is made to remark on seeing a Revenue vessel's flag, "Revenue stripes, by the Lord." It has been suggested that the bars of the castle port and portcullis in the seal were called "stripes" by the sailors of that day, in as much as they called the East India Company's flag of genuine stripes the "gridiron."

But to me it seems much more likely that the following is the explanation for calling a Revenue cutter's flag "stripes." The signal flags Nos. 7 and 8, which were used by the Royal Navy in 1746 to order a chase both consisted of stripes.[1] No. 7 consisted of eleven horizontal stripes, viz. six red and five white. Flag No. 8 had nine horizontal stripes, viz. red, white, blue repeated three times, the red being uppermost. I submit that in sailor's slang these signals would be commonly referred to as "stripes." Consequently whatever flags subsequently would be used to signal a chase would be known also as "stripes." Therefore whatever signal might be flown in the Revenue service when chasing would be known as "stripes" also.

But by an Order in Council of the 1st of February 1817, the pendant and ensign were to be thus:

> The pendant to have a red field having a regal crown thereon at the upper part next the mast. The ensign to be a red Jack with a Union Jack in a canton at the upper corner next the staff, and with a regal crown in the center of the red Jack. This was to be worn by all vessels employed in the prevention of smuggling under the Admiralty, Treasury, Customs or Excise.

---

[1] I am indebted to a suggestion made on p. 183, Vol. I, No. 7 of *The Mariner's Mirror*.

Now during an interesting trial at the Admiralty Sessions held at the Old Bailey in April of 1825, concerning the chasing of a smuggler by a Revenue cruiser, Lieutenant Henry Nazer, R.N., who was commanding the cutter, stated in his evidence that when he came near this smuggling vessel the former hoisted the Revenue pendant at the masthead, which he described as "a red field with a crown next the mast at the upper part of it." He also hoisted the Revenue ensign at the peak-end, the "Union at the upper corner in a red field," the field of the ensign being also red. It had a Jack in the corner. This, then, was exactly in accordance with the Order in Council of 1817 mentioned above.

But my own opinion relative to the firing of the first gun is in favor of the proposition that this was not necessarily unshotted. I shall refer in greater detail to some actual incidents on a later page, but for now the following is strong proof in favor of this suggestion.

During a trial in the year 1840 (Attorney-General v. William Evans) it transpired that Evans had entered the Medway in a smack without heaving-to, and the following questions and answers respectively were made by counsel and Richard Braddy, a coast-guard who at the time of the incident was on duty at Garrison Fort (*Sheerness*):

Question. "Is the first signal a shot always?"

Answer. "A blank cartridge we fire mostly."

Q. "Did you fire a blank?"

A. "No, because she was going too fast away from me."

Q. "Did you hit her?"

A. "No."

To me it seems certain from this evidence of the coast-guard that though the first signal was "mostly" blank, yet it was not always or necessarily so.

It was frequently discovered that smuggling vessels lay off the coast some distance from the shore and unshipped their cargoes into smaller craft by which they were brought to land. This practice was often observed by the Naval officers at the signal stations. Thus, these smuggling runs might be prevented if those officers were enabled to apprise the Admiralty and Revenue cruisers whenever observed, so the Treasury put themselves in communication with the Customs Board with regard to so important a matter.

In 1807 the Admiralty was requested to specify some signals by which Naval officers stationed at the various signal-posts along the coasts might be able to convey information both to his Majesty's and the Revenue cruisers whenever vessels were observed illegally discharging cargoes. The Admiralty accordingly did as requested, and these signals were sent on to the commanders of the cutters.

This, of course, opened up a new matter in regard to the apportioning of prize-money, and it was decided that when any vessel or goods discharged therefrom should be seized by any of the cruisers in consequence

The Fine Art of Smuggling:

of information given by signal from these stations, and the vessel and her goods afterwards were condemned, one-third of the amount of the King's share was to be paid to the officer and men at the signal-post whence such information was first communicated. The obvious intention of this regulation was to incite the men ashore to keep a smart look-out.

The coast signal-stations[1] had been permanently established in the year 1795, and were paid off at the coming of peace but re-established when the war broke out again, permission being obtained from the owners of the land and a code of signals prepared. The establishment of these signal-stations had been commenced around the coast soon after the Revolutionary war. Those at Fairlight and Beachy Head were established about 1795.[2] Each station was supplied with one red flag, one blue pendant, and four black balls of painted canvas. When the Sea Fencibles, to whom we referred earlier, were established, the signal-stations were placed under the district captains. This was done in March 1798, and the same thing was done when the Sea Fencibles had to be re-established in 1803. The signal-stations at Torbay and New Romney (East Bay, Dungeness) had standing orders, says Captain Hudleston, to report all arrivals and departures direct to the Admiralty.

The Customs Board advanced another step forward when, in the year 1808, they considered whether "benefit might not arise to the service by establishing certain signals by which the commanders of the several cruisers in the service of the Revenue might be enabled to make their vessels known to each other, on meeting at sea, or to distinguish each other at a distance, and also to make such communications as might be most useful, as well as to detect any deception which might be attempted to be practiced by the masters of vessels belonging to the enemy, or of smuggling vessels." They therefore consulted "the proper officers on the subject," and a code of tabular signals was drawn up and approved and sent to the commanders of the cruisers in a confidential manner.

Each commander was ordered to pay the strictest attention to such signals as might be made, and to co-operate by every means in his power. These commanders were also to apprise the Customs Board of any matter which might arise in consequence thereof "fit for our cognizance." These signals were also communicated to the commanders of the several Admiralty cruisers.

We must remember that although naval signaling had in a crude and elementary manner been in vogue in our Navy for centuries, and the earliest code was in existence as far back as 1340, yet it was not until the eighteenth century that it showed any real development. During the early years of the nineteenth century a great deal of interest was taken in the matter by such men as Mr. Goodhew, Sir Home Popham, Captain Mar-

---

[1] See article by Captain R. Hudleston, R.N., in *The Mariner's Mirror*, Vol. I, No. 7.

[2] Victoria County Hist.: Sussex, Vol. II p. 199.

ryat, and others. It was the atmosphere of the French and Spanish wars which gave this incentive, and because the subject was very much in the Naval minds at that time it was natural that the Revenue service should appreciate the advantage which its application might bestow for the prevention of smuggling.

Further means were also taken in the early nineteenth century to increase the efficiency of the cruisers.

In 1811, in order that they should be kept as constantly on station as possible, and that no excuses might be made for delays, it was decided that in the future the Inspecting Commanders of Districts be empowered to incur expenses up to £35 for the repairs which a cutter might need, and £5 for similar repairs to her boats. The commanders of the cruisers were also permitted to incur any expenses up to £20 for the cutter and boats under their command. Such expenses were to be reported to the Board, with information as to why this necessity had arisen, where and by what tradesmen the work had been done, and whether it had been accomplished in the most reasonable manner.

At the end of the following year, in order was given to further prevent the occurrence of two specific situations. The first was cruisers being absent from their stations "at the season of the year most favorable for smuggling practices, and when illegal proceedings are generally attempted," (i.e. in the dark days of autumn and winter and spring). And the second was in order to keep several cutters from being in the Port of London at the same time, "whereby the part of the coast within their respective districts would be left altogether without guard."

The commanders of these cruisers were to give warning when it was apparent that extensive repairs were needed, or a general refit, or any other cause which compelled the craft to come up to London. Timely notice was to be given to the Board so that the necessity and propriety thereof should be inquired into. It was done also with a view to bringing in the cruisers from their respective stations only as best they might be spared consistent with the good of the service. But they were to come to London for such purposes only between April 5 and September 5 of each year. By this means there would always be a good service of cruisers at sea during the bad weather period, when the smugglers were especially active.

In our quotation from *The Three Cutters* in another chapter we gave the colors of the paint used on these vessels. I find an interesting record in the Custom House dated November 13, 1812, giving an order that, to avoid the injury which cruisers sustain from the use of iron bolts, the decks in future were to be fastened with composition bolts, "which would eventually prove a saving to the Revenue." After ordering the commanders to cause their vessels to be payed twice every year either with paint or bright varnish, and not to use scrapers on their decks except after caulking, and then only to remove the unnecessary pitch, the instruction goes on to stipulate the only paint colors which are to be employed for cruisers. These are such as were then allowed in the Navy, viz. black, red, white, or yellow.

But apart from all the manifold difficulties and anxieties, both general and detailed, which arose in connection with these cruisers so long as they were at sea or in the shipwrights' hands, in commission or out of commission, there were others which applied more directly to their crews. Such an incident as occurred in the year 1785 needed very close attention.

In that year the English Ambassador at the Court of France had been informed by Monsieur de Vergennes that parties of sailors belonging to our Revenue cruisers had recently landed near Boulogne in pursuit of some smugglers who had taken to the shore. Monsieur de Vergennes added that if any British sailors or other armed men should be taken in such acts of violence the French Government would unhesitatingly sentence them immediately to be hanged.

Of course the French Government was well within their rights in making such representations for, as natural as it was to chase the smugglers when they escaped ashore, the trespass was indefensible. The Board of Customs therefore instructed their cruisers, as well as those of the Admiralty "whose commanders are furnished with commissions from this Board," to make a note of the matter, so that neither they nor their men might inadvertently expose themselves to the severity of the French laws.

In 1812 one of the mariners belonging to a cruiser happened to go ashore, and while there was seized by the press-gang for his Majesty's Navy. Such an occurrence as this was highly inconvenient not only to the man but to the Board of Customs. So the board resolved that henceforth the commanders of cruisers were not to allow any of their mariners shore leave unless in case of absolute necessity "until the protections which may be applied for shall have been received and in possession of such mariners."

Another matter that required rectification was the practice of taking on board some of their friends and relatives who had no right to be there. Whether this was done for pleasure or profit the carrying of these passengers was deemed to be to the great detriment of the service, and the Board put a stop to it.

It was not merely confined to the cruisers, but the boats and galleys of the Waterguard were just as badly abused. The one exception allowed was, that when officers of the Waterguard were moving from one station to another, they might use such a boat to convey their families with them provided it did not interfere with the duties of the other officers. So also some of the commanders of the cruisers had even taken on board apprentices and been dishonest enough to have them borne on the books as able seamen, and drawn their pay as such. The Board not unnaturally deemed this practice highly improper, and to be discontinued immediately. No apprentices were to be borne on the books except the boy allowed to all cruisers.

After a smuggling vessel's cargo had been seized and it was decided to send the goods to London, it was done by placing the tobacco, spirits, etc., in a suitable coaster and dispatching her to the Thames. But in order to prevent her from being attacked on the sea by would-be rescuers she was ordered to be convoyed by the Revenue cutters. The commander of whatever cruiser was in the neighborhood was ordered "to accompany and guard" her to the Nore or Sea Reach as the case might be.

Every quarter the cruisers were also to send a list of the seizures made, giving particulars of the cruiser—her name, burthen, number of guns, number of men, commander's name, number of days at sea during that quarter, how many days spent in port and why, the quantity of goods and nature of each seizure, the number and names of all smuggling vessels captured, both when and where. There was also to be sent the number of men who had been detained, how they had been disposed of, and if the men had not been detained how it was they had escaped.

"Their Lordships are induced to call for these returns," ran the instruction, "in order to have before them, quarterly, a comparative view of the exertions of the several commanders of the Revenue cruisers... They have determined, as a further inducement to diligence and activity in the said officers, to grant a reward of £500 to the commander of the Revenue cruiser who, in the course of the year ending 1st October 1808, shall have so secured and delivered over to his Majesty's Naval Service the greatest number of smugglers; a reward of £300 to the commander who shall have secured and delivered over the next greatest number, and a reward of £200 to the commander who shall be third on the list in those respects." That was in September of 1887.

During the year ending October 1, 1810, Captain Gunthorpe, commander of the Excise cutter *Viper*, succeeded in handing over to his Majesty's Navy thirteen smugglers whom he had seized. As this was the highest number for that year he thus became entitled to the premium of £500. Captains Curling and Dobbin, two Revenue officers, were together concerned in transferring six men to the Navy, but in as much as Captain Patmour had been able to transfer five men during this same year it was he to whom the £300 were awarded. Captain Morgan of the *Excise* cutter and Captain Haddock of the Custom House cutter *Stag* each transferred four men during that year.

"But my Lords," states a Treasury minute of December 13, 1811, "understanding that the nature of the service at Deal frequently requires the Revenue vessels to co-operate with each other, do not think it equitable that such a circumstance should deprive Messrs. Curling and Dobbin of a fair remuneration for their diligence, and are therefore pleased to direct warrants likewise to be prepared granting to each of those gentlemen the sum of £100."

The Fine Art of Smuggling:

In spite of the above numbers, however, the Treasury was not satisfied, and did not think that the number of men by this means transferred to the Navy had been at all proportionate to the encouragement which they had held out. They therefore altered the previous arrangement so as to embrace only those cases in which the exertions of the cruisers' commanders had been of an exceptionally distinguished nature. Thus during 1812 and the succeeding years, until some further provision might be made, it was decided that "the sum of £500 will be paid to such person commanding a Revenue cutter as shall in any one year transfer to the Navy the greatest number of smugglers, not being less than twenty." The sum of £300 was to be paid to the persons commanding a Revenue cutter who in any year should transfer the next greatest number of smugglers, not being less than fifteen. And £200 were to be paid to the commander who in one year should have transferred the third largest, not being less than ten.

This decision was made in January of 1812, and in the following year it was directed that in future the rewards granted to the commanders of the Revenue cruisers for delivering the greatest number of smugglers should be made not exclusively to the commanders but distributed among the commander, officers, and crew according to the scale which has already been given on an earlier page in this volume. At the end of 1813 it was further decided that when vessels and boats of above four tons measurement were seized in ballast and afterwards broken up, not owing to their build, their construction, or their denomination, but simply because they had been engaged in smuggling, the seizing officers should become entitled to 30s. a ton.

There was also a system instituted in the year 1808 by which the widows of supervisors and surveyors of Riding officers and commanders of cruisers were allowed £30 per annum, with an additional allowance of £5 per annum for each child until he or she reached the age of fifteen. The widows of Riding officers, mates of cutters, and sitters of boats specially stationed for the prevention of smuggling were allowed £25 per annum and £5 for each child until fifteen years old. In the case of the widows of mariners they were to have £15 a year and £2, 10s. for each child until the age of fifteen. And one finds among those thus rewarded Ann Sarmon, the widow, and the three children of the commander of the *Swan* cutter stationed at Cowes; the one child of the mate of the *Tartar* cutter of Dover; the widow of the mate of the *Dolphin of St. Ives*; the widow of the Riding officer at Southampton; the widow and children of the commander of the cutter *Hunter* at Yarmouth; and likewise of the *Hunter*'s mate.

After the 10th of October 1814 the allowance for victualing the crews of the Revenue cruisers was augmented as follows: For victualing commander and mate, 3s. a day each and 1s. 6d. per lunar month for fire and candle. For victualing, fire, and candle for mariners, 1s. 10d. a day each. The daily rations to be supplied to each mariner on board the cruisers were to consist of 1-1/2 lbs. of meat, 1-1/2 lbs. of bread, and two quarts of beer. If flour or vegetables were issued, the quantity of bread was to be reduced, and if cheese were supplied then the amount was to be reduced in proportion to the value and not to the quantity of such articles. And, in order to obtain uniformity, a table of the rations as above was to be fixed up against the fore side of the mast under the deck of the cruiser, and also in some conspicuous place in the Custom House.

Very elaborate instructions were also issued regarding the use of the tourniquet, which "is to stop a violent bleeding from a wounded artery in the limbs until it can be properly secured and tied by a surgeon." The medicine chest of these cruisers contained the following twenty articles: vomiting powders, purging powders, sweating powders, fever powders, calomel pills, laudanum, cough drops, stomach tincture, bark, scurvy drops, hartshorn, peppermint, lotion, Friar's balsam, Turner cerate, basilicon (for healing "sluggish ulcers"), mercurial ointment, blistering ointment, sticking-plaster, and lint.

In short, with its fleet of cruisers well armed and well manned, well found in everything necessary both for ship and crew; with good wages, the offer of high rewards, and pensions; with other privileges second only to those obtainable in the Royal Navy; the Customs Board certainly did their best to make the floating branch of its Preventive service as tempting and efficient as it could possibly be. And that there were not more captures of smugglers was the fault at any rate not of those who had the administration of these cutters.

A very good idea as to the appearance of a nineteenth century Revenue cruiser may be obtained by regarding the accompanying photo-

H.M. Cutter Wickham This shows an early Nineteenth Century King's Cutter (a) running before the wind with square sails and stuns'ls set, (b) on a wind with big jib set.

graphs of his Majesty's cutter *Wickham*. These have been courteously supplied to me by Dr. Robertson-Fullarton of Kilmichael, whose ancestor, Captain Fullarton, R.N., had command of this vessel.

The original painting was made in 1806, and shows a fine, able vessel with ports for seven guns a-side, being painted after the manner of the contemporary men-of-war. To facilitate matters the central portion of the picture has been enlarged, and thus the rigging and details of the *Wickham* can be closely examined. It will be observed that this cutter has beautiful bows with a fine, bold sheer, and would doubtless possess both

H.M. CUTTER WICKHAM Commanded by Captain John Fullarton, R.N. From a contemporary painting in the possession of Dr. Robertson-Fullarton of Kilmichael.

speed and considerable seaworthiness essential for the west coast of Scotland, her station being the Island of Arran. In the picture before us it will be seen that she has exceptionally high bulwarks and appears to have an additional raised deck forward. The yard on which the squaresail was carried when off the wind is seen lowered with its foot-ropes and tackle. The mainsail is of course loose-footed, and the tack is seen well triced up.

Two things especially strike us. First, the smallness of the yard to which the head of the gaff-topsail is laced; and secondly, the great size of the headsail. She has obviously stowed her working jib and foresail and set her balloon jib. When running before a breeze such a craft could set not merely all plain sail, but her squaresail, square-topsail and even stun'sls. Therefore, the smuggling vessel that was being chased needed to be pretty fleet of foot to get away.

Campbeltown in those days was the headquarters of no fewer than seven large Revenue cruisers, all being commanded by naval officers. They were powerful vessels, generally manned by double crews. Each had a smaller craft to act as tender, their chief duties being to intercept those who smuggled salt, spirits, and tea from the Isle of Man.

The officers and men of the cutters made Campbeltown their home, and the houses of the commanders were usually built opposite to the buoys of the respective cutters. The merits of each cutter and officer were the subject of animated discussion in the town, and how "Old Jack Fullarton had carried on" until all seemed to be going by the board on a coast bristling with sunken rocks, or how Captain Beatson had been caught off the Mull in the great January gale, and with what skill he had weathered the headland—these were questions which were the subjects of many a debate among the enthusiasts.

This Captain John Fullarton had in early life served as a midshipman on a British man-of-war. On one occasion he had been sent under Lord Wickham to France on a certain mission in a war-vessel. The young officer's intelligence, superior manners, and handsome appearance so greatly pleased Lord Wickham, that his lordship insisted on having young Fullarton alone to accompany him ashore.

After the mission was over Lord Wickham suggested procuring him some advancement in the service, to which Fullarton replied, "My lord, I am sincerely grateful for your undesired kindness, and for the interest you have been pleased to show in regard to my future prospects. Since, however, you have asked my personal views, I am bound to say I am not ambitious for promotion on board a man-of-war. I have a small property in Scotland, and if your lordship could obtain for me the command of one of his Majesty's cutters, with which I might spend my time usefully and honorably in cruising the waters around my native island of Arran, I should feel deeply indebted to you, and I should value such an appointment above all others."

Soon afterwards, the cutter Wickham was launched, and Mr. Fullarton obtained his commission as captain, the mate being Mr. Donald Fullarton, and most of the crew Arran men.[1]

---

[1] For these details I am indebted to the kindness of Dr. Robertson-Fullarton, who has also called my attention to some information in an unlikely source: *The Memoirs of Norman Macleod*, D.D., by Donald Macleod, 1876.

CHAPTER TEN
The Increase in Smuggling

By an Order in Council, dated September 9, 1807, certain rewards were to be paid to the military for aiding any officer of the Customs in making or guarding any seizure of prohibited "or uncustomed goods." It was further directed that such rewards should be paid as soon as possible, for which purpose the Controllers and Collectors were to appraise with all due accuracy all articles seized and brought to his Majesty's warehouse within seven days of the articles being brought in. The strength of all spirits seized by the Navy or Military was also to be ascertained immediately on their being brought into the King's warehouse, so that the rewards might be immediately paid. The tobacco and snuff seized and condemned were ordered to be sold. But when these articles at such a sale did not fetch a sum equal to the amount of the duty chargeable, then the commodity was to be burnt.

Great exertions were undoubtedly made by the soldiers for the suppression of smuggling, but care had to be taken to prevent wanton and improper seizures. The men of this branch of the service were awarded 40s for every horse that was seized by them with smuggled goods.

Everyone is aware of the fact that, not once but regularly, the smugglers used to signal to their craft at night from the shore as to whether the coast were clear, or whether it were better for the cutter or lugger to run out to sea again. From a collection of authentic incidents I find the following means were employed for signaling purposes:

1. The most common signal at night was to wave a lantern from a hill or some prominent landmark, or from a house suitably situated.

The Fine Art of Smuggling:

2. To take a flint and steel and set fire to a bundle of straw near the edge of a cliff.

3. To burn a blue light.

4. To fire a pistol.

5. All the above were night-signals, but for day-work the craft could signal to the shore or other craft by lowering and raising a certain sail so many times.

There were very many prosecutions for signaling to smuggling craft at many places along the coast. A sentence of six months imprisonment was usually the result. Similarly, the Preventive officers on shore used to fire pistols or burn a blue light in signaling to themselves for assistance. The pistol-firing would then be answered by that of other Customs men in the neighborhood.

In 1805 the Attorney-and Solicitor-General gave the following opinion with regard to signals being given by the friends of smugglers. In effect they said that it was not even necessary for the prosecution to prove that there was at that time a smuggling craft hovering anywhere off the coast. The justice and jury need only be satisfied from the circumstances that the fire was lit for the purpose of giving a signal to some smugglers.

By the summer of 1807 smuggling in England and Wales had increased to what the Commissioners of Customs designated as an "alarming extent." An Act was therefore passed to ensure the more effective prevention of this crime, and once again the Revenue officers were exhorted to perform their duty to its fullest extent. Further, they were threatened with punishment in the case of any dereliction, while rewards were held out as an inducement to zealous action.

Under this new Act powers were given to the Army, Navy, Marines, and Militia to work in concert with each other for the purpose of preventing smuggling, for seizing smuggled goods, and all implements, horses, and persons employed or attempting to bring these ashore. The lack of vigilance, and even the collusion with smugglers, on the part of Revenue officials was still too real to be ignored. Between Dover and Rye, especially, were tobacco, snuff, spirits and tea run into the country to a very considerable extent. And the Government well knew that "in some of the towns on the coast of Kent and Sussex, amongst which are Hastings, Folkestone, Hythe, and Deal, but more especially the latter, the practice of smuggling is carried on so generally by such large gangs of men, that there can exist no hope of checking it but by the constant and most active vigilance of strong military patrols, with parties in readiness to come to their assistance." So wrote Mr. W. Huskisson, Secretary of the Treasury, to Colonel Gordon in August 1807.

The Deal smugglers went to what Mr. Huskisson called "daring lengths," and for this reason the Treasury suggested that patrols should be established within the town of Deal, and for two or three miles east and west of the same. And the Treasury also very earnestly requested from the Commander-in-chief every possible assistance from the Army.

It was observed, also, that so desperate were these smugglers, that even when they had been captured and impressed, they frequently escaped from the men-of-war and returned to their previous life of smuggling. To put a stop to this the Treasury made the suggestion that such men when captured should be sent to ships cruising at distant foreign stations.

Some idea of the violence which was always ready to be used by the smugglers may be gathered by the incident which occurred on the 25th of February 1805. On this day the cutter *Tartar*, in the service of the Customs, and the Excise cutter *Lively* were at 10 P.M. cruising close to Dungeness on the look-out for smuggling craft. They saw a large decked lugger which seemed to them indeed to be a smuggler. If it stayed on its course it would eventually run its nose ashore. So a boat's crew, consisting of men from the *Tartar* and the *Lively*, got out their oars and rowed to the spot where the lugger was evidently about to land her cargo. They brought their boat right alongside the lugger just as the latter took the ground. But the lugger's crew, as soon as they saw the Revenue boat come up to her, promptly scrambled on to the beach. It was noticed that her name was *Diana*, and the Revenue officers had from the first been pretty sure that she was no innocent fishing-vessel, for they had seen flashes from the shore immediately before the *Diana* grazed her keel on to the beach.

Led by one of the two captains out of the cutters, the Revenue men got on board the smuggler and seized her, when she was found to contain a cargo of 665 casks of brandy, 118 casks of rum, and 237 casks of Geneva. Besides these, she had four casks, one case and one basket of wine, 119 bags of tobacco, and 43 lbs. of tea. It was truly a very fine and valuable cargo.

But the officers had not been in possession of the lugger and her cargo more than three-quarters of an hour before a great crowd of infuriated people came down to the beach, armed with firearms and wicked-looking bludgeons. The lugger's crew had evidently rushed to their shore friends and told them of their bad luck. Some members of this mob were on horseback, others on foot, but on they came with oaths and threats to where the lugger and her captors were remaining. "We're going to rescue the lugger and her goods," exclaimed the smugglers, as they stood round the bows of the *Diana* in the darkness of the night. The Revenue men warned them that they had better keep off, or violence would have to be used.

But it was impossible to expect reason from an uncontrolled mob raging with fury and indignation. Soon the smugglers had opened fire, and ball was whistling through the night air. The *Diana* was now lying on her side, and several muskets were leveled at the Revenue men. One of the latter was a man named Dawkins, and the smugglers had got so close that one villainous ruffian presented a piece at Dawkins' breast, though the latter smartly wrested it from him before any injury had been re-

The Fine Art of Smuggling:

A great crowd of infuriated people came down to the beach.

ceived. But equally quickly, another smuggler armed with a cutlass brought the blade down and wounded Dawkins on the thumb.

A general engagement now proceeded as the smugglers continued to fire, but unfortunately the powder of the Revenue men had become wet, so only one of their crew was able to return the fire. Seeing that they were no match for their aggressors, the crews were compelled to leave the lugger and retreat to some neighboring barracks where the Lancashire Militia happened to be quartered, and a sergeant and his guard were requisitioned to strengthen them. With this squad the firing was more evenly returned and one of the smugglers was shot, but before long, unable to resist the military, the smugglers ceased firing and the beach was cleared of the mob.

The matter was in due course reported to the Board of Customs, who investigated the affair and ordered a prosecution of the smugglers. No one had been captured, however, so they offered a reward of £200. That was in the year 1805; but it was not until 1814 that information came into their hands, for no one would come forward to earn the reward.

In 1814, however, a search was made for the wanted men, and two persons, named respectively Jeremiah Maxted and Thomas Gilbert, natives of Lydd, were arrested and put on trial. They were certainly the two ringleaders of that night, and incited the crowd to a frenzy, although these two men did not actually themselves shoot, but they were heard to offer a guinea a man to any of the mob who would assist in rescuing the seized property. Still, in spite of the evidence that was brought against these men, such was the condition of things that they were found not guilty.

King's Cutters vs Smugglers -1700-1855

But it was not always the case that the Revenue men acted with so much vigor, or with so much honesty. It was towards the end of the year 1807 that two of the Riding officers stationed at Newhaven, Sussex, attempted to bribe a patrol of dragoons who were also on duty there for the prevention of smuggling. The object of the bribe was to induce the military to leave their posts for a short period, so that a cargo of dutiable goods, which were expected to arrive soon, might be smuggled ashore without the payment of the Crown's duties.

For such a suggestion to be made by Preventive men was in itself disgraceful, and showed not merely a grossly dishonest purpose but an extraordinary failure of a sense of duty. However, the soldiers, perhaps not altogether displeased at being able to give free rein to some of the jealousies which existed between the Revenue men and the Army, did not respond to the suggestion. Instead they promptly arrested the Riding officers and conducted them to Newhaven. Of these two it was afterwards satisfactorily proved that one had actually offered the bribe to the patrol, but the other was acquitted of that charge. Both, however, were dismissed from the Customs service, while the sergeant and soldiers forming the patrol were rewarded with the sum of £20.

It was not merely the tobacco, spirits, and tea which in the early years of the nineteenth century were being smuggled into the country, although these were the principal articles. In addition to silks, laces, and other goods, the number of gloves which clandestinely came in was so great that the manufacture of English gloves was seriously injured.

By 1811 it was clear that the existing shore arrangements were so ineffective that an entirely new plan was tried for suppressing smuggling. The Riding officers no doubt had a difficult and even dangerous duty to perform, but their conduct left much to be desired. Under the new system, the office of Supervisor or Surveyor of Riding officers was abolished, and that of Inspector of Riding officers was created in its stead. The coast of England was divided into three districts:

No. I - London to Penzance.
No. II - Penzance to Carlisle.
No. III - London to Berwick.

There were seven inspectors appointed, three being for the first district, two for the second, and two for the third. The first district was of course the worst, because it included the English Channel and especially the counties of Kent and Sussex. Hence the greater number of Inspectors. Hence, also, these three officers were given a yearly salary of £180, with a yearly allowance of £35 for the maintenance of a horse. The Inspectors of the other two districts were paid £150 each with the same £35 allowance for a horse. In addition, the Inspectors of all districts were allowed 10s. a day when upon inspections, which were not to last less than 60 days in each quarter in actual movement, "in order by constant and unexpected visitations, strictly to watch and check the conduct of the Riding officers within their allotted station."

The Fine Art of Smuggling:

Under this new arrangement, also, the total number of Riding officers was to be 120, and these were divided into two classes—Superior and Inferior. Their salaries and allowances were as follows:

First District

Superior Riding Officer	£90
Inferior Riding Officer	£75
Allowance for horse	£30

Second And Third Districts

Superior Riding Officer	£80
Inferior Riding Officer	£65
Allowance for horse	£30

The general principle of promotion was to be based on the amount of activity and zeal which were displayed. The Superior Riding officers were to be promoted from the Inferior, and the Inspectors of Districts being promoted from the most zealous of the Superior Riding officers.

And there was, too, a difficulty with regard to the smugglers when they became prisoners.

In the year 1815 there were some smugglers in detention on board one of the Revenue cutters. At that time the cutter's mate was acting as commander, and he was foolish enough to allow some of the smugglers' friends from the shore—themselves of the same trade—to have free communication with two of the prisoners without anyone else being present. The result was that one of the men succeeded in making his escape. As a result of this, smugglers were not permitted to have communication with their friends except in the presence of a proper officer.

There was also a great laxity in the guarding of smugglers sent aboard his Majesty's warships. In several cases the commanders actually declined to receive these men when delivered by the Revenue department. They didn't want the rascals captured by the cutters, and they were not going to take them into their ship's complement. This went on for a time, until the Admiralty sent down a peremptory order that the captains and commanders were to receive these smugglers, and when an opportunity arose they were to send them to the flagship at Portsmouth or Plymouth.

As illustrative of the business-like methods with which the smugglers at this time pursued their calling, the following might be mentioned.

In the year 1814 several of the chief smuggling merchants at Alderney left that notorious island and settled at Cherbourg. But those small craft, which up until then had been wont to run across to the Channel Isles, began instantly to make for the French port instead. From Lyme and Beer in West Bay, from Portland and from the Isle of Wight they sailed, to load up with their illicit cargoes. As soon as they arrived they found, awaiting them in the various stores near the quays, vast quantities of "tubs," as the casks were called. So great was the demand, that several coopers were kept busily employed making new ones.

The English craft were loaded with spirits, hoisted sail and sped away to the English shores, though many there must have been which foundered in bad weather, or, swept on by the dreaded Alderney Race and its seven-knot tide, had an exciting time. Nevertheless, many were followed by the English Revenue cutters, or captured under the red cliffs of Devonshire in the act of taking the tubs ashore. The Customs Board well knew of this change of market to Cherbourg, and lost no time in informing their officers at the different outports and the cruiser-commanders as well.

A large number of the merchant-smugglers from Guernsey at the same time migrated to Coniris, about eight miles from Tregner, in France, and ten leagues east of the Isle of Bas, and twelve leagues S.S.W. from Guernsey. Anyone who is familiar with that treacherous coast, and the strength of its tides, will realize that in bad weather these little craft, heavily loaded as they always were on the return journey, must have been punished pretty severely. Some others, doubtless, foundered altogether and never got across to the Devonshire shores.

Those people who had now settled down at Coniris were those who had previously dealt with the smugglers of Cawsand, Polperro, Mevagissey, and Gerrans. To these places were even sent circular letters inviting the English smugglers to come over to Coniris, just as previously they had come to fetch goods from Guernsey. Another batch of settlers from Guernsey made their new habitation at Roscore (Isle of Bas), from which goods were smuggled into Coverack (near the Lizard), Kedgworth, Mount's Bay, and different places "in the North Channel."

Spirits, besides being brought across in casks and run into the country by force or stealth, were also frequently at this time smuggled in via the French boats which brought vegetables and poultry. In this case the spirits were also in small casks, but the latter were concealed between false bulkheads and hidden below the ballast. But this method was practically a new departure, and began only about 1815.

This was the smuggling-by-concealment method, as distinct from that which was carried on by force and by stealth. We shall have a good deal more to say about this later.

Commanders of cruisers were of course on the look-out for suspected craft, but they were reminded by the Board that they must be careful to make no seizures within three miles of the French and Dutch coasts. That was why, as soon as a suspected vessel was sighted, and a capture was about to be made, some officer on the Revenue cutter was most careful to take cross-bearings and fix his position precisely. If no land was in sight he would reckon the number of leagues the ship had run since the last "fix" had been made.

This information naturally was placed in evidence in the trials when the captured smugglers were being prosecuted. At the same time, it was the business of the defending counsel to do their best to upset the officers reckoning, and prove that the suspected craft was within her proper and legitimate limits.

Another trick which sprang up also about 1815, was that of having the casks of spirits fastened, the one behind the other, in line on a rope. One end of this rope would be passed through a hole at the aftermost end of the keel, where it would be made fast. As the vessel sailed along she would thus tow a whole string of barrels like the tail of a kite, but in order to keep the casks from bobbing above water, sinkers were fastened. Normally, of course, these casks would be kept on board, for the resistance of these objects was very considerable, and lessened the vessel's way. Any one who has trailed even a fairly thick rope astern from a small sailing craft must have been surprised at the difference it made to the speed of the vessel.

But as soon as a Revenue cutter appeared, the end of the rope that was merrily pulling the casks behind was tossed overboard. The cutter would run down to her, and order her to heave-to, which she could afford to do quite willingly. She would be boarded and searched, but the officer would, to his surprise, find nothing at all and be compelled to release her. Away would go the cruiser to chase some other craft, and as soon as she was out of the range of the commander's spy-glass, in would come the tubs again to be stowed dripping in the hold.

This trick was played many a time with success, but at last the cruisers got to hear of the device and the smugglers were caught. I shall in due course illustrate this by an actual occurrence. For now what I want the reader to bear in mind is that, while the age of smuggling by violence and force took a long time to die out, it had reached its zenith about the middle or the last quarter of the eighteenth century. Right until the end of the grand period of smuggling violence was certainly used, but the year 1815 inaugurated a period that was characterized less by force and armed resistance than by artfulness, ingenuity, and all the inventiveness that it is possible to employ on a smuggling craft.

"Smugglers," says Marryat in one of his novels, "do not arm now—the service is too dangerous; they effect their purpose by cunning, not by force. Nevertheless, it requires that smugglers should be good seamen, smart, active fellows, and keen-witted, or they can do nothing.... All they ask is a heavy gale or a thick fog, and they trust to themselves for success." It was after 1816, when the Admiralty reorganized the cruiser service and the Land-guard was tightened up, that the smugglers distinguished themselves by their great skill, resourcefulness, enterprise, and their ability to simply hoodwink the Revenue men.

The wars with France and Spain had come to an end, and the Government could devote her full attention to rectifying the smuggling evil. This increased watchfulness plus the gradual reduction of duties brought the practice of smuggling to such a low point that it became unprofitable, and the increased risks were not equal to the decreased profits. This same principle, at least, is pursued in the twentieth century. No one is so foolish as to try and run whole cargoes of goods into the country without paying Customs duty. But those ingenious persons who smuggle spirits in foot-warmers, saccharine in the lining of hats, tobacco and cigars in false bottoms carry out their plans not by force but by ingenuity and skill.

CHAPTER ELEVEN
The Smugglers at Sea

    Had you been alive and afloat in June of 1802 and been cruising near Falmouth Bay, or taken up a position on the top of one of those glorious high cliffs anywhere between St. Anthony and the Dodman, and remembered to take your spyglass with you, you would have witnessed a very interesting sight. Between those two headlands are two fine bays, named respectively Gerrans and Veryan, while away to the southwest the land runs out to sea until it ends at the Lizard. A whole history could be written of the smuggling which took place in these two bays, but we must content ourselves with the following instance.

    On this day it happened that his Majesty's frigate *Fisgard* was proceeding up Channel under the command of Captain Michael Seymour, R.N. The time was three in the afternoon. In spite of the intermittent haziness, an hour earlier he had been able to fix his position by St. Anthony, which then bore north by west distant six or seven miles. He was then sailing by the wind close-hauled lying S.S.E.1/2E. In other words, he was standing away from the land out into mid-channel, the breeze being steady.

    By three o'clock the *Fisgard* had only traveled another six or seven miles, so that she was now about 12-1/2 miles from St. Anthony or just to seaward of the Lizard. It was at this time that the frigate sighted a smaller craft, fore-and-aft rigged and heading N.N.W., also on a wind, the breeze being on the larboard-beam. This subsequently turned out to be the *Flora*, and the course the cutter was taking would have brought her towards the Dodman.

    The haze had now lifted for a time and, although the *Flora* was still eight miles away, she could clearly be seen. Knowing that this cutter had no right to be within a line drawn between the Lizard and Prawl Point, the *Fisgard* starboarded her helm and went in pursuit. But the Flora's crew were also on the look-out, though not a little displeased that the fog had lifted and revealed her position.

When she saw that the *Fisgard* was coming after her she began to make off, bore up, and headed due North. But presently she altered her tactics and hauled round on the starboard tack, which would of course bring her away from the land, make her travel faster because her headsails would fill, and she hoped also no doubt to get clear of the Prawl-to-Lizard line. Before this she had been under easy sail, but now she put up all the canvas she could carry.

But unfortunately the *Flora* had not seen another frigate which was also in the vicinity. This was the *Wasso*, and the haze had hidden her movements. But now, even though the weather was clearing, the bigger ship had been hidden from view because she had been just round the corner in Mevagissey Bay. And at the very time that the Flora was running away from the *Fisgard* and traveling finely with every sail drawing nicely and getting clear of the cliffs, the *Wasso* was working her way round the Dodman.

As soon as the latter came into view she took in the situation—the cutter *Flora* foaming along out to sea and the *Fisgard* coming up quickly under a mountain of canvas. So now there were two frigates pursuing the cutter, and the *Flora's* skipper must have cursed his bad luck for being caught in this trap. But that unkind haze was favoring the King's ships that day, for before the chase had continued much longer, yet a *third* frigate came in sight, whose name was the *Nymph*.

The Flora with the Fisgard, Wasso, and Nymph.

King's Cutters vs Smugglers -1700-1855

This was too much for the *Flora* to be chased by three ships each bigger and better armed than herself. The *Nymph* headed her off, and the cutter seeing it was all up reluctantly hove-to. On examination she was found to have a cargo of gin, brandy, and tobacco, which she would have succeeded in running ashore had the haze not played such tricks. However, she had done her best for three exciting hours, for it was not until six on that wintry evening that she was captured by the *Nymph*, and if she had been able to hold on a little longer she might have escaped in the night, gotten completely away and landed her cargo elsewhere before the sun came up. But, as it was, her skipper James Dunn had to stand trial, when a verdict was given in favor of the King, and Dunn was fined £200.

We must pass over the next two years and travel from one end of the English Channel to the other until we find ourselves again in Kentish waters. The year is 1804, and the 14th of June. On this summer's day at dawn the gun-brig *Jackal*, commanded by Captain Stewart, R.N., was cruising about to the North of the Goodwins. As day broke he was informed that three smuggling vessels had just been seen in the vicinity. One of them was not more than three miles from the land, and it was fairly certain what their intention was. When Captain Stewart came on deck and convinced himself of their identity he ordered out his boats. He took command of one, while one of his officers took command of another, each boat having about half-a-dozen men on board.

We mentioned just now how important it was in such cases as this that the position should be defined as accurately as possible. As soon as the boats had left the *Jackal* the pilot and one of the crew took bearings from the North Foreland and found the *Jackal* was about 7-3/4 miles from this landmark. They also took bearings of the position of the three smuggling luggers, and found these were about three or four miles off and bore from the *Jackal* E. by S.

To return to Captain Stewart and the two boats: for the first twenty minutes these oared craft gained on the luggers owing to the absence of wind, and the smugglers could do nothing. The dawn had revealed the presence of the *Jackal* to the smugglers no less than the latter had been revealed to the gun-brig. And as soon as the illicit carriers realized what was about to happen they, too, began to make every effort to get moving. The early morning calm, however, was less favorable to them than to the comparatively light-oared craft which had put out, so the three luggers just rolled in the swell under the cliffs of the Foreland as their canvas and gear slatted idly from side to side.

But soon, as the sun rose in the sky, a little breeze came forth which bellowed the lug-sails and enabled the three craft to stand off from the land and endeavor, if possible, to get out into the Channel. In order to accelerate their speed the crews laid on to the sweeps and pulled manfully. Every sailor knows that the tides in that neighborhood are exceedingly strong, but the addition of the breeze did not improve matters for the *Jackal's* two boats, although the luggers were getting along just fine.

The Fine Art of Smuggling:

However, the wind on a bright June morning is often fitful and light, so the boats kept up a keen chase urged by their respective officers, and after three hours of strenuous rowing Captain Stewart's boat came up with the first of these named the *IO*. But before he had come alongside her and was still 300 yards away, the master and pilot of this smuggler and six of her crew was seen to get into the lugger's small boat and row off to the second lugger named the *Nancy*, which they boarded. When the *Jackal's* commander, therefore, came up with the *IO* he found only one man aboard her. He stopped to make some inquiries, and the solitary man produced some Bills of Lading and other papers to show that the craft was bound from Emden to Guernsey, and that their cargo was destined for the latter place.

The reader may well smile at this barefaced and ingenuous lie. Not even a child could be persuaded to imagine that a vessel found hovering about the North Foreland was really making for the Channel Isles from Germany. It was merely another instance of employing these papers if any awkward questions should be asked by suspecting Revenue vessels or men-of-war.

The truth, however, was that the *IO* was bound not to but from Guernsey, where she had loaded a goodly cargo of brandy and gin, all of which was found on board, and no doubt would shortly have been got ashore and placed in one of the caves not far from Longnose. Moreover, the men were as good as convicted when it was found that the spirits that were in those small casks were the kind only employed by the smugglers. Indeed, such a cargo of spirits to Guernsey would never have been carried in such small-sized kegs, for Guernsey always required its spirits in much larger vessels.

It was further pointed out at the trial that the luggers could not have been bound on the voyage alleged, for they had not enough provisions on board. The Solicitor-General also demonstrated the fact that when these luggers were approached in deep water—that is, of course after the three hours' chase—they could not possibly have been making for Guernsey. The farther they stood from the shore the greater would be their danger, for they would be likely at any hour to fall in with the enemy's privateers which were known to be cruising not far off.

But to return to the point in the story.

Captain Stewart, a quarter of an hour before finally coming up with the *IO*, had fired several times to cause her to heave-to, but this they declined to do, and all her crew but one deserted her as stated. Leaving one of his own men on board her the naval officer, after marking her with a broad arrow to indicate she had been seized, went with his four remaining men in pursuit of the second lugger, which was rowing away with all haste, and alongside which the *IO's* boat was lying. But, as soon as Stewart began to approach, the men now quitted the lugger and rowed back to the *IO*. He opened fire at them, but they persisted, and seeing this he continued to pursue the second lugger, boarded her and seized her, the time being now about 6.30 A.M.

Afterwards he waited until his other boat had come up, and left her crew in charge of this second lugger, and then rowed off to the first lugger again, but once more the *IO's* people deserted her and rowed towards the shore. Undaunted he then went in pursuit of the third lugger, but as a breeze came up she managed to get away. Presently he was able to hail a neutral vessel who gave him a passage back, and at midday he rejoined the *IO*, which was subsequently taken captive into Dover, and at a later date ordered to be condemned. She had belonged to Deal and was no doubt in the regular smuggling industry.

Then there was the case of the lugger *Polly*, which occurred in January of 1808. Because vessels of this kind were, from their construction, their size, and their rig especially suitable for running goods, they were now compelled to have a license before being allowed to navigate at all. This license was given on condition that she was never to be found guilty of smuggling, nor to navigate outside certain limits, the object of course being to prevent her from running backwards and forwards across the English and Irish Channels.

In the present case the *Polly* had been licensed to navigate and trade, to fish and to carry pilots between Bexhill and coastwise round Great Britain, but not to cross the Channels. To this effect her master, William Bennett, had entered in a bond. But on the date mentioned she was unfortunately actually discovered at the island of Alderney, and it was obvious that she was there for the purpose of loading the usual cargo of goods to be smuggled into England.

Six days later she had taken on board all that she wanted, but just as she was leaving the Customs officer examined her license; and as it was found that she was not allowed to "go foreign," and that to go to Alderney had always been regarded a foreign voyage, she was promptly seized. Furthermore, as there was no suggestion of any fishing-gear found on board it was a clear case, and after due trial the verdict was given for the King and she was condemned.

There is existing an interesting application from the boat-masters and fishermen of Robin Hood's Bay (Yorkshire) in connection with the restrictions which were now enforced regarding luggers. These poor people were engaged in the Yarmouth herring-fishery, and prayed for relief from the penalties threatened by the recent Act of Parliament, which stipulated that luggers of a size exceeding 50 tons burthen were made liable to forfeiture. As their North Sea craft came under this category they were naturally in great distress. However the Customs Board pointed out that the Act allowed all vessels and boats of the above description and tonnage "which were rigged and fitted at the time of the passing thereof and intended for the purpose of fishing" to be licensed.

Whenever those tubs of spirits were seized from a smuggling craft at sea they were forwarded to the King's warehouse, London, by those coasting vessels, whose masters were "of known respectability." And by a different conveyance a sample pint of every cask was to be transmitted to the same address.

The bungs of the casks were to be secured with a tin-plate, and under a seal of office, each cask being branded with the letters "G.R.," and the quantity given at the head of each cask. But those spirits which were seized on land and not on sea were to be sold by public auction. All smuggling transactions of any account, and all seizures of any magnitude, and especially all those which were attended by any attempt to rescue, were to be reported separately to the Customs Board. Small casks which had contained seized spirits were, after condemnation, sometimes allowed to fall into the hands of the smugglers, who used them again for the same purpose. To put a stop to this it was ordered that these tubs were in future to be burnt or cut to pieces "as to be only fit for firewood."

Even as early as 1782 considerable frauds were perpetrated by stating certain imports to be of one nature when they were something entirely different. For instance a great deal of starch had been imported under the denomination of flour from Ireland. The Revenue officers were therefore instructed to discriminate between the two articles by the following means.

Starch "when in flour" and real flour could be differentiated by putting some of each into a tumbler of water. If the "flour" were starch it would sink to the bottom and form a hard substance, if it were real flour then it would turn into a paste. Starch was also much whiter than flour. And a good deal of spirits, wine, tea, and tobacco brought into vessels as ship's stores for the crew were also frequently smuggled ashore. Particularly was this the case in small vessels from Holland, France, Guernsey, Jersey, and Alderney.

One day in the month of May, 1814, a fine West Indian ship named the *Caroline* set sail from the Island of St. Thomas with a valuable cargo of dutiable goods, and in due time entered the English Channel. Before long she had run up the coast and found herself off Fairlight (between Hastings and Rye). The people on shore had been on the look-out for this ship, and as soon as the *Caroline* hove in sight a boat put off to meet her. Someone threw down a line which was made fast to the boat, and from the latter several men clambered aboard.

After the usual salutations they accompanied the master of the ship and went below to the cabin, where some time was spent in bargaining. To make a long story short, they arranged to purchase from the *Caroline* 25 gallons of rum and some coffee, for which the West Indiaman's skipper was well paid, the average price of rum in that year being about 20s. a gallon. A cask of rum, 3 cwt. of coffee in a barrel and 2 cwt. in a bag were accordingly lowered over the ship's side into the boat and away went the little craft to the shore, having, as it was supposed, cheated the Customs. The *Caroline* continued her course and proceeded to London. The Customs authorities, however, had got wind of the affair and the matter was brought to a conclusion before one of his Majesty's judges.

"The Caroline continued her course and proceeded to London."

But East Indiamen were just as bad, if not a great deal worse, for it was their frequent practice to arrive in the Downs and sell quantities of tea to the men who came out from Deal in small craft. The commodity could then be kept either for the use of their families and sold to their immediate friends, or sent up to London by the "duffers" in the manner we spoke of in an earlier chapter. In the instances when spirits were smuggled into the country there was usually some arrangement between the publicans and the smugglers for disposing of the stuff.

But, you may ask, how did the Deal boatmen manage to get the tea to their homes without being seen by the Customs officers? In the first place it was always difficult to prove that the men really were smugglers, for they would be smart enough not to bring obvious bales ashore; and, secondly, the Deal men had such a reputation as desperate characters that no officer, unless he was pretty sure that a smuggling transaction was being carried on and could rely, too, on being well supported by other Customs men and the soldiers, would think of meddling in the matter. But, lastly, the men who came ashore from the East Indiamen had a smart little dodge of their own for concealing the tea.

The Fine Art of Smuggling:

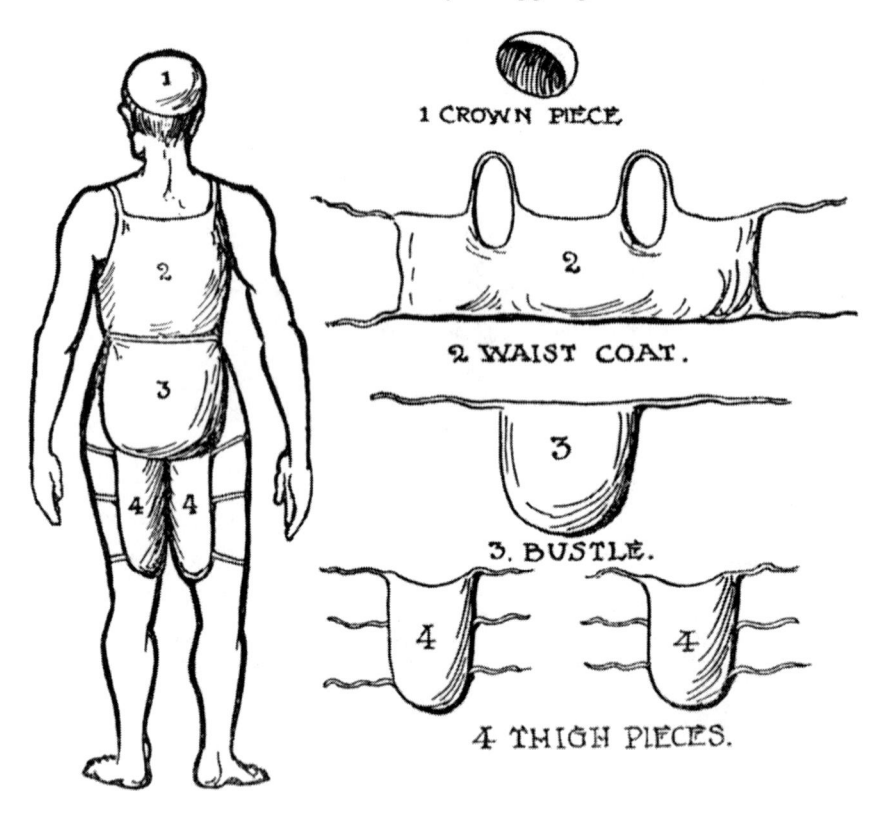

1 CROWN PIECE

2 WAIST COAT.

3. BUSTLE.

4 THIGH PIECES.

How the Deal Boatmen used to Smuggle Tea Ashore

The above picture is no imaginary instance, but is actually taken from an official document.

The figure is supposed to represent one of these Deal boatmen, and the numerals will explain the methods of secreting the tea. (1) Indicates a cotton bag which was made to fit the crown of his hat, and herein could be carried 2 lbs. of tea. He would, of course, have his hat on as he came ashore, and probably it would be a sou'wester, so there would be nothing suspicious in that. (2) Cotton stays or a waistcoat tied round the body. This waistcoat was fitted with plenty of pockets to hold as much as possible. (3) This was a bustle for the lower part of the body and tied on with strings. (4) These were thigh-pieces also tied round and worn underneath the trousers. When all these concealments were filled the man had on his person as much as 30 lbs. of tea, so that he came ashore and smuggled with impunity. And if you multiply these 30 lbs. by several crews of these Deal boats you can guess how much loss to the Revenue the arrival of an East Indiamen in the Downs meant to the Revenue.

Another old dodge, though different in kind, was employed by a smuggling vessel when at sea and being chased towards evening, or on one of those days when the atmosphere is hazy or foggy.

To prevent her canvas from being seen against the horizon, the lugger would lower her sail, and her black hull was very difficult to distinguish in the gathering gloom. This happened once when the smuggling cutter *Gloire*, a vessel of 38 tons burthen belonging to Weymouth, was being chased about midnight in January of 1816 by the Revenue cutter *Rose*. The smuggler had hoped to have been able to run his goods ashore at Bowen Bottom, Dorset, but the *Rose* was too smart for him, launched her galley, and seized her with a full cargo of half-ankers.

CHAPTER TWELVE
The Work of the Cutters

If the reader will recall, in 1787 we saw a reformation in the system of the Revenue cruisers, and the practice of employing hired craft was discontinued. This reformed system went on until the year 1816, when a very important change occurred in the administration of these vessels.

On the 5th of April in that year all the Revenue cruisers which previously had been under the control of the Board of Customs now passed into the hands of the Admiralty. The general object was to adopt more effective means for putting a stop to the smuggling, and these vessels were of course to be employed in co-operation with the ships of his Majesty's Navy afloat and the Revenue officers on shore. Notice was accordingly sent from the Customs office informing the commanders of cruisers that they were to place themselves under the orders of the Admiralty in the future. But the cost of these cruisers was still to be borne by the Customs as before.

It may seem a little curious that this sudden change should have been made when the Board of Customs had controlled these vessels for about a hundred and fifty years. But any customs organization must primarily belong to the shore. The employment of cruisers was in its origin really an afterthought to prevent the Crown being cheated of its dues. In other words, the service of sloops and cutters was a kind of off-shoot from the service on land. It was only because the smuggling was so daring, because the Crown was so regularly robbed, that some means of dealing with these robbers on sea had to be devised. But, of course, with the Admiralty the case was quite different.

For centuries the admiralty had to deal with ships and everything connected with them. Therefore to many it seemed that the department that controlled the larger Navy should also control the smaller navy comprised of the Revenue cruisers.

We must remember that the Battle of Waterloo had been won only a few months before. Once and for all Napoleon had been crushed and broken, and at last there had come peace and an end of those wars which had seemed interminable. From this return of peace followed two facts.

First, the European ports were now re-opened not merely to honest traders, but to the fleets of smugglers who could go about their work with greater safety—with less fear of being captured by privateers. Thus it was most probable that as the English Channel was now a safe place there would be renewed activity on the part of these men.

But, secondly, it also followed that the Admiralty was now free to devote its attention, most especially their organizational abilities, for the benefit of the Revenue department. At one and the same time, then, there was the chance of greater smuggling activity, and a more concentrated effort to put it down.

Furthermore, because the wars had ended, the Navy needed fewer men. We know how it was in the case of Naval officers, many of whom found themselves unemployed. But it was no less bad for the seamen, many of whom had drifted into the service by the way we have seen—through being captured smuggling and then impressed.

Returned once more to their native haunts after long separation, was it likely that having done so much roving, fought so many battles, sailed so many miles, passed through so many exciting incidents that they would quietly take up tilling the fields or gathering the crops? Some, no doubt, did; others applied themselves to some other industries for which they were fitted. But there were many who went back to the occupation of the smuggler. They had heard the call to sea, and since fishing was in a bad way they must resume running illicit cargoes again. Agriculture and the like have few fascinations for men who have fought and roamed the sea most of their lives. So, when some enterprising rascal with enough ready capital came along, they were more than prepared to take up the practice once more.

That was how the matter was viewed from their side. But the Government was determined that an evil which had been a great worry for at least a century and a half should be stamped out. The only way to do that was to make the smuggling unprofitable. In As Much as these men for the most part made their profits through being able to undersell the fair trader (because there were no Custom duties paid) the most obvious remedy would have been to lower the rates of import duties. But since that was not practicable, the only possible alternative was to increase the dangers and risk to which a smuggler must expose himself.

Instantly the first step, then, must be towards establishing "such a system of discipline and vigilance over the Revenue cruisers and boats as shall give the country the benefit of their constant and active services." These smuggling pests must be sought out, they must never be allowed to escape, to laugh defiantly at the Crown's efforts, and they must be punished severely when captured. It was therefore deemed by the Treasury that there would be a greater efficiency in these cruisers if "put under naval watchfulness and discipline, controlled by such authority as the Department of the Admiralty may think fit."

The change came about as stated, and the Admiralty retained in the service those officers and crews of the Revenue cruisers as by length of service and in other ways had shown that they were fit and efficient. Those, however, who had grown too old for the work were superannuated. Similarly, with regard to the Preventive boatmen, these were also taken over by the Admiralty, but here again, only those who were capable were accepted, while for the others "some moderate provision" was made.

On the last day of July the regulations were sent out that the Admiralty had drawn up regarding the salaries, wages, victualing, etc., of the Revenue cruisers. These may be summarized as follows, and compared with rates which have been given for previous years. They were sent addressed in each case to the "Commander of His Majesty's Cruiser employed in the prevention of smuggling."

And first as to payment:

(I) Cruisers of the First Class, i.e. of 140 tons burthen and upwards.
   Commander to have £150 per annum
   1st Mate   80 per annum
   2nd Mate   45 per annum

(II) Cruisers of the Second Class, i.e. of 100 tons and upwards but under 140 tons.
   Commander to have £130 per annum
   1st Mate   70 per annum
   2nd Mate   40 per annum

(III) Cruisers of the Third Class, i.e. of less than 100 tons.
   Commander to have £110 per annum
   1st Mate   60 per annum
   (No 2nd Mate)

The wages of the following persons were to remain the same in all classes, viz.:
   Deputed Mariners £2 8s. per lunar month
   Seamen   2 0 per lunar month
   Boys   10 0 per lunar month

Accurate muster books were ordered to be kept, and the sum of 1s. 6d. a day was allowed to the commander for each man borne on the books and actually victualed. This was to provide for the following provisions: 1-1/2 lbs. of meat, 1-1/2 lbs. of bread, 1/2 gallon of beer. The commander was also allowed 3s. a day for his own victuals, and a like sum for each of his mates. Allowance was made for a medicine chest to the extent of £3 annually. All expenses of pilotage were to be paid by the

The Fine Art of Smuggling:

Navy, "but the commanders and mates are to make themselves acquainted with the coasts, etc., and no general pilot will be allowed for more than two months after a cruiser's arrival on any new station."

There was now a notable innovation which marked the advent of a new age. Instead of the prevailing hemp cables with which these cruisers had been supplied and had been in use for centuries, these cutters were ordered to be furnished with chain cables "in order that the vessels may have the less occasion for going to a King's Port to refit or make purchases." If a man were injured or became sick whilst in the service so as to need surgical aid, the expense was to be allowed. And in order still further to make the cruisers independent of the shore and able to offer no excuse for running into harbor they were ordered never to proceed to sea without three weeks provisions and water. As to the widows of mariners, they were to receive £10 per annum.

So much, then, for the new conditions of service. Let us now obtain some idea of the duties that were attached to these officers and vessels.

The commanders were directed by the Admiralty to make themselves familiar with the Acts of Parliament for the prevention of smuggling, Orders in Council, Proclamations, etc. They were also to obey the instruction of whatever admiral they were placed under, as well as the commanders of any of his Majesty's ships whom they might fall in with "diverting you from the cruise on which you are employed."

Each commander was assigned his own particular station for cruising, and he was never to lie in any harbor, bay, or creek unless by stress of weather or other unavoidable necessity. He was to keep a look-out for vessels of a suspicious appearance, which, in respect of size and build, appeared to be adapted for smuggling. He was especially to look for French craft of this description. Having arrested them he was to hand them over to the nearest man-of-war. He was also to keep a smart look-out for the smugglers' practice of sinking goods and afterwards creeping for them. The cruisers were to visit the various creeks and bays; and whenever weather permitted the commander was to send a boat and crew to examine such places at night. If necessary, the crew were to remain there until the cruiser came to fetch them back in the morning.

Care was to be taken that the smugglers themselves no less than their craft and goods were to be captured. The commanders of these cruisers were to co-operate with the Land-guard and keep in close touch with the Riding officers ashore as well as the Sitters of Preventive boats. They were also to agree upon a code of signals between them, as, for example, by making false fires at night or the hoisting of proper colors in the different parts of the vessel by day, so that the shore officers might be informed of any suspicious vessels on the coast.

These cruisers were to speak with all the ships with which they fell in, and to direct any ships subject to quarantine to proceed to quarantine stations. If they came across some merchantman or other vessel, which they suspected of smuggling, the cruiser was to accompany such craft

King's Cutters vs Smugglers -1700-1855

into port. And they were warned to be particularly careful to guard East India ships to their moorings, or until, the next station having been reached, they could be handed over to the next cruiser.

The commanders of the cruisers were also to be on their guard against the practice in vogue among ships that had been to Holland and France with coals. These craft were especially prone on their return to put dutiable goods into light craft from London, or on the coast, but chiefly into cobbles or small fishing craft at sea. Even when it should happen that a cruiser had to be detained in port for repairs, the commander was to spare as many officers and seamen as possible to keep a regular watch on the high grounds near the sea, so as to watch what was passing, and, if necessary, dispatch a boat and part of the cruiser's crew. The commanders were reminded that the cruisers were not to fly the colors of the Royal Navy, but to use the same ensigns and pendants as provided by the Revenue Board under 24 Geo. III c. 47, sect. 23.

Earlier we went into the matter of firing at the smuggling craft with shotted or with un-shotted guns. Now among the instructions which were issued by the Admiralty was the clear order that no officer of a cruiser or boat was justified in shooting at a suspected smuggling vessel until the former shall have first hoisted his pendant and ensign, and unless a gun shall have been first fired as a signal.

The date of this order, of course, was 1816. But among the documents preserved at the Swansea Custom House there is an interesting letter dated July 1806, written by the Collector to Mr. Hobhouse. It stated that a Mr. Barber, the sailing-master of the *Cleveland*, had been committed for trial on a charge of willful murder, he having fired a shot to cause a boat to bring-to and thus killed a man. This, taken in conjunction with the testimony of the Sheerness Coast-Guard, seems to me fairly conclusive that in practice at least there was no fixed rule as to whether the first gun were shotted or un-shotted. At the same time the above quoted instruction from the Admiralty, although loosely worded, would seem to have meant that the first gun was merely to be of the nature of a warning signal and no shot fired in this first instance.

And then, again, among these instructions there was the reminder that in times past commanders of cruisers had not been wont to keep the sea in bad weather—a period when the conditions were most favorable for smugglers. But now the Admiralty remarked that if the commander should be deficient in "this most essential part of your duty" he would be superseded. On the west coasts of England and especially Scotland some of the commanders had been accustomed in former years to pass the night in some harbor, bar, or creek instead of cruising on their station. Consequently the Admiralty now strictly charged the commanders to cruise during the night, and no matter of private concern must serve as a pretext for any intermission.

They were also to maintain a regular communication with the commander of any other vessel with which they had been instructed to cruise.

And cruisers were to be furnished with the laws relative to smuggling and not to exceed the powers vested in the commanders by law. As to any uncustomed or prohibited goods, these were to be secured in the King's Warehouse at the next port, and care was to be taken that these goods remained undamaged or pilfered by the crew. After the goods had been thus put ashore both the commander and mate were to carefully search the smuggling vessel, the boxes, and bedding of her crew to see if anything had been kept back.

Whenever a vessel was seized at sea precautions must be taken to ascertain the distance from the shore "by causing two points of land to be set, and the bearings thereof to be noted by two or more of your officers and mariners who are acquainted with those points of land, so that each of them may be in condition to swear to the bearings from the note taken by him at the time, to be produced by him upon the trial of the vessels."

Any papers found on board the smuggling craft were to be immediately initialed by the persons present, and no cruiser or any of her boats should be employed in carrying passengers or pleasure parties. The commander and mate were to keep separate journals of all the proceedings of the cruiser relative to wind and weather, bearings, and distances from the land, soundings, etc., every twenty-four hours so that the admiral could tell whether the cruisers had used every exertion to suppress smuggling, or had been negligent and slack in their duties.

For this purpose the twenty-four hours were divided into three parts thus: Midnight to 8 A.M., 8 A.M. to 4 P.M., and 4 P.M. to midnight. In each of these three divisions the commander was to fix his position by cross-bearings and soundings if in less than 30 fathoms. This was to be done a little before sunrise, at noon, and a little before sunset, provided that if the land were not seen or the cruiser be chasing a vessel, this fact was to be noted in the journal, and the bearings and soundings were to be taken whenever the land should be seen. An exact copy of this journal was to be sent after the end of each month to the admiral under whose command the cruiser happened to be placed.

The table on the following page is an example of the journal of one of these craft, and will show instantly the kind of record which was kept.

On the 1st of January, 1817, the Preventive boats were put under the control of Captain Hanchett, R.N., who was known as the Controller-General of the Preventive Boat Service. There was an effort made also in this department to obtain increased efficiency.

The following articles were ordered to be supplied to each Preventive boat: one small flat cask to hold two gallons of fresh water, one small water-tight harness cask to hold provisions, one chest of arms and ammunition, one Custom House Jack, two "spying-glasses" (one for the watch-house, the other for the boat), one small bucket for baling, one "wall piece," forty rounds of cartridges, thirty muskets or carbines, preference being given to carbines with musket-ball bore where new ones are to be purchased, twenty light pistols, balls in proportion to the above,

King's Cutters vs Smugglers -1700-1855

Day of the Week and Month.	Wind	Weather	At Sea or in Port	Land Seen	Bearings and Distances in Miles	Soundings in Fathoms	Occurrences and Remarks
July Monday 1st., Morning or first part	E.S.E.	Moderate	At sea	Red Head Light, Bell Rock	W.N.W. 9 miles S.W. by S. 12 miles	Above 30	Cruising in station spoke a vessel from the Baltic laden with hemp, etc., but sea running high, did not board her. Saw H.M. sloop Cherokee to the N.E. at 9 A.M.
Noon or second part				Fifeness Isle of May	W.N.W. 5 miles S.W. by W. 6 miles	23	Nothing remarkable occurred.
Evening or third part				Fifeness Light, Bell Rock	S. by E. 8½ miles E. by S. 9 miles	12	Lost sight of the Cherokee standing off and on in St. Andrews Bay. Sent out the boat with Mr. Jones, second mate, to visit the creeks.

Journal of His Majesty's Revenue Cruiser the "*Vigilant*,"
John Smith, Commander, for the Month of July 18—

bayonets, cutlasses, pouches, tucks, small hand hatchets for cutting away rigging, musket flints, pistol flints, a set of implements for cleaning arms, a set of rummaging tools, and a dark "lanthorn." With this full inventory these open, oared boats could go about their work for long spells in bays, up creeks and estuaries, on the prowl for the smugglers by night.

Whenever any vessels were seized and condemned a full, descriptive account was sent to London regarding their size, breadth, depth, burthen, age, where built, draught, scantlings, the nature of the wood, how fastened, whether the craft appeared strained, how many guns she carried, what was the probable expense of having her refitted, how long she would last when this had been done, whether she had the reputation for rowing or sailing quickly, and what was her value. If it was recognized that she was a serviceable vessel she was not to be destroyed but employed in the Preventive service.

Among the names of the Revenue cutters about this time were the *Scorpion, Enchantress, Jacobus,* and *Rattlesnake.* There was a good deal of smuggling now going on in Essex, and the last-mentioned was employed to watch the river Blackwater in that district. Lieutenant Neame,

The Fine Art of Smuggling:

R.N., was also ordered to proceed to the Blackwater with the lugger *Fortune*, and arrived there to take charge of the *Rattlesnake*. This was in September 1818.

The Preventive Water-guard originally had charge of the whole coast of England; but a few months before the above date—it occurred actually in July 1817—the staff between the North and South Forelands was withdrawn, and this part of the coast was placed under the charge of the Coast Blockade. Under the arrangement of 1816, the cruisers had been put under the care of the Admiralty, the Preventive Waterguard had come under the authority of the Treasury, but now, in 1817, came the this change. Towards the close of 1818 the Coast Blockade, instead of being confined merely to that coast between the two Forelands, was extended until it reached on the one side Shellness by the mouth of the East Swale, and on the other all the away down Channel to Cuckmere Haven (between Newhaven and Beachy Head).

The history of this change may be summed up as follows.

In 1816 it was suggested by Captain M'Culloch of H.M.S. *Ganymede* (which was one of the vessels employed in the prevention of smuggling between Dungeness and North Foreland) that it would be advantageous to land the crews of the vessels. The men were to be put ashore every day just after sunset and so form a guard along the coast during the night. In the morning, just before sunrise, the men were to be put on board their ships once more.

So the experiment was tried and was found to be so successful that this method of guarding the coast was adopted by a Treasury Minute of June 19, 1817. The district between the Forelands was assigned to Captain M'Culloch, who had with him the officers and crew of H.M.S. *Severn*. Those boats and men which had belonged to the Preventive service stationed between the Forelands were withdrawn, and the entire protection of this district was left to Captain M'Culloch's force. This was known as the Coast Blockade, and was afterwards extended as just mentioned to Sheppey and Seaford.

If we may anticipate for a moment in order to preserve continuity, let us add that in the year 1821 this span of coast was divided into three divisions, and each division was subdivided into four districts. The divisions were under the superintendence of a senior lieutenant, a midshipman, one petty officer of the first class and one of the second. The districts, on the other hand, were under the superintendence of a junior lieutenant.

The men were divided into parties of ten, each party having about a mile of coastline, and guard-houses were established along the coast at a distance of about every four miles. The seamen volunteered into the service, and, if found effective, of good character, but had no relatives in the neighborhood, they were accepted. The object of this last condition was to prevent their showing any sympathy with the smugglers. These men undertook to serve for three years, and for payment of wages they were borne on the books of any of his Majesty's ships.

King's Cutters vs Smugglers -1700-1855

We can thus see how gradually the influence of the Admiralty had been exerted over the Preventive work which had been carried on by the Customs. There are then three steps. First in assisting the Revenue cruisers, and, lastly, by taking charge of the Land-guard. The proof of the wisdom of this change was seen in the results, for the Revenue derived better protection because of the Admiralty influence. There was better discipline, greater activity, and a smarter look-out was kept.

Thus it came about that in that very south-eastern district which had been for so long a time notorious for its nefarious trade, the smugglers found their calling a very difficult one. And both these changes in respect of cruisers and Land-guard had been made without the support of the Board of Customs, who had indeed expressed their doubts as to whether such a transformation were prudent.

Some idea of the number of his Majesty's ships and vessels which were employed in the prevention of smuggling in the year 1819 may be gathered from the following list. It should, however, be mentioned that these did not include the numbers of Custom House cruisers which the Admiralty had begun to control, but were actually the Naval ships which aided those of the Revenue:

> Plymouth supplied 10 ships and 4 tenders
> Portsmouth supplied 8 ships and 3 tenders
> Sheerness supplied 8 ships and 2 tenders
> Leith supplied 7 ships and 1 tender
> Ireland supplied 12 ships and 1 tender

at a total cost of £245,519. But it should also be borne in mind that these ships of the Navy, or at any rate by far the greater number of them, would have been in commission whether employed or not in the prevention of smuggling. In certain cases these ships were employed in the Preventive service for only a part of the year. Without the Revenue cutters the Navy could not possibly have dealt with the smugglers, and this was actually admitted in a Treasury Minute of January 15, 1822. The total number of Revenue cruisers employed in Great Britain and Ireland during the year 1819, as distinct from the ships of the Royal Navy, amounted to 69. The following year this number had increased to 70. These were apportioned thus:

> 20   under the Commander-in-Chief at Sheerness
> 11   under the Commander-in-Chief at Portsmouth
> 14   under the Commander-in-Chief at Plymouth
> 12   under the Commander-in-Chief at Leith
> 11   were employed in Ireland
> 2   were employed by the Commissioners of Customs

To sum up then with regard to the Preventive Water-guard, let us state that this had been constituted in 1809 to supplement the efforts of the cruisers and Riding officers. The coast of England and Wales was divided into three parts, and placed under the control of Inspecting Commanders. Under this arrangement were included the Revenue cruisers themselves. Then in 1816 the Admiralty had taken over these cruisers from the Preventive Water-guard, and the following year the Coast Blockade had taken over that portion of the coast between the Forelands, to be extended in 1818 to Shellness and Seaford respectively.

By 1819 the sphere of activity of the Preventive Water-guard was thus considerably curtailed. From the instructions which were now issued to the Inspecting Commanders we can see how the rest of the coastline other than that section just considered was dealt with.

Each station consisted of one chief officer, one chief boatman, two commissioned boatmen, and four established boatmen. There was a six-oared boat with her rudder and wash-boards—"wash-streaks" they are officially called—a five-fathom rope as a light painter, eight good ash oars, and two boat-hooks. She was a sailing craft, for she was provided with a fore-mast, main-mast, and mizzen-mast, with "haul-yards," travelers, down-hauls, sheets, etc. Her canvas consisted of foresail, mainsail, and mizzen with a yard for each. She carried also a jib, the casks for water and provisions, a boat's "bittacle" (i.e., binnacle), with compass and lamp. She was further furnished with a couple of creeping irons for getting up the smugglers' kegs, a grapnel, a chest of arms and ammunition, the Custom House Jack and spy-glass as already mentioned.

This vessel was rigged as a three-masted lugger with a jib. There is no mention of a bowsprit, so either one of the oars or a boat-hook would have to be employed for that purpose. In addition to this larger boat there was also on the station a light four-oared gig fitted with mast, yard (or "spreet"), a 7 lb. hand lead, 20 fathoms of line for the latter, as well as ballast bags to fill with stones or sand. If the established crews were inadequate during emergency extra men could be hired. The boats were painted twice a year, but "always to be completed before the bad weather sets in, and the colors to be assimilated as near as possible to those used by the natives and smugglers which frequent the coast which are least conspicuous."

If any of the established boatmen intermarried with families of notorious smugglers the Inspecting Commander was to send information to the Controller-General. Furthermore, no one was to be appointed to any station within twenty miles of his place of birth or within twenty miles of the place where he had resided for six months previous to this appointment.

The name, color, rig, and other description of any vessel about to depart on a smuggling trip or expected to arrive with contraband goods on the coast were to be given by the Inspecting Commander both to the admirals commanding the men-of-war off the coast in that neighborhood, and to the captains and commanders of any men-of-war or Revenue cruisers. They were also to be given to the Inspecting Commander of the Preventive Water-guard on either side of him. And in order to keep the men up to their duties the Preventive stations were to be inspected often, and at certain times by day and night. The Inspecting Commanders were to perform their journeys on horseback and to proceed as much as possible by the sea-coast, so as to become well acquainted with the places where the smugglers resort.

The officers and boatmen were ordered to reside as near their duty as possible and not to lodge in the houses of notorious smugglers. Officers and men were also to be private owners of no boats nor of shares in public-houses or fishing-craft. The Inspecting Commanders were to report the nature of the coast, the time, the manner, and the method in respect of the smuggling generally carried on in the district. If there were any shoals or rocks, not generally laid down or known, discovered when sounding to possess a different depth of water, or if anything should occur which might be useful for navigating the coasts of the kingdom, then cross bearings were to be taken and noted. These men were also to render every assistance in case of wrecks and to prevent goods being smuggled therefrom into the country. If any of these Preventive boatmen were wounded in fighting with a smuggler they were to be paid full wages for twenty-eight days or longer, and a reasonable surgeon's bill would also be paid.

To prevent any possible excuse for discontinuing a chase, the boat was never to leave the beach without the two-gallon keg of fresh water. And to prevent any obvious possibility, this boat was never to be left by day or night without one of the boat's crew to guard it. The latter was always to have ready some sort of floating buoy, "loaded at one end and a piece of bunting at the other," for marking the place where goods might be thrown overboard in a chase. The Inspecting Commanders were also to be on their guard against false information, which was often given to divert their attention from the real place where the smuggling was occurring.

"As night is the time when smugglers generally run their cargoes, it is expected that the boat, or her crew, or the greater part of them will be out, either afloat or on land, as often as circumstances will permit, which must be, at least, five nights a week." They were ordered generally to co-operate with the Revenue cruisers and to keep a journal of all proceedings. When out at night time they were to have a candle and "lanthorn" in the boat as well as the boat's "bittacle," and not to rummage a vessel without the candle being carefully secured in the lanthorn to prevent accident by fire.

All suspicious ships were to be rummaged, and whenever the weather would not permit the boat keeping at sea, the crew and Inspecting Commander were to keep a look-out by land. Even as late as 1819, when the great wars had come to an end, it was found that the transfer of smugglers to the Navy had continued to be the most effective means of protecting the Revenue. The sum of £20 was granted for each smuggler taken, and this was paid to the individual or individuals by whom or through whose means the smuggler was secured, and it was not to be paid to the crew in general. But when chasing a smuggling craft, whether

The Fine Art of Smuggling:

by night or day, they were not to fire at the delinquents until the Custom House Jack had been displayed. The salary of each Inspecting Commander, it may be added, was now £200 per annum and £60 for the first cost and upkeep of an able horse.

CHAPTER THIRTEEN
The Period of Ingenuity

Just as there had been a great improvement in the reorganization brought about by the advent of the Coast Blockade, so the Preventive service on shore generally was smartened up. That this was so is clear from the existing correspondence. For instance, five more Preventive boats were to be stationed between Shellness and Southwold, and three between Cuckmere Haven and Hayling Island. Another boat was sent to Newton (Yorkshire), another to Dawlish (Devonshire), and another to Happisburgh (Norfolk) or, as it was then spelt, Hephisburg.

Some idea of the activity of the cruisers may be seen from the number of smugglers which these craft had been able to capture. The reader will recollect that during the year ending October 1, 1810, the highest number of smugglers handed over to the Navy was thirteen, and this was done by Captain Gunthorpe of the Excise cutter *Viper*. He thus became entitled to the sum of £500. It will be remembered also that it was afterwards decided that, beginning in 1812, £500 would be paid only if the number captured was not less than twenty. But now from a Treasury Minute of October 20, 1818, we find that, although the former number of captures was over thirteen, it was just under twenty.

Again, Captain Matthew Gunthorpe, this time commanding the Excise cutter *Vigilant*, and Captain Robert Hepburn of the Excise cutter *Regent*, in the year 1816 seized nineteen smugglers each, or a total of thirty-eight. As neither captain had reached the twenty and both were equal, it was decided to add the second and third rewards together (i.e. £300 plus £200) and to give £250 to Captain Gunthorpe, officers and crew, and £250 to Captain Hepburn, officers and crew. There is on record at this time a memorial from one W. Blake, the son of W. Blake, sen-

The Fine Art of Smuggling:

ior. The last-mentioned had been commander of the cutter *Nimble*, but was drowned in 1816. His son now applied for the reward of £300 to be paid to the family of the deceased, as he had captured sixteen smugglers.

After the Admiralty had taken over the Revenue cruisers they did not neglect to sanction a pension system, and the following scheme was enacted: Commanders of cruisers on retiring were to have from £91, 5s. to £155, 2s. 6d. per annum, according to their length of service; and for any wound received they were to have an additional £91, 5s. per annum. First mates were pensioned after five years' service at the rate of £35 a year, but after thirty years' service they were to have £85 a year as pension. And so it was arranged for all ratings down to the boys. The widow of a commander killed or drowned in the service was allowed £65 a year.

Now that we are in that period after the year 1815 we must not fail to bear in mind that this is the epoch when the smugglers were using ingenuity in preference to force. The busiest part had yet to come and did not occur until the third decade of the nineteenth century. But even from the time of the Battle of Waterloo (1815) until, say, about 1825 there were ten years in which the smugglers left no device untried which they could conceive to enable them to outdo the Revenue authorities. We may now proceed to give actual instances of these ingenious attempts.

We begin with the early part of 1816. At this time the Tide-Surveyor at one of the out-ports had reason to suspect that the French market-boats which used to sail across to England were in the habit of bringing also a good deal of silks and other prohibited goods. He finally went on board one of these craft and, immediately after she had arrived, he caused the whole of her cargo to be put ashore. He then searched her thoroughly from deck to keelson, but he found nothing at all. However, he was determined not to give up his quest, and had part of her ceiling examined minutely, and was then surprised to note that some fresh nails had apparently been driven. He therefore caused the ceiling to be ripped off, when he discovered that a large variety of contraband goods had been neatly stowed between the ship's timbers.

It was only a few months later in that same year that another Revenue officer boarded a Dutch schuyt which was bound from Amsterdam to London. Her cargo consisted of 500 bundles of bulrushes, but on making his examination these innocent articles were found to conceal between the rushes forty-five boxes of glass in illegal packages, and also some other prohibited goods which had been shipped from the United Kingdom for exportation and were intended to have been clandestinely relanded.

The reader will remember our mentioning the name of Captain M'Culloch in connection with the coast blockade. Writing on the 2nd of April, 1817, from on board H.M.S. *Ganymede* lying in the Downs, this gallant officer stated that, although it was known that the smugglers had constructed places ashore for the concealment of contraband goods under the Sand Hills near to No. 1 and No. 2 batteries at Deal, these hiding-places were so ingeniously formed that they had baffled the most rigid search. However, his plan of landing crews from his Majesty's ships to guard this district (in the manner previously described) had already begun to show good results. For two midshipmen, named respectively Peate and Newton, commanding the shore parties in that neighborhood, had succeeded in locating five of those places of concealment.

"This discovery," continued the dispatch, "I am assured will be a most severe blow to the smugglers, as they were enabled to remove their cargoes into them in a few minutes, and hitherto no person besides themselves could form any idea of the manner in which their store-holes were built. They are generally 4 feet deep, of a square form and built of a 2-inch plank, with the scuttle in the top, into which a trough filled with shingle is fitted instead of a cover to prevent their being found out by pricking; and I understand they were built above two years ago. I have ordered them to be destroyed, and parties are employed in searching for such concealments along the other parts of the beach." Thus, thanks to the Navy, the smugglers had been given a serious reversal in the most notorious district.

Then there was also the danger of collusive smuggling. For instance, when a smuggler had been frustrated from successfully landing a cargo of spirits from a small foreign vessel or boat he might go and give information to a Custom officer so that he might have the goods seized by the latter, the arrangement being that the smuggler should be paid a fair portion of the reward which the officer should receive for the seizure. In as much as the officers' rewards were by no means inconsiderable this method might fully indemnify the smuggler against any loss.

Just before Christmas of 1819 the Custom officers at Weymouth seized on board a vessel named *The Three Brothers* sixteen half-ankers and seven small kegs or flagons of foreign spirits. These were found to be concealed under a platform of about nine feet in length fitted on either side of the keelson, and of sufficient height for one cask. Its breadth was such as to allow two casks and a flagon. When full, this secret hiding place would contain about thirty casks in all. The whole concealment was covered with stone and iron ballast. The platform was fitted with false bulkheads and filled up with large stones so as to avoid suspicion. The entrance was made (after removal of the ballast) from the bottom of the forecastle through two bulkheads about two feet apart.

Another instance was that of a consignment of four cases which had come over from France. These cases contained plaster figures and appeared to be hollow. However, the Custom officers had their suspicions and decided to perforate the plaster at the bottom with an auger. After making still larger holes there were extracted from inside the following amazing list of articles:Two clock movements, six pieces of bronze, thirty-two pieces of porcelain, and two small paintings.

A certain other French craft was boarded by the Revenue officers who, on measuring her range of deck and also under it including the bulkheads, found a greater difference than the rake would fairly account for. They were naturally highly suspicious and proceeded to take down part of the bulkhead aft, when they discovered that this bulkhead was not single but double, being between the cabin and the hold. This bulkhead was made of solid oak planking and was 2 feet 10 inches thick. It was securely nailed, and the cavity thus made extended from one side of the hull to the other, giving a breadth of 7 feet 2 inches, its length being about 2 feet 2 inches, and the height 3 feet 6 inches. It will thus be readily imagined that a good quantity of spirits, wine, and plums from France could easily be contained therein and brought ashore when opportunity presented itself.

At another port a vessel was actually discovered to have false bows. One might wonder how it was that the officer ever found this out, but he was smart enough to measure the deck on the port side, after which he measured the ship below. He found a difference of over a foot, and so he undertook a thorough search of the ship. He first proceeded to investigate the forepeak, but he was unable to discover any entrance. He therefore went to the hold, examined the bulkhead, and observed that the nails of the cleats on the starboard side had been drawn. He proceeded to force off the cleats, whereupon one of the boards of the bulkhead fell down, and a quantity of East India silk handkerchiefs came tumbling out. Needless to say, this proved a serious matter for the vessel's skipper.

Sometimes too, cases used to come over from France containing carton boxes of artificial flowers. These boxes, it was found, were fitted with false bottoms affording a space of not more than a quarter of an inch between the real bottom and the false. But into this space was squeezed either a silk gauze dress or some parcels "very nicely stitched in," containing dressed ostrich feathers. The flowers were usually stitched down to the bottom of the boxes to prevent damage, so it was difficult to detect that there was any false bottom at all. However, after this practice had been in vogue for some time it was discovered by the Revenue officers and the matter made generally known among the officials at all the ports, so that they could be on the alert for such ingenuity.

Sometimes when a Revenue officer was on her station she would come across a sailing craft, which would be found to have quite a considerable number of spirits in small casks together with a number of other prohibited goods. If the master of such a craft were told by the cruiser's officer that they would have to be seized as they were evidently about to be smuggled, the master would reply that they were nothing of the kind. He would say that while they were on the fishing grounds working their nets they happened to bring these casks up from the sinkers and warp which had kept them below water; or they had found these casks floating on the sea, and had no doubt been either lost or intentionally thrown overboard by some smuggling vessel while being chased by a Revenue cruiser. It became a very difficult matter to ascertain whether the master was speaking the truth or not, for it was not altogether rare for the kegs to be picked up by fishermen in the manner indicated. So the only way out of this dilemma was for the commanders of the cruisers to bring such craft as the above to the nearest Custom House, where the master could be brought ashore and subjected to a cross-examination as to where they found these casks and what they proposed doing with them.

A seizure was made at Deal about the year 1818 consisting of thirty-three packages of China crape and silk. These had been very artfully concealed in the ballast bags of a lugger called the *Fame*, belonging to London. One package was found in each bag completely covered up with shingles or small stones, so that even if a suspicious officer were to feel the outside of these bags he would be inclined to believe that they contained nothing but ballast. If he opened them he would think there was nothing but stones, for the goods were carefully squeezed into the center of the bags and surrounded with a good thickness of shingle.

Another dodge which was discovered at Shoreham on a vessel which had come from Dieppe was to have the iron ballast cast in such a form that it was not solid but hollow inside. By this means a good deal of dutiable stuff could be put inside the iron and then sealed up again. There was a ship, also, named the *Isis*, of Rye, which fell into disgrace in endeavoring to cheat the Customs.

She was a smack of 26-16/94 tons burthen, her master being William Boxhall. It was while she was lying at her home port that one of the Revenue officers discovered a concealment under her ballast, the entrance to which was obtained by unshipping two bulkhead boards forward. There was one concealment on each side of the keel, and each contained enough space to hold from twenty to twenty-four ankers of spirits.

Along the Kentish coast a good deal of smuggling used to go on by means of galleys which were rowed by six, ten, and even twelve oars. As these were navigated by foreigners and sailed under foreign papers, the Customs officers were a little puzzled as to what exactly could be done. Could such craft be seized even when found with no cargoes on board, when they were either hauled up the beach or were discovered hovering off the coast?

After applying to the Board of Customs for guidance they were referred to the Act,[1] which provided that any boat, wherry, pinnace, barge, or galley that was built so as to row with more than four oars, if found within the counties of Middlesex, Surrey, Kent, or Essex, or on the River Thames, or within the limits of the Port of London, Sandwich, or Ipswich, or the creeks thereto belonging, should be forfeited together with her tackle. The object of this was clearly to prevent the shortest cross-Channel route being traversed from Holland or France by big, seaworthy but open, multiple-oared craft, with enough men to row them and enough space to carry cargo that would make the smuggling journey worth while.

The following fraud was detected at one of the out-ports in 1819. An

---

[1] 8 George I cap. 18.

entry had been made of twenty-seven barrels of pitch which had been imported in a ship from Danzig. But the Revenue officers discovered that these casks were peculiarly constructed. Externally each cask resembled an ordinary tar-barrel. But inside there was enclosed another cask properly made to fit. Between the cask and the outside barrel pitch had been run in at the bung so that the enclosure appeared at first to be one solid body of pitch. But after the affair was properly looked into it was found that the inner cask was filled with such dutiable articles as plate glass and East India china.

Sometimes tubs of spirits were packed up in sacks and packs of wool and thus conveyed from the coast into the interior of the country. In the seizing of some goods at Guernsey it was found that tea had been packed into cases to resemble packages of wine which had come out of a French vessel belonging to St. Malo. Nor was the owner of a certain boat found at Folkestone any novice at this high-class art. Of course those were the days when keels of iron and lead were not so popular as they are today. Inside ballast was almost universal, being a relic of the mediaeval days when so much valuable inside space was wasted in ships.

In this Folkestone boat half-a-dozen large stones were used as ballast, which was a very natural thing for such a craft. But when these stones came to be examined they were found to have been hollowed out and to have been fitted with tin cases which were filled with spirits. One cannot acquit the owner of any fraudulent intent, but one certainly can admire both his ingenuity and the great patience which must have been necessary to have hollowed a cavity from such an unyielding material as stone.

This was equalled only by the cargo from Guernsey. Four sacks said to contain potatoes from the Channel Isles were opened by the Revenue officers at a certain port, and, on being examined, it was found that these were not potatoes at all. They were so many rolls of tobacco which had been fashioned to resemble the size and form of the vegetable, and then artfully covered over with a thin skin and finally clayed over so cleverly that they had every appearance of the potatoes they pretended to be.

But the Channel Isles were still notorious. In twelve sacks of flour imported from Jersey were found hidden in the middle twelve bales of tobacco weighing 28 lbs. each. A few weeks later three boxes of prunes also from Jersey were opened, when it was discovered that the prunes were not more than three inches deep at the top and three inches deep at the bottom. But between there was a space in which were concealed—in each box—a paper parcel of silk, some scarves and gloves, etc. But in order to make the total weight of the box approximate to that which would have existed had it been full of prunes a square piece of lead was placed above and another underneath these dutiable articles.

But to me the most ingenious method of all was that which was employed in 1820 for smuggling tobacco. The offending ship was one of the

King's Cutters vs Smugglers -1700-1855

vessels employed in the transport service, and the man who thought of the device was not far from being a genius.

He first of all obtained the quantity of tobacco which he proposed—no doubt with the assistance of more than one confederate—to smuggle ashore. He then proceeded to divide this into two, each of which formed one strand. Afterwards he made these strands into a rope, every bit of it being tobacco. But then he took a three-strand hawser and laid this over the tobacco, so that when the hawser was finished no one could suspect the tobacco without first cutting or unlaying the rope. I have not been able to discover how this trick was ever suspected. Nothing less than an accident or the information of a spy could possibly lead to detection in such a clever case.

There were all sorts of varieties of concealments now practiced since the "scientific" period of smuggling had come in. And since those wicked old days have passed, and with them a good many of the old-fashioned types of craft, it may be well that examples of these misdirected efforts should be collected herewith.

There was a smack, for instance, which was found to have under her ballast a large trunk that was divided into four separate compartments each about 15 feet long and could contain twelve half-ankers. One end of the trunk was fixed against the bulkhead of the cabin, and extended the whole length of the hold opening at the forward end close to the keelson by unshipping two pieces of the bulkhead.

Another instance of the employment of false bows to a craft was found on searching the fishing smack *Flower*, of Rye, whose master's name was William Head. It was observed that this false section would hold as much as forty to fifty half-ankers, the entrance being on the port side of the false bow. There a square piece could be taken out, being fastened by a couple of screws, the heads of which were concealed by wooden bungs imitating treenails.

The *Flower* was further discovered to have a false stern, the entrance to this being by means of the upper board of the stern on the port side in the cabin. She was a vessel 39 feet 2-1/2 inches long, 12 feet 1-1/2 inches beam, 5 feet 9-1/2 inches deep, and of 23-1/2 tons burthen, being fitted with a standing bowsprit and sloop-rigged. An almost identical set of concealments was found in the smack *Albion* at Sandwich, a vessel of over 42 tons burthen. The entrance to her false stern was through a small locker on the port and starboard sides. She was further fitted with a false stern-post and false timbers.

A considerable amount of ingenuity must have been exercised in the case of an open four-oared boat which was seized at Dover together with twelve ankers of spirits. The device was as follows: Across the bow end of the boat was the usual thwart on which an oarsman sat. At the after end where the stroke sat was another thwart. Under each of these thwarts was an ordinary stanchion for supporting the thwart. But each of these two stanchions had been made hollow. Thus, through each a rope could be inserted, and in as much as the keel had also been pierced it was possible to pass one rope through at the bow-thwart and another at the stern-thwart, these ropes penetrating the boat from thwart to keel. The inboard ends of these two ropes were carelessly lashed round the thwarts or covered with gear, so there was no untoward appearance. But at the other ends of the ropes were fastened the twelve ankers, which were thus towed along under the keel of the craft, and not trailing out astern as was sometimes done in the case of bigger boats. Thus, because the whole body of the boat covered the floating casks it was very unlikely that their presence would be suspected.

The smack *Strawberry of Deal*, on being searched, was found to have a false bottom, capable of containing a considerable quantity of goods. This bottom was constructed by two leaden cases fixed on the timbers the whole length of the hold, one on each side of the keelson, and covered over with the usual ceiling, having the ballast placed over it. The cases opened on each side of the hold by taking out a plank from the temporary ceiling. In the case of the lugger *Fox* (as usual belonging to Rye), a vessel over 16 tons, with John Souden, master. There were found to be double bottoms underneath the bed cabins, the entrance being made from underneath the cabins, and then, by unshipping a small piece of board about a foot square, each concealment was able to hold from fifty to sixty pieces of bandana silks.

Another smuggling device in vogue during this ingenious period had to be employed in such places as Ramsgate harbor, where it would have been utterly impossible to have used ordinary methods. It resembled very much the method employed at Dover, mentioned just now. A rowing-boat would come into the harbor, apparently with nothing in her nor anything towing astern. But there were fifteen or so half-ankers underneath her hull, spirits of course being contained in these casks.

Now the latter were all fastened to a long iron bar, the ropes to the boat being fastened to this bar. Consequently, after the boat had reached her corner of Ramsgate harbor, all she had to do was to let go the ropes and the iron bar would keep the kegs on the sandy bottom and prevent them from disclosing their identity by floating. At low water the smugglers could have gone to get them up again, for they would not move far even with the ebb tide. Unfortunately, however, the Revenue Tide Surveyor at this port preceded the smugglers, and by creeping for the bar and tubs with grapnels succeeded in locating what he wanted.

On another occasion at one of the out-ports, or rather along the neighboring beach, thirty-three gallons of spirits, contained in nineteen small casks, were recovered in a startling manner.

Going along the beach were noticed among the chalk rocks and stones of the neighborhood some other objects. These were the casks, but they had been so cleverly covered over with a cement of chalk, to which was fastened seaweed in the most natural manner, that seeing them there among the rocks of the shore they would never have been discovered by the Revenue men, had not it been (as one may guess) for a hint given by an informer. Otherwise there they would have remained until the smugglers found it convenient to come and fetch them.

We called attention just now to the concealing of tobacco in rope. This device evidently became a fine art, and had succeeded on many an occasion. At any rate in Flushing tobacco was openly on sale in the shops ready for smuggling into England already made up into ropes. You could get anything as big as a hawser and as small as a sail-tyer done up so ingeniously as to deceive almost any one. In fact on washing these slightly with a little rum they had every appearance of hempen rope.

CHAPTER FOURTEEN
Some Interesting Encounters

Rowing about on the night of Lady Day, 1813, a six-oared boat, which had been launched from the Custom House cutter *Lion*, was on the prowl in that bay which extends all the way from Dungeness to Folkestone. When the watchers in this craft were off Hythe, and only about a quarter of a mile from the shore, they saw coming along over the dark waters a lugsail boat with foresail and mizzen making towards Dymnchurch, which is just to the west of Hythe. It was about an hour before midnight, and as this suspicious craft did not come near to the *Lion*'s boat the latter rowed towards her and hailed her.

"What boat is that?" they asked.

"A Folkestone boat," came back the answer.

Thereupon John Wellar, a deputed mariner in the Customs boat, shouted to the lugger to heave-to, for he guessed what the game was.

"Heave-to!" roared the lugger's master. "We'll see you d——d first!"

But the rowing-boat was not to be put off with mere insults, and quickly pulled up alongside the craft. One of the men in the Customs boat then stood up and looked into the lugger and remarked that she was full of kegs. Wellar therefore immediately jumped into her, followed by three or four of his men, and seized her. On board he found three men, and them also he secured. He further discovered 144 half-ankers of spirits, consisting of brandy and gin from across the Channel, which were subsequently taken to the Custom House at Dover. A little more than a year later, Robert Baker, the lugger's master, was brought before the judge and fined £100.

There was an interesting incident which occurred a few years later in

The Fine Art of Smuggling:

the eastern corner of England, which led to trouble for a man named Henry Palmer of Harwich. This man was master and owner of a yawl named the *Daisy*, which belonged to Ipswich. About midday on the 22nd of March 1817, one of the Preventive officers, named Dennis Grubb, observed the *Daisy* sailing up the Orwell, which flows from Ipswich past Harwich and out into the North Sea. Grubb was in a six-oared galley, and about three-quarters of a mile below Levington Creek, which is on the starboard hand about a third of the way up the river between Harwich and Ipswich. With Grubb was another man, and on seeing the *Daisy* they began rowing towards her. Whether Grubb had any reason for suspecting her more than any other craft, whether he had received warning from an informer, we don't know. But what is true is that he was determined to have her examined.

While Palmer must have known perfectly well that this was a preventive boat, and that he was duty bound to stop when hailed, it was obvious that, as soon as the galley came near, the *Daisy* instantly went about on the other tack and stood away from the boat. The latter in turn pulled after the yawl and was again approaching when the *Daisy* once more tacked and ran away. But at last the galley came up, and just as Grubb was in the act of stepping aboard, Palmer coolly remarked that he had some tubs aboard, following this up by the explanation that he had got them on the trawling ground. This was too obvious a lie to be believed for a moment.

Grubb accordingly inquired how it was that Palmer had come past Harwich since the latter was his home, to which he answered that he was bound for Ipswich, as there his vessel was registered. But in as much as there were two of the Revenue cutters as well as a guardship lying at the entrance to the river, how was it that he had not stopped to hand the tubs over to them? For either the Customs cutter *Griper*, or the Excise cutter *Badger*, would have been the ordinary receptacle, instead of waiting until a Preventive galley overtook the *Daisy*. When Grubb asked how Palmer had come by all these tubs he said that he had caught them in his trawl, whereupon the preventive man examined the net and found it damp but certainly not wet, as it would have been had Palmer's version been the truth. Furthermore, if these tubs had been caught in the trawl there would have been a number of holes torn, but Grubb found there to be no holes. There were no fewer than forty-eight of these tubs found on the *Daisy*—all half-ankers, and fitted with slings ready for landing—and in as much as it was clear that the net had not been lately used Palmer was obviously lying. The iron which, had it been dragged along the sea-bed, would have been polished bright with the sand, was actually not bright but rusty, thus proving that it had not been recently used.

Grubb therefore felt justified in arresting the yawl, and taking her and her tubs to the Custom House. Later on he made a thorough search of her, and found a creeping-iron which had five prongs and a long shank. The reader is well aware that such an implement was used by the smugglers but never found on board a genuine fishing-craft. For getting up sunken tubs it was essential, and for that purpose it was evidently on board the *Daisy*. Moreover, it was found to be both wet and polished bright as to its prongs, and there was still some wet mud sticking thereto.

The case, of course, duly came on to be tried, and the Attorney-General suggested that at that time, in nine cases out of every ten, the tubs of smuggled spirits were not brought directly to port but sunk at different places in the sea, located by landmarks and buoys, fishing-boats being sent out later on to get them by these creepers, and to bring them in by small quantities as opportunity permitted. Palmer's defense was that they had found the tubs just outside Harwich harbor, opposite to Landguard Fort, at about seven o'clock the previous evening. But it was a somewhat strange fact that though this fishing-vessel should have been out all night not a single fish was found on board. And when Palmer was asked how it was that if he had found these tubs, and had intended to hand them over to the Customs authorities, he had been so careful to stow them all below and not leave them on deck to be visible to the *Griper* and *Badger* as he passed? His reply, that he had put the tubs below lest a puff of wind might blow them overboard, somehow did not convince the judge, and the verdict went against him.

A curious instance of an abuse of office was seen in the occurrence which centered round a certain Mr. Thomas Moore Slade. Mr. Slade was Agent Victualer for the Chatham Victualing Office, and from his connection with that department he had the power of employing some of his Majesty's vessels belonging to the department. This gentleman got to know that a splendid collection of pictures was about to be dispersed in France. They were of great value both artistically and intrinsically, and had belonged to the late Duke of Orleans. Slade therefore, quite unjustifiably, determined to make use of one of the craft under his charge for the purpose of fetching these pictures into the country, and thus cheating the Government of its dues, which would have been very heavy in this transaction.

The way he went about it was to direct a man named Thomas Cheney, who commanded the sloop *Grace* (belonging to the King's Victualing Office), to get under way and proceed a certain distance from Chatham. After he had come out of the Medway and had reached the Nore he was to open a letter which Slade had given him, wherein he would find his instructions. The *Grace* in due course hoisted sails and anchor and found herself out by the Nore. On opening the letter, Cheney was surprised to find he was directed to proceed to Calais. He informed the crew, who were very indignant, as they had all thought they were bound for Deptford. So that night they put back to Sheerness and let go anchor. The following day, with a reluctant company on board, they started off again and reached Ramsgate, where they lay all night. On the third day they crossed the Channel and got into Calais Roads, anchored, and remained there all night.

It should be added that Slade had taken the precaution to put on board this sloop before she left England a Mr. Thomas Aldridge, an ex-

The Fine Art of Smuggling:

pert judge of pictures. His exact role for this voyage was as supercargo, a term which signifies an officer in a trading vessel whose duty it is to manage the sales and superintend all the commercial concerns of the voyage. Having arrived, then, off Calais, Cheney, Aldridge, and some of the crew proceeded ashore and, guided by the art expert, went to a certain Monsieur Dessein, who kept a hotel in that town. From him they obtained a large number of cases containing the Orleans collection, and brought them off to the *Grace*. Altogether there were no less than fifteen of these cases, and although the *Grace* was a vessel of some thirty-two tons burthen, the weight of these paintings was sufficiently great to lower her water-line a good six inches.

After this valuable cargo had been got aboard and stowed, a gale of wind sprang up and detained them for a few days, but at length they cleared the French coast and steered for the Downs. From there they rounded the North Foreland, and after running up the Thames entered the Medway and let go at Gillingham until it was dark. But as soon as night had fallen they got going once more, and ran alongside the Victualing Wharf at Chatham. The pictures were brought up from the sloop and taken ashore by means of a crane, and then quietly carried to Mr. Slade's house. By this he had thus saved the cost both of carriage and of duty, the pictures being afterwards sold for a very large sum. However, this dishonest business at length leaked out, an action was brought against Slade, and a verdict was given for the King and for six pictures of the single value of twenty guineas.

On the evening of a November day in the year 1819, the Revenue cutter *Badger*, under the command of Captain Mercer, was cruising in the English Channel between Dungeness and Boulogne. About seven o'clock it was reported to the commander that about a quarter of a mile away there was a lugger steering about N.W. by W. towards the English coast. The *Badger* thereupon gave chase, but as she drew nearer and nearer the lugger altered her course many times. Carrying a smart press of canvas, the *Badger*, which was one of the fastest vessels employed in the Revenue, came up rapidly. As usual she fired her warning gun for the lugger to heave-to, but all the notice taken by the chased ship was to go about on the other tack and endeavor still to escape. But presently the cutter, running with the wind on her quarter and doing her eight knots to the lugger's four or five, came up to her foe so quickly as to run right past her. But before the *Badger* luffed up she hailed the lugger (whose name was afterwards found to be the *Iris* of Boulogne) and ordered her to heave-to.

"I be hove-to," answered back one of the lugger's crew in unmistakable English.

Meanwhile the *Badger* was hoisting up the galley in the rigging preparatory to launching, and the crew stood by ready to get in. As soon as the *Badger* had shot past, down went her helm and she came alongside the *Iris* as the galley was dropped into the leaden waters. But just at that moment the *Badger*'s people overheard some men on the lugger exclaim, "Now's your time," whereupon the crew of the lugger also launched their

"The Badger was hoisting up the galley in the rigging."

boat, forsook the *Iris*, and began to row off as fast as they could. The *Badger* called to them—among whom was a man named Albert Hugnet—ordering them under pain of being shot to come alongside the cutter. They replied that they were coming, but that they could not find their thole-pins, saying that they had only two oars on one side and one oar on the other. This was said in English, and was obviously a mere excuse to gain time. Meanwhile the cutter's galley and men had come alongside the lugger, in which they found 110 half-ankers, containing 382 gallons of brandy, and 157 half-ankers of Geneva, 55 bags of tea, and 19 bags containing 355 lbs. of manufactured tobacco.

As the men of the *Iris* showed no signs of coming back, the prize-crew on the lugger hailed the *Badger*, giving information that the smugglers were escaping. "Lie close," came the command, so the cutter trimmed her sheets and went in pursuit, and fired some shots in the direction of the retreating boat. But it was no use, for the boat was quickly lost from sight among the waves and disappeared entirely. There was some sea on at the time, so no one among the Revenue men envied the *Iris*'s crew their task of rowing across to Boulogne, a distance of somewhere about twenty-seven miles, in that weather and against very strong tides. Moreover they were certain of having an even worse time as the Ridens and the neighborhood of Boulogne was approached. In fact the chief mate of the cutter remarked, some time after, though he had seen these tub-boats go across the sea in all weathers, and were splendidly

The Fine Art of Smuggling:

seaworthy, yet he considered it was not very wise of the *Iris*'s crew to risk it on such a night as that.

Convinced, then, that the men were making for France, the lugger, with her prize crew on board, presently sailed after the cutter, hoping to come across their captives. But neither cutter nor lugger could find the men, and concluded, no doubt, that the tub-boat had foundered. But, at a later date, Albert Hugnet was arrested, and in the following June was brought to trial and punished. It then came out that the whole boat-load had escaped with their lives. For Andres Finshaw was called as evidence for the defense. He had been one of the lugger's crew, and showed that after rowing away that night they had not fetched across to the French coast, but having the good luck to find a French fishing-craft only a quarter of a mile away, they were taken aboard her and thus returned to France.

It was also brought out very clearly by the other side that when first seen the *Iris* was within nine miles of the English coast, and afterwards the *Badger* steered N.W. by W. towards the south of Dungeness, and after five and a half miles saw the Dungeness light and the South Foreland light, took cross-bearings of these, and having marked them off on the chart, fixed their position as about three miles from the coast. Thus when the lugger was first encountered the latter was about nine miles from the land.

The date of that incident, then, was the 12th of November, and Hugnet was not then captured. We may now pass over the next four weeks until we come to the 10th of December in that same year.

At eight o'clock in the morning the Revenue cutter *Eagle* was cruising off the coast of Kent when she observed a lugger bearing about N.W. by N. from them. The lugger was under all sail and heading S.E. for Boulogne, having come out from East Dungeness Bay. The weather was thick, it was snowing, and no land was in sight, Dungeness being the nearest portion of the English coast.

It did not take long for the *Eagle*'s commander to guess what was happening, especially when that bay was so notorious, and the cutter began to give chase, the wind being roughly N.W. But as the *Eagle* pursued, the lugger, as was the approved custom, hauled up and came on a wind, hoping to get away and outpace the cutter. But in this the smugglers were not successful, and eventually the *Eagle* overhauled her. The cutter's galley was now launched, and after having been for three-quarters of an hour rowed quickly by the aid of her eight men, the lugger was reached and hailed. The usual warning signal was fired from a musket in the boat and colors shown. The lugger, however, declined to heave-to as requested.

"If you don't heave-to," roared the chief mate of the *Eagle*, as he looked towards the helmsman, "we'll fire right into you." On this the lugger lowered her sails, the galley bumped alongside, and the chief mate and crew, pistols in hand, leapt aboard.

"Where are you from?" asked the chief mate. The answer came in French, which the latter did not understand, but he thought they said they were bound from Bordeaux to Calais. If so, it was an obvious and foolish lie. The mate, Mr. Gray, then inquired how many men were aboard, and the answer returned that there were seven. Gray then called the lugger's men aft, and separated the English from the foreign, and found there were five French and two English. The two latter, said the Frenchman (who was none other than Albert Hugnet, whom we spoke of earlier), were just passengers. A few minutes later, the skipper contradicted himself and said there were not seven but nine, all told. Gray then proceeded to look for the other two, and jumped down forward into the forepeak. As the place was dark he put his cutlass in first and rummaged about. In a moment the cutlass brought up against something soft. Gray had struck a man, hiding there, on the legs and thighs.

He was called upon by the cutter's mate to come out, and instantly obeyed, fearing no doubt that the cutlass would assail him again if he didn't. As he emerged he was followed by another man, and another, and yet another; in fact from that dark hole there came out a procession of seven, all of whom were found to be Englishmen.

It was noticeable that most, if not all, were dressed in short jackets and petticoat trousers. They were clearly sailors, and not landsmen—passengers or anything else. In plain language they were out-and-out smugglers. What was especially to be noted was the fact that their trousers were quite wet right up to their middles. In some cases their jackets were also wet up to their elbows. All this clearly pointed to the fact that they had not long since put off from the shore, where they had succeeded in landing a contraband cargo by wading from the lugger to the beach. Thick weather, such as there was on the previous night must have made it highly convenient for them. Nevertheless, even for these weather-hardened seamen, it cannot have been altogether pleasant penned up in sopping clothes in a dark forepeak with an unseen cutlass waving about in their midst and a seizure pending.

Gray also ordered these men to go aft, and put them together so that he might see how many were English and how many French. It was found that there were nine English and five French. Taking possession of the helm, Gray let the sails draw and ran down to the *Eagle*, telling his prisoners he was going to get further instructions from his commander.

There were no tubs found on the lugger, which was to be expected, but there was a solitary hoop which had evidently come off whilst these tubs were being hauled out, and there were also found two pairs of slings which were universally employed for getting the half-ankers ashore. These slings were made of small line, and were passed round the circumference of the cask at its "bow" and "stern," sufficient line being left so that there were two lines, one to pass over each of a man's shoulders. These two lines could be joined to other two on another cask, and so each smuggler could land with one tub on his back and another on his chest, in much the same way as you see a sandwich-man carrying boards in the street.

On examining this lugger there was no bilge-water found in the forepeak, so those seven shivering men could not have made the excuse that the vessel was damp in that portion. To cut a long story short, the lugger was eventually taken into Harwich, having been discovered seventeen miles from the French coast and eleven from the English shore. Assuming the lugger had traveled at about four knots an hour, this would mean that she had started off from the English beach on her return journey about 5 A.M., the previous hours of the night having doubtless been spent in unloading the tubs somewhere between Folkestone and Dungeness or perhaps Rye. Thus Hugnet, having at last been caught, had to stand his trial for both this and the occurrence of the previous month. And a verdict in each case having been returned against him, his activities in running backwards and forwards across the English Channel were, for a time at least, considerably modified.

These tub-boats, which we have had cause to mention more than once, were usually not towed but carried on the lugger's deck. A tub-boat got its name from the fact that when the lugger was too big to run her nose on the beach the tubs were landed in these boats. For that reason they were made very deep, with plenty of high freeboard, and were accordingly wonderfully good sea-boats, though they were somewhat heavy to row even without their spirituous cargoes.

As one looks through the jail-books and other smuggling records, one finds that there was a kind of tradition that this running of contraband goods should pass on from father to son for generations. Thus there are constant repetitions, in different ages, of men bearing the same surname engaged in smuggling and becoming wonderfully notorious in this art.

Among such family names must be mentioned that of Rattenbury. The man of whom we are about to speak was flourishing during the second decade of the nineteenth century, and his christian name was John. In November 1820—it is significant how often this dark month crops up in the history of smuggling, when the weather was not likely to tempt those Revenue cruisers' commanders, who preferred the snug shelter of some creek or harbor—John Rattenbury happened to find himself at Weymouth. Into that port also came a vessel named the *Lyme Packet*, which was accustomed to trade between Lyme and Guernsey. But on this occasion the ship had just received the misfortune of carrying away her bowsprit—possibly in the Portland Race—and her master, John Cawley, decided to run into Weymouth for repairs.

Whilst these were being taken in hand what should be more natural than that the *Lyme Packet*'s master should drift into a local public-house? Having brought up comfortably in that haven of rest, he was promptly discovered by his old friend Rattenbury, who had also made for the same house of refreshment. The usual greetings took place, and Rat-

King's Cutters vs Smugglers -1700-1855

tenbury inquired how it was that Cawley came to be there, and an explanation of the accident followed.

According to the skipper's version, they got into a conversation, and, over a glass of grog, Rattenbury said that if Cawley would be willing to sail across to Cherbourg to fetch a cargo of spirits he would pay him at a rate that would make it much more profitable than trading between Lyme and Guernsey. In fact he was willing to pay Cawley as much as twelve shillings a cask, adding that in one voyage this skipper, who happened also to be the owner, would make more money than in a year of regular trade.

Such a proposition was more than a tempting one, and Cawley gave the matter his attention. Unable to resist the idea, he acquiesced. It was agreed that Rattenbury would accompany him to France, where they would take in a cargo of spirits. Cawley to be paid twelve shillings for every cask they were able to bring across. So, as soon as the bowsprit was repaired and set in its place, the *Lyme Packet* cast off her warps and ran out of Weymouth harbor. She made direct for Cherbourg, where they anchored in the roadstead.

Rattenbury now went ashore and returned accompanied by 227 casks of spirits made up in half-ankers. These were put on board and the voyage back to England commenced, the intention being to make for West Bay and land the goods somewhere near Sidmouth. Having arrived off the Devonshire coast, Rattenbury took the *Lyme Packet*'s boat and rowed himself ashore, landing at Beer Head, his object being to get assistance from the men of Sidmouth for landing his goods. It was then about one A.M.

The captain of the *Lyme Packet* kept his ship standing off and on during the night, and hovered about that part of the coast until daybreak. But as Rattenbury had not returned by the time the daylight had come back, Cawley became more than a little nervous and feared he might be detected. Before very long—the exact time was 6:30 A.M.—Robert Aleward, a mariner on the Revenue cutter *Scourge*, on turning his eye into a certain direction not more than three miles away, saw the *Lyme Packet*, informed his commander, and a chase was promptly begun. Cawley, too, saw that the *Lyme Packet* had been observed, and began to make preparations accordingly.

He let draw his sheets, got the *Lyme Packet* to foot it as fast as she could, and as the three intervening miles became shorter and shorter he busied himself by throwing his casks of spirits overboard as quickly as he and his crew knew how. The distant sail he had noticed in the early morning had truly turned out to be the Revenue cutter, but he hoped yet to escape or at any rate to be found with nothing contraband on board. It was no good, however, for the cruiser soon came up, and as fast as the *Lyme Packet* had dropped over the half-ankers, so quickly did the *Scourge*'s men pick them up again in the cutter's boats.

The Fine Art of Smuggling:

Having come up alongside, the cutter's commander, Captain M'Lean, went on board, seized Cawley and his ship as prisoners, and eventually took both into Exmouth. Judicial proceedings followed with a verdict for the King, so that what with a broken bowsprit and the loss of time, cargo, ship, and liberty the voyage had in no way been profitable to Cawley.

CHAPTER FIFTEEN
A Tragic Incident

And now we must turn to an occurrence that was rather more tragic than the last, though the smugglers had only themselves to blame.

The reader is already aware of the practice existing at this time of actually rowing contraband across from France to England in large boats pulling four or more oars. As one who have myself rowed a craft most of the way from Calais to Dover in a flat calm, I cannot altogether envy the smugglers their job.

On May 11, 1818, Captain Hawtayne, commanding H.M.S. *Florida*, was cruising in the English Channel on the look-out for contraband craft. Evidently he had received advance information, for at eight o'clock that evening he ordered Mr. Keith Stewart, the master's mate, to man one of the ship's boats and to intercept any boat that might leave the French coast that looked at all of a suspicious nature.

This order was duly obeyed. A galley was observed some time before, which had no doubt aroused Captain Hawtayne's suspicions. This galley had been seen to come out of Calais harbor and to be rowed towards the west. But she must have spotted the *Florida*, for she very shortly put back. But before long Mr. Stewart's boat fell in with another craft—a long white galley named the *St. Thomas*. This was now about 1:00 A.M., and for a time the *St. Thomas* had the impudence to pretend she was a French police boat.

When spotted she was about five or six miles to the N.N.W. of Cape Blanc Nez, and was steering to the west. The night was dark, for the moon had disappeared behind a cloud as Mr. Stewart's boat came up alongside and hailed the strange craft. He began by asking what boat she

The Fine Art of Smuggling:

"Fire and be damned."

was. The steersman replied by inquiring what boat Mr. Stewart's was. The latter answered that it was the King's boat.

At that time the *St. Thomas*'s sails were up, and now Mr. Stewart ordered the steersman to lower them. He made no answer, but, turning round to his crew exhorted them to pull quickly, saying, "Give way, my boys, give way." Thereupon the smugglers cheered and pulled as hard as they could.

Mr. Stewart again ordered the steersman to lower sail, adding that should he fail to do so he would fire at him. But this did not awe the *St. Thomas*. "Fire and be damned," answered the steersman. "If you fire, I will fire. We are as well armed as you are." Stewart held his hand and did not fire, but ordered his men to pull closer. Coming alongside, he addressed the steersman, saying it was absolutely essential that he should examine the *St. Thomas* and that he knew they were Englishmen, adding that he was unwilling that there should be any bloodshed by firing into the boat.

With this the *Florida*'s boat pulled up on the other's quarter, and the bowmen hooked on with the boat-hook. The *St. Thomas*' steersman knocked the boat-hook away and threatened to shoot the bowman if he did not let go. For a short time thereafter the boats separated and drifted apart. But a second time his Majesty's boat pulled up alongside, and Mr. Stewart jumped forward into the bows and ordered one of his own men to stand by ready to accompany him on board. The steersman of the other, however, was determined, and resisted Stewart's attempt. At the same time he presented a pistol and threatened to shoot the officer if he advanced one step further. On that the men of *St. Thomas* ceased rowing, drew in their oars, and rushed aft to where the steersman was standing in the stern.

Matters began to look ugly, and being convinced that these men were bent on desperate resistance, Mr. Stewart was compelled to fire with his pistol at the steersman, who immediately fell. Stewart instantly leapt aboard, but was nearly jostled into the sea by two of the enemy. He ordered the whole of this crew to go forward, but they declined to obey, and followed this up by threatening that if they still refused he would have to use his sword and cut them down.

The only member of his own crew who had already got aboard was his coxswain, and owing either to himself or the action of the coxswain in stepping from one boat to the other, the two craft had drifted apart. For a time there was considerable risk that the men, who were obvious smugglers, would fall on these two. But the naval officer had already cut down two of their number with his sword, and after that the rest went forward and were obedient.

The *St. Thomas* was rather a large craft of her kind. In addition to her sails, she rowed five on one side, six on the other, and also had a steersman. The additional oarsman was no doubt placed according to the tide so that his work might in some measure counteract the great leeway which is made by small vessels crossing the strong tidal stream of the English Channel.

As all was now quiet on board, Mr. Stewart searched her and found she was laden with kegs, which, said the crew, were filled with tea and tobacco, these kegs being as usual already slung for putting ashore or sinking. Later on it was found that out of this crew no less than six were English, besides one man who had been born at Flushing of English parentage, though he called himself a Dutchman. The rest were all foreigners.

No one can read such an incident as this without regretting that they should have ever led to slaughter. It is a serious thing to take any man's life when there is no warfare, and it is still more dismal if that man is of the same nationality as the one who deals death. If the whole of the *St. Thomas*'s crew had been killed there could have been no blame on Mr. Stewart, for he was only carrying out his orders and acting in self-defense. The smugglers were fully aware they were in the wrong, and they were responsible for any consequences that might accrue. The officer had given them ample warning, and he had only used severe measures when absolutely compelled.

But there is a more satisfactory side to this regrettable incident, which one is only too glad to be able to record. The man who had been so badly wounded desired to speak to Mr. Stewart, and when the latter had approached him he turned to him and said:

"You've killed me; sir, I'm dying."

Mr. Stewart saw that this was perfectly true, and that the man was in no sense exaggerating.

"Well, I'm sorry for it," he said, "but it was your own fault."

The Fine Art of Smuggling:

"Yes," answered the dying man, "I know that, but I hope you won't make things worse than they are. I freely forgive you."

This was the steersman who had so strenuously opposed the boarding of the *St. Thomas*. We can quite sympathize with the feelings of Mr. Stewart, and be thankful that those lawless days of violence have long since passed. If you talk with any of the Revenue officers still living who were employed in arresting, lying in wait for, receiving information concerning, and sometimes having a smart fight with the smugglers, you will be told how altogether hateful it was to have to perform such a duty.

It is such incidents as the above which knock all romance out of the smuggling incidents. An encounter with fisticuffs, a few hard blows, and an arrest after a smart chase or a daring artifice, whilst not lessening the guilt of smuggling, cannot take away our interest. Our sympathies all the time are with the Revenue men, because they have right on their side, and in the long-run right must eventually conquer might. But, as against this, the poorer classes in those days were depressed in ignorance with low ideals, and lacking many of the privileges which no thinking man today would refuse them. And because they were so daring and so persistent, because they had so much to lose and (comparatively speaking) so little really to gain, we extend to them a portion of our sympathy and a large measure of our sympathy. They were entirely in the wrong, but they had the right stuff in them for becoming the best kind of English sailormen, the men who helped to win our country's battles, and to make her what she is today as the owner of a proud position in the world of nations.

Ten of these twelve men were taken as prisoners to the *Florida*, and the *St. Thomas* with her cargo still aboard were towed by the *Florida* into Yarmouth Roads, and there delivered to the Collector of Customs. She was found to be a 54-foot galley—a tremendous length for an oared craft—with no deck, and rigged with three lugsails and jib, her size working out at about 11 tons burthen. On delivering the cargo at Yarmouth it was found that there were altogether 207 kegs. The ten uninjured prisoners were taken before the Yarmouth magistrates, and the two whom the officer had cut down were sent on shore as soon as the *Florida* arrived in that port. The English steersman died, two others were fined £100 each, two were sent to jail, and one, who was the son of the man who died, was liberated, as it was shown that he had only been a passenger. The man who had been born of English parents at Flushing was also set free, as the magistrates had not sufficient proof that he was a British subject.

A few months prior to the above occurrence Lieutenant John Wood Rouse was in command of his Majesty's schooner *Pioneer*. On the 11th of January 1817 he was cruising between Dungeness and Point St. Quintin, when his attention was drawn to a lugger whose name was the *Wasp*. She appeared to be making for the English coast on a N.W. bearing, and was about six miles out. In order to cut her off and prevent her from making the shore Lieutenant Rouse sent one of his men named Case with a galley to cross her bows. At the same time he also dispatched another of his boats under the care of a Mr. Walton to make directly for the lugger. This occurred about 10 A.M., and the chase continued until about 3.45 P.M., when the schooner came alongside the lugger that had, by this time, been seized by Mr. Case. Lieutenant Rouse was then careful to take bearings of the land, and fixed his position so that there should be no dispute as to whether the lugger were seized within the legal limits.

On capturing the lugger, only two persons were found on board, and these were at once transferred to the *Pioneer*. To show what liars these smugglers could become, one of these two said he was a Frenchman, but his name was the very British-sounding William Stevenson. The other said he was a Dutchman. Stevenson could speak not a word of French, but he understood English perfectly, and said that part of the cargo was intended for England and part for Ireland, which happened to be the truth, as we shall see presently. He also added that of the crew of eight, three were Dutchmen and five English, for he had by now forgotten his own alleged nationality.

Prior to the arrival of Mr. Case's boat the lugger had hoisted out her tub-boat and rowed away as fast as the waves would let her, with all the crew except these two. She was found to have a cargo of tobacco and tea, as well as Geneva, all being made up into suitable dimensions for landing. On examining the ship's papers it was indicated that she was bound for Bilbao in Spain. But these papers had evidently been obtained in readiness for such an occurrence as the interception by the the schooner. When it is mentioned that this lugger was only a large galley with absolutely no deck whatever, and capable of being rowed by ten men, it was hardly credible that she would be the kind of craft to sail round Ushant and across the Bay of Biscay. "Was she calculated to carry a cargo to Spain?" asked counsel at the trial two years later. "I will risk my experience as a sailor," answered one of the witnesses, "that I would not have risked my life in a boat of that description."

But, unfortunately for the smugglers, there was discovered on board a tin box which absolutely gave their case away. In this tin box was found an instructive memorandum which it requires no very great ingenuity to decipher, and ran something as follows:

For B. Valden.

From Tusca Tower to Blackwater Hill, allowing half a point for the tide.

For W. Martensons Glyn.

From Tusca N.E. until Tara Hill bears N.W.

    10 pieces of chocolate 10 gulders.
    10 pieces of gays[1] 10 ditto.

---

[1] "Gays" was evidently trade slang to denote bandanna silk handkerchiefs, which were frequently smuggled, and some of which were found on board.

The Fine Art of Smuggling:

> A proportion of G., say one-third, and let it be strong as possible. A vessel coming in the daytime should come to anchor outside the banks.
>
> At Clocker Head, Bryan King.
>
> At the Mountain Fort, Henry Curran.
>
> And Racklen, Alexander M'Donald.

Now anyone on consulting a chart or map of the southwest and west of the British Isles can easily see that the above was just a crude form of sailing directions to guide the ship to land the goods at various places in Ireland, especially when the box also contained a paper to the following effect:

> The Land's End to Tusca 135 miles N.N.E.
>
> A berth off Scilly 150 N.E.3/4N.

The ship was to take such goods as mentioned to the above individuals, and here were the landmarks and courses and the division of the goods. "A proportion of G," of course, referred to the amount of Geneva, but the gentleman for whom it was intended did not get it "as strong as possible." Not one of these places mentioned was within hundreds of miles of Bilbao, but all the seamarks were to guide the mariners to Ireland. Tara Hill, Tuscar Rock and so on were certainly not Spanish. But these instructions were by no means uncommon. They were technically known among smugglers as "spot-notes," that is to say, indications of the spots where the goods were to be landed. When Stevenson found that his captors had become possessed of these papers he was considerably confused and embarrassed, even going so far as to ask for them to be given back to him—a request which was naturally declined.

The lugger was taken captive into Dover, and Stevenson, being an Englishman, was committed to jail in the Dover town prison, from which he succeeded in escaping. The Dutchman was let off, as he was a foreigner. The men who had rowed away in the tub-boat escaped to France, having taken with them out of the galley one parcel of bandanna handkerchiefs. The rule in these cases was to fine the culprit £100 if he was a landsman; but if he was a sailor he was impressed into the Navy for a period of five years.

There must be many a reader who is familiar with some of those delightful creeks of Devonshire and Cornwall, and has been struck with the natural facilities which are offered to anyone with a leaning for smuggling. Among these there will rise to the imagination that beautiful inlet on whose left bank stands Salcombe. Towards the end of June in the year 1818 William Webber, one of the Riding officers, received information that some spirits had been successfully run ashore at the mouth of this harbor, "a place," remarked a legal luminary of that time, "which is very often made the spot for landing" this class of goods.

Webber therefore obtained the assistance of a private in the 15th Regiment, and early in the evening, as he had been informed that the goods were not yet carried away, but still were lying deposited somewhere near the beach, proceeded to the spot. He and the hussar arrived at the place about nine o'clock on this June evening and managed to conceal themselves behind a hedge. They had not very long to wait before they heard the sound of some men talking, and a man named James Thomas was observed to remark:

"We couldn't have had a better time for smuggling if we had lain a-bed and prayed for it."

Through the openings in the hedge Webber and the hussar could see the outline of the delinquent, and the voice was more than familiar to the Riding officer. We can readily appreciate Thomas's ecstasy when we remark that it had now become rather dark and a sea-haze such as frequently comes up in fine weather after a hot day was beginning to spread itself around. For some time longer the two men continued to remain in their hiding-place, and then heard that Thomas and his accomplice had become joined by a number of other people. The sound of horses' hoofs being led down to the beach was also distinctly heard, and there were many signs of accelerated activity going on. Presently there came upon the ears of the Riding officers the noise which proceeds from the rattling of casks, and from some convenient hiding-place, where they had remained, these were at last brought forth, slings were prepared, and then the load was placed on the backs of the several horses.

At this point, deciding that the time had come to interfere, the Riding officer and the hussar crept out from their place of concealment and advanced towards the band of smugglers. But, alert as hares, the latter, as soon as they realized their own danger, took to their heels and ran away in all directions. Thomas, however, was too upset to hasten, and began to curse his men. He began by complaining that the kegs which had been brought forth were amazingly "slack," that is to say they were not as full as they might have been, hinting that someone had been helping himself to their contents of spirits. "If you had brought these a little sooner," referring doubtless to both horses and casks, "we should have been three miles on our way home."

But scarcely had he finished his sentence than the last of his band had fled, leaving him behind with both horses and casks. He was promptly arrested and eleven months later prosecuted by the Attorney-General.

Because the smugglers were so frequently assisted in their work by those night signals to which we alluded some time back it had been made a penal offense to show a light for the purpose of signaling within six miles of the coast. Arising out of such an offense, John Newton and another found themselves prosecuted for an incident that occurred about the middle of December 1819.

The comparative seclusion of that big bight which extends from the Bill of Portland to the promontory well known to many readers as Hope's or Pope's Nose, was much favored by the smuggling fraternity. This West

The Fine Art of Smuggling:

Bay was well out of the English Channel and the track of most of his Majesty's ships, and there were plenty of hills and high ground from which to show friendly signals to their comrades. Rattenbury and Cawley, as we related, had in vain tried to land their cargo hereabouts, though there were many others who, before the Revenue cutters became smarter at their duty, had been able to run considerable quantities of dutiable goods in the vicinity of Sidmouth and Lyme.

On the afternoon of this winter's day two small sailing craft had been noticed by the Preventive shore officers to be tacking about near the land, but did not appear to be engaged in fishing. It was therefore reasonably supposed they were about to run some contraband ashore after dark. A Mr. Samuel Stagg and a Mr. Joseph Pratt, stationed at Sidmouth in the Preventive service, at this time keeping a smart look-out on these boats, and somewhere about five o'clock in the evening launched their oared-cutter and rowed off towards them.

After a chase they came alongside the first, which was named the *Nimble*, and boarded her. They found therein three men consisting of John Newton, John Bartlett, and Thomas Westlake; but as they searched her and found no trace of any casks or packages of tobacco, the Preventive men left her to row after the other craft. It was now, of course, quite dark, and there was blowing a nice sailing breeze. Scarcely had they started to row away before the *Nimble* hoisted sail and by means of flint and steel began to make fire-signals, and kept on so doing for the next half hour. This was, of course, a signal for the second boat, and as soon as the latter observed these signs she also made sail and hurried away into the darkness of the bay.

It was impossible for the officers to get up to her, for they would stand every chance of losing themselves in the vast expanse of West Bay, and the craft might take it into her head to run down Channel perhaps into Cornwall or eastwards round to Portland, where goods often were landed. Viewing one craft under arrest to be worth two sailing about in West Bay, they went back and seized the *Nimble*. The three men, whose names we have given, were taken ashore, tried, and found guilty. But as illustrative of the times it is worth noting that John Bartlett had before this occurrence actually been engaged for some time as one of the crew of that Revenue cutter about which we spoke some time back in this very bay. And so, now, "for having on the high seas, within six miles of the coast, made a certain light on board a boat for the purpose of giving a signal to a certain person or persons," he was, in company with his two colleagues, condemned.

That the age of lawless mobs was by no means past, may be seen from the following incident. It had been thought that the Act which had been passed, forbidding any boat built to row with more than four oars, would have put a considerable check to activities of the smugglers. But these boats not only continued to be built, but also to be navigated and used for the contraband purposes. The Revenue officers of the district of Christchurch Head, had reason in April of 1821 to believe that a boat was being constructed in their neighborhood of such dimensions and capable of being rowed with such a number of oars as made her liable to seizure. Therefore, taking with them a couple of dragoons, two of these Revenue officers proceeded on their way to the district near Milton, which is, roughly speaking, the center of that bay which is bounded on one side by Christchurch Head, and on the other by Hurst Point. They had not arrived long at their destination before it was found that about thirty men had concealed themselves in an adjoining wood. The officers had found the boat they were looking for in a meadow, and were about to seize it.

It was found to be covered over with sails, having been hidden in the meadow for safety's sake, for since it was made to row seven aside it was clearly liable to forfeiture. One of the two officers now went off to fetch assistance, and whilst he was away two of the smugglers came forth and fraternizing with the two dragoons, offered them some brandy which they drank. In a short while both soldiers had taken such a quantity of the spirits that they became utterly intoxicated and helpless. One of the two smugglers then gave a whistle, and about thirty men issued forth from the wood, some of them in various forms of disguise. One had a deer's skin over his face, others had their faces and hands colored with blue clay and other means. These men angrily demanded from the solitary officer the sails which he had removed from the boat, but their requests were met by refusal. The mob then seized hold of the sails, and a tussle followed, whereupon the officer threatened to shoot them. He managed to retain hold of one sail, while the mob held the other and took it away.

About three o'clock in the afternoon the other officer returned with the Lymington Preventive officer, two Custom House men, and three dragoons. They found the intoxicated soldiers, one of whom was lying prostrate on the field, while the other was ludicrously and vainly endeavoring to mount his horse. The seven men now united, and got a rope by which they began to remove the boat from its hiding-place, when a great many more people came on to the scene in great indignation. As many as fifty, at least, were now assembled, and threats and oaths were bandied about. During this excitement some of the crowd cut the rope, while a man named Thomas Vye jumped into the boat, and rather than see her fall into the hands of the enemy, endeavored to stave her in.

The remainder of the story is but brief. For, at last, the seven men succeeded in pulling the boat away in spite of all the crowd's efforts, and dragged it even across a couple of fields, where there was a road. Here a conveyance was waiting ready, and thus the boat was taken away, and at a later date Vye was duly prosecuted by the Crown for his share in the proceedings.

CHAPTER SIXTEEN
Administrative Reforms

By an Order in Council of May 5, 1821, it was directed that henceforth all sums which were awarded for arrests on shore of any person concerned in smuggling should be paid in the following proportions.

He who made the arrest was to have three-quarters of the reward, which was to be divided into equal proportions if there were more than one person. If there were any officer or officers present at the time of arrest, these were to have one quarter of the reward. The officer commanding the party was to have two shares, each of the other officers having one share. The reward payable for a smuggler convicted and transferred to the Navy amounted to £20. And here let it be added that the persons liable to arrest in regard to smuggling were: (1) Those found on smuggling vessels; (2) Those found unloading or assisting to unload such craft; (3) Those found to be carrying away the landed goods or concerned in hiding the same. But before conviction it was essential to prove that the seized spirits were foreign; that the vessel had come from foreign parts; that the party who detained the smugglers was a Customs Officer; and that the offenders were taken before a proper magistrate.

We now come to the year 1821, when the Commissioners of Inquiry made an important report touching the Revenue service. They suggested that the Riding Officers were not valuable in proportion to their cost, and so it came about that the Inspectors and superior officers, as well as a large number of the inferior classes, were dispensed with, but a small percentage of the lowest class was retained as a Preventive Mounted Guard, the annual cost of this being only the modest sum of £5000. This Preventive Guard was to be employed in watching for any gatherings of smugglers, and whenever any goods might be landed and carried up into

The Fine Art of Smuggling:

the country, they were to be followed up by the members of this guard. They were also to maintain a communication between the different stations.

Up to the year 1821, from those early days of the seventeenth century and earlier, the Revenue cruisers were the most important of all the means employed for suppressing smuggling. But the same body that had made its recommendations regarding the Riding Officers also reported that the effectiveness of the vessels employed in protecting the Revenue was not proportionate to the expense incurred in their maintenance. They advised, therefore, that their numbers should be reduced, and that, whereas they had in 1816 come under the care of the Admiralty, they should now be restored to the control of the Customs. But the officers and crews of these cruisers were still to be selected by the Admiralty. And thus in the year 1822 these recommendations were carried into effect, and a new order inaugurated.

It was by a Treasury Minute of February 15, 1822, that it was directed that the whole of the force employed for the prevention of smuggling "on the coast of this kingdom," was to be consolidated and transferred, and placed under the direction of the Customs Board. This force was to consist of the cruisers, Preventive Water-guard, and Riding Officers. And henceforth the commanders of cruisers were to receive their orders from the Controller-General of the Coast-Guard, who was to be responsible to the Board of Customs. The one exception to this change was that the Coast Blockade on the coast of Kent and Sussex, which had shown itself so satisfactory that it was left unaltered. The Preventive Water-guard became the Coast-Guard, and this—rather than the cruisers—should form the chief force for prevention of smuggling, the Riding Officers, or Preventive Mounted Guard, being merely auxiliary by land, and the cruisers merely auxiliary by sea.

To what extent the number of cruisers were reduced can be estimated by stating that whereas there were forty-seven of these Revenue craft employed in England in 1821, there were only thirty-three two years later, these consisting of the *Mermaid, Stag, Badger, Ranger, Sylvia, Scout, Fox, Lively, Hawk, Cameleon, Hound, Rose, Scourge, Repulse, Eagle, Tartar, Adder, Lion, Dove, Lapwing, Greyhound, Swallow, Active, Harpy, Royal George, Fancy, Cheerful, Newcharter, Fly, Seaflower, Nimble, Sprightly, Dolphin.*

The first-class cruisers were of 140 tons and upwards, the second class of from 100 to 140 tons, and the third class were under 100 tons. In 1824 the cruisers on the Irish coast and the Scotch coast were also transferred to the Customs Board, and from that date the entire Coast-Guard service, with the exception of the Coast Blockade, was directed, as stated, by the Controller-General.

In the year 1829, the instructions were issued to the Coast-Guard. Afloat, these applied to the commanders, mates, gunners, stewards, carpenters, mariners, and boys of the cruisers. Ashore, they were applicable to the Chief Officers, Chief Boatmen, Mounted Guard, Commissioned Boatmen, and Boatmen, both sections being under their respective commanders. Each member of the Mounted Guard was provided with a good horse and sword, with an iron scabbard of the Light Cavalry pattern, as well as a couple of pistols and ammunition. The cruiser commanders were again enjoined to keep the sea in bad weather and at night, nor were they permitted to come to harbor except when really necessary.

In 1831 came the next change, when the Coast-Guard took the place of the Coast Blockade, which had done excellent duty for so many years in Kent and Sussex. The aim was to make the Coast-Guard service national rather than departmental. To promote the greatest efficiency it was to become naval rather than civil. It was to be for the benefit of the country as a nation, than for the mere protecting of its revenues. Thus there was a kind of somersault performed; and the whole of the original idea capsized. Whereas the Preventive service had been instituted for the benefit of the Customs, and then, as an after-thought, became employed for protection against the enemy across the Channel, so now it was to be exactly the other way around. The Revenue was to be subservient to the greater and national force.

In this same 1831, the number of cruisers had risen to thirty-five in England, but many of them had tenders. There were altogether twenty-one of these latter and smaller craft, their tonnage varying from twenty-five to sixty. And the next year the Mounted Guard was reorganized and the Riding Officers disappeared. With the cordon of cruisers afloat, and the more efficient Coast-Guard service ashore, there was a double belt round our coasts, which could be relied upon both for both national and Revenue services.

By this time, too, steam was invading the domain of the ship, and in 1839, besides the old-fashioned sailing cutters and tenders, there was a steamer named the Vulcan, of 200 tons, taken into the service. Her duty was to cruise about and search for suspicious vessels. In some parts of the country, also, there was assistance still rendered by the Mounted Guard for watching the roads leading inland from the beach to prevent goods being brought up.

With this increased efficiency it was only natural that a change should come over the character of the smuggling. Except for a number of rather startling occasions, force was fast going out of fashion. But because of the increased vigilance along the coast the smuggler was hard put to devise new methods of running his goods into the country without being surprised by the officials. Most, if not all, of the old syndicates of French and Englishmen, who made smuggling a roaring trade, had died out. The armed cutters had long since given way to the luggers as the smuggling craft. Stealth had taken the place of violence, concealments and sunken goods were favored rather than daring and outrageous incursions.

And yet, just as a long-standing illness cannot be cured at once, but

The Fine Art of Smuggling:

keeps recurring, so there were periods when the smuggling disease kept breaking out and seemed to get worse. Such a period was that between 1825 and 1843, but it was pointed out to the Treasury that so long as the high duties continued, "Your Lordships must look only to the efficiency of the Coast-Guard for the continued absence of successful enterprises, and that smuggling would immediately revive upon the slightest symptom of relaxation on the part of the Commissioners of Customs." The service was therefore glad to encourage Naval Lieutenants to serve as Chief Officers of the Coast-Guard.

Among the general instructions issued to the Coast-Guard of the United Kingdom in 1841, were definite orders to the commanders of cruisers. Thus, if ever a cruiser ran aground the commander was to report it, with full particulars of the case and extent of damage. During the summer season the Inspecting Commanders were to take opportunities for trying the comparative speeds of these cruisers. And, whenever cruisers should meet at sea, in any roadstead or in any harbor, they were to hoist their ensigns and pendants as an acknowledgment that each had seen the other. When both had thus hoisted their colors they might immediately be hauled down. This was also to be done when one cruiser should pass another at anchor.

Cruisers were again reminded that they were to wear only the ensigns and pendants appointed for the Revenue service, and not such as are used in the Royal Navy. Nor were salutes to be fired by cruisers except on particular and extraordinary occasions. It was further ordered that no alteration was to be made in the hull, masts, yards, sails, or fittings of the cruisers, without the sanction of the Controller-General. To prevent unnecessary expense on fitting out or refitting of any of the cruisers, the use of leather was to be restricted to the following: the leathering of the main pendants, runners in the wake of the boats when in tackles, the collar of the mainstay, the nip of the main-sheet block strops, leathering the bowsprit traveler, the spanshackle for the bowsprit, topmast iron, the four reef-earings three feet from the knot. All old copper, copper-sheathing, nails, lead, iron and other old materials which were of any value, were to be collected and allowed for by the tradesmen who perform the repairs. New sails were to be tried as soon as received in order to ascertain their fitness. Both boats and cruisers were also to be painted twice a year, above the water-line, this to be done by the crews themselves.

A general pilot was allowed for two months when a cruiser arrived on a new station, and an occasional pilot was permissible in cases of necessity, but only licensed pilots were to be employed. General pilots were paid 6s. a day as well as the usual rations of provisions. The cruisers were provided with charts of the coast off which they were employed. Naval officers holding appointments as Inspecting Commanders of cruisers, Chief Officers of stations and Mates of cruisers were ordered to wear the greatcoat established by any Admiralty regulation in force for the time being, with epaulettes, cap, and side-arms, according to their ranks. Commanders of cruisers, if not naval officers, were to wear a blue lapel-coat, buttoned back with nine Coast-Guard uniform buttons and notched button-holes, plain blue stand-up collar with gold lace loop and button on each side thereof—the loop to be five inches long, and the lace three-quarters of an inch in breadth. There were also to be three buttons and notched button-holes on each cuff and pocket, as well as three buttons in the folds of each skirt.

The waistcoat was to be white or blue kerseymere, with uniform buttons, white or blue pantaloons or trousers, with boots, a blue cloth cap similar in shape to those worn in the Royal Navy, with two bands of gold lace three-quarters of an inch broad, one at the top and the other at the bottom of the headpiece. The sword was to have a plain lace knot and fringe tassel, with a black leather belt. White trousers were worn on all occasions of inspection and other special occasions between April 23 and October 14. Blue trousers were to be worn for the other months.

In 1849 the Select Committee on the Board of Customs expressed the opinion that the number of cruisers might be reduced, and the Land-guard practically abolished; but it was deemed advisable that these protections being removed, the coastline of defense ought to be strengthened by securing the services of Naval Lieutenants who had retired from the Navy on half-pay. So the number of cruisers and tenders which in 1844 had reached seventy-six, and in 1849 were fifty-two, had now sunk to fifty in the year 1850. In 1854, on the outbreak of war with Russia, 3000 men were drafted into the Navy from the Coast-Guard, their places being filled by pensioners. During the war considerable service was also rendered by the Revenue cruisers, by capturing the Russian ships in the Northern Seas, for we must remember that, just as in the wars with France, there were two centers to be dealt with, viz., in the north and south. The war with Russia, as regards the sea service, was prosecuted both in the Narrow Seas and in the Black Sea, and the Russian trade was badly cut up. As many as eleven Russian ships were captured by means of these British cutters, and no less than eight of these prizes were condemned. The fact is worthy of being borne in mind when considering the history of these craft which have long since passed from performing active service.

The next modification came in 1856, when it was resolved to transfer the control of the Coast-Guard to the Admiralty; for in spite of the great change which had been brought about in 1831, all the Coast-Guard officers and men while being appointed by the Admiralty, were none the less controlled by the Customs. However, this condition was now altered, but in the teeth of opposition on the part of the Customs, who represented to the Treasury that considerable inconvenience would result from this innovation. But on the 1st of October 1856, the control of the Coast-Guard was transferred to the Admiralty, as it had been foreshadowed. And with that we see practically the last stage in the important development which had been going on for some years past. It was practically the finale of the tendency towards making the service naval rather than civil.

The Fine Art of Smuggling:

For the moment, I am seeking to put the reader in possession of a general idea of the administrative features of the service, which is our subject, during the period between 1822-1856. At the last-mentioned date our period devoted to cutters and smugglers practically ends.

But before proceeding to deal with the actual incidents and exciting adventures embraced by this period, it may be convenient just to mention that these changes were followed in 1869, when the services of civilians employed in any capacity in the Coast-Guard were stopped altogether. Since then the general basis of the Coast-Guard development has been for the better defense of our coasts, so as to be vigilant against any disembarkation by a foreign power, at the same time providing to a certain extent for the manning of the ships of the Royal Navy when required. Thus, the old organization, with which the Customs Board was so closely and for so long a time connected, changed its character when its sphere became national rather than particular. Its duty henceforth was primarily for the protection of the country than for the prevention of smuggling.

But between 1822—when the Admiralty yielded up their responsibilities to the Customs Board—and the year 1856, when again the control was returned to the Admiralty, no material alterations were made in the methods of preventing smuggling. The most important event during that period—apart altogether from the actual smuggling incidents—was the change which had been brought about in 1831.

During the different reigns and centuries in which the smuggling evil had been at work, all sorts of anti-smuggling acts had been passed. We can well understand that a certain amount of hasty, panic-driven legislation had from time to time been created according to the sudden increase of contraband running. But all these laws had become so numerous, and their accumulation had made matters so intricate, that the time had come for some process of unravelling, straightening out, and summarizing.

The systematizing and clarification were affected by the Act of January 5, 1826 (6 Geo. IV. cap. 108). And one of the most important features of this was to the effect that any vessel belonging wholly or in part to his Majesty's subjects, found within four leagues of the coast of the United Kingdom, with prohibited goods on board, and not proceeding on her voyage, was to be forfeited. Any vessel or boat, not square-rigged, belonging wholly or in part to his Majesty's subjects, and found in the British (as it was then frequently designated) Channel or Irish Channel, or elsewhere within 100 leagues of the coast, with spirits or tobacco in casks or packages of less size than 40 gallons; or tea, tobacco, or snuff, in any package containing less than 450 lbs. in weight, was to be forfeited. And vessels (not square-rigged), if found unlicensed, were also to be forfeited. But whale-boats, fishing-boats, pilot's boats, purely inland boats, and boats belonging to square-rigged ships were exempt.

Smuggling was, of course, still very far from being dead, and the Revenue cruisers had always to be on the alert. Some idea of the sphere of activity belonging to these may be gathered from the following list of cruiser stations existing in the early twenties. The English cruiser stations consisted of: *Deptford, Chatham, Sheerness, Portsmouth, Cowes, Weymouth, Exmouth, Plymouth, Fowey, Falmouth, Penzance, Milford, Berwick, Grimsby, Boston, North Yarmouth, Harwich, Gravesend, Dover, Poole, Brixham, Ilfracombe, Douglas (Isle of Man), Alderney, Dover, Seaford, Dartmouth, Holyhead, Southend* (in the port of Leigh). In Scotland there were: *Leith, Montrose, Stranraer, Stornoway, Aberdeen, Cromarty, Campbeltown, Greenock*. In Ireland there were: *Kingstown, Larne, Killibegs, Westport, Galway, Cork, and Dunmore East*.

It was to such places as the above that the cruisers repaired for their provisions. When smugglers had been captured and taken on board these cruisers they were allowed not to fare as well as the crew, but to have only two-thirds of the victuals permitted to the mariners. In 1825 additional instructions were issued relating to the victualing of his Majesty's Revenue Cruisers, and in future every man per diem was to have: One pound of biscuit, 1/3 of a pint of rum (wine measure), until the establishment of the imperial measure, when 1/4 of a pint was to be allowed, the imperial gallon being one-fifth greater than the wine gallon. Each man was also to have 1 lb. beef, 1/2 lb. flour, or in lieu thereof 1/2 pint of oatmeal, 1/4 lb. suet, or 1-1/2 oz. of sugar or 1/4 oz. of tea, also 1 lb. of cabbage or 2 oz. of Scotch barley.

They were to be provided with pure West India rum, of at least twelve months age. Further regulations were also taken as to the nature of the men's grog. "As it is considered extremely prejudicial to the health of the crew to suffer the allowance of spirits to be drank raw, the Commanders are to cause the same to be served out to them mixed with water, in the proportion of three parts water and one part spirits, to be so mixed and served out in presence of one of the mates, the boatswain, gunner, or carpenter, and one or two of the mariners."

Smugglers detained on board were not to have spirits. Before proceeding to sea each cruiser was to have on board not less than two months' supply of salt beef, spirits; suet or sugar and tea in lieu, as well as Scotch barley. With reference to the other articles of food, they were to carry as large a proportion as could be stowed away, with the exception of fresh beef and cabbages. But two years prior to this, that is to say on April 5, 1823, the Board of Customs had reduced the victualing allowances, so that Commander and mates and superintendents of Quarantine received 2s. 6d. a day each; mariners 1s. 3d.; and mariners of lazarettes (hospitals 1s. for quarantine) 1s. 3d. a day.

As to the methods of the smugglers, these continued to become more and more ingenious, though there was a good deal of repetition of successful tricks until the Revenue officers had learned them, then some other device had to be thought out and employed. Take the case of a craft called the *Wig Box*, belonging to John Punnett. She was seized at Folkestone in the spring of 1822 by a midshipman of the Coast Blockade.

The Fine Art of Smuggling:

There were found on her six gallons of spirits, which were concealed in the following most ingenious manner.

She was quite a small vessel, but her three oars, her two masts, her bowsprit, and her bumpkin, had all been made hollow. Inside these hollows tin tubes had been fitted to contain the above spirits, and there can be little doubt but that a good many other small craft had successfully employed these means until the day when the *Wig Box* had the misfortune to be found out. There is still preserved in the London Custom House a hollow wooden fend-off which was slung when a ship was alongside a quay. No one for a long time ever thought of suspecting that this innocent-looking article could be full of tobacco, lying as it was under the very eyes of the Customs officers of the port. And in 1820 three other boats were seized in one port alone, having concealed prohibited goods in a square foremast and outrigger, each spar being hollowed out from head to foot and the ends afterwards neatly plugged and painted. Another boat was seized and brought into Dover with hollow yards to her lugsails, and a hollow keel composed of tin but painted to look like wood, capable of holding large quantities of spirits.

But there was a very notorious vessel named the *Asp*, belonging to Rye, her master's name was John Clark, her size being just under 24 tons. In 1822 she was seized and found to have a false bow, access to which was by means of two scuttles, one on each side of the stem. These scuttles were fitted with bed-screws fixed through false timbers into the real timbers, and covered with pieces of cork resembling treenails. The concealment afforded space for no fewer than fifty flat tubs besides dry goods.

But in 1824 another vessel of the same name and port, described as a smack, was also arrested at Rye, and found to have both tobacco and silk goods concealed. This was effected by means of a false bottom to the ship, which extended as far aft as the ballast bulkhead. The entrance to the concealment was by means of a couple of scuttles on each side of her false keelson, these scuttles being screwed down in such a manner as also to be imperceptible. Also on either side of her cabin there were other hiding-places underneath the berths, and so constructed that they deceived more than one Revenue officer who came aboard to rummage her. The latter had bored holes through the lining, so as to try the distance of that lining from the supposed side of the vessel. Finding this distance not to exceed the fair allowance for the vessel's scuttling, the officers had gone ashore quite satisfied. From the number of gimlet-holes in the lining it was clear that the officers had been imposed upon considerably. But what these officers had taken for the side of the ship was only an intermediary planking, the actual concealment being between that and the vessel's side.

To get to the entrance of these concealments, the bedding had to be taken out, which they had no doubt omitted to do. But if they had done this they would have been able properly to get to the lining, when two small pieces of wood about an inch square let into the plank made them-

King's Cutters vs Smugglers -1700-1855

selves apparent. And these, if removed with the point of a knife or chisel, allowed small pieces of cork (circular in shape) to become visible. As soon as these corks were removed, the heads of bed-screws were observable, and these being unscrewed allowed two boards running the whole lengths of the berths to be taken up, by which means were revealed the concealments capable of containing a considerable quantity of dry goods.

Somewhat reminiscent of this ship was the French vessel, *St. Antoine*, which was seized at Shoreham. She had come from Dieppe, and her master was named A. Fache. The after part of her cabin was fitted with two cupboards which had shelves that took down, the back of which was supposed to be the lining of the transom. But on taking up the same, timbers showed themselves. On examining the planks closely, it was noticed that they overlapped each other, the timbers being made to act as fastenings. On striking the lower end of the false timbers on one side, it moved round on a bolt, and one plank with a timber was made to shift on each side of the false stern-post, forming a stern-frame with the other. Below the cupboards down to the run of the vessel the same principle was followed. The entrance to this was by taking down the seats and lockers in the cabin, and a false stern-post appeared to be fastened with a forelock and ring, but by unfastening the same, the false stern-post and middle plank could be taken down.

Two ingenious instances of the sinking of contraband goods were found out about the year 1823, and both occurred within that notorious southeast corner of England. The first of these belongs to Sandwich, where three half-ankers of foreign spirits were seized floating, being hidden in a sack, a bag of shingle weighing 30 lbs. being used to act as a sinker. Attached to the sack were an inflated bladder and about three fathoms of twine, together with a small bunch of feathers to act as a buoy to mark the spot. When this arrangement was put into use it was found that the bladder kept the sack floating one foot below the surface of the water. The feathers were to mark the spot where the sack, on being thrown overboard, might bring up in case any accident had occurred to the bladder.

At spring tides the rush of the water over the Sandwich flats causes a good deal of froth which floats on the surface. The reader must often have observed such an instance on many occasions by the sea. The exact color is a kind of dirty yellow, and this color being practically identical with that of the bladder, it would be next to impossible to tell the difference between froth and bladder at any distance, and certainly no officer of the Revenue would look for such things unless he had definite knowledge beforehand.

The second occurrence took place at Rye. A seizure was made of twelve tubs of spirits which had been sunk by affixing to the head of each a circular piece of sheet lead which just fitted into the brim of the cask, and was there kept in its place by four nails. The weight of the lead was 9 lbs., and the tubs, being lashed longitudinally together, rolled in a tideway unfettered, being anchored by the usual lines and heavy stones. The

The Fine Art of Smuggling:

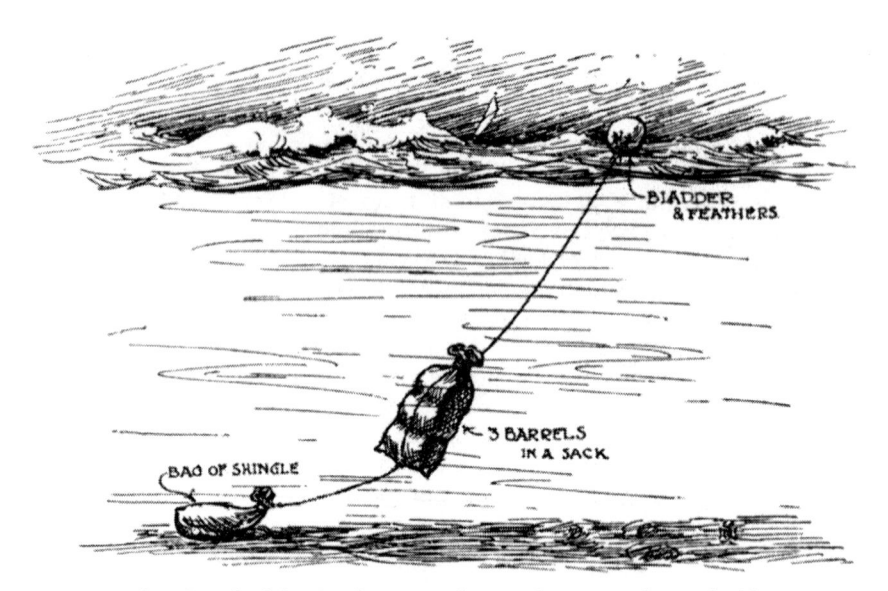

The Sandwich Device. In the sack were three half-ankers. A bag of shingle acted as sinker, and the bladder kept the sack floating.

leads sank the casks to the bottom in 2-1/2 fathoms of water, but at that depth in specific gravity they so nearly approximated to their equal bulk of fluid displaced that they could scarcely be felt on the finger. The leads were cast in moulds to the size required, and could be repeatedly used for the same purpose, and it was thought that the smuggling vessels, after coming across the Channel and depositing their cargoes, would on a later voyage be given back these pieces of lead to be affixed to other casks.

A clinker-built boat of about 26 tons burthen named the *St. Francois,* the master of which was named Jean Baptiste La Motte, of and from Gravelines, crossed the North Sea and passed through the Forth and Clyde Canal in the year 1823 to Glasgow. Nominally she had a cargo of apples and walnuts, her crew consisting of six men besides the master. She was able to land part of her cargo of "apples" at Whitby and the rest at Glasgow, and afterwards, repassing safely through the canal again, returned to Gravelines. But some time after her departure from Scotland it was discovered that she had brought no fruit at all, but that what appeared to be apples were so many portions of lace made up into small boxes of the size of apples and ingeniously painted to resemble that fruit.

Even as late as the year 1824, the last of the armed cutters had not been yet seen. We may call attention to the information which was sent to the London Custom House through the Dublin Customs. The news was to the effect that in February of that year there was in the harbor of Flushing, getting ready for sea in three or four days, a cutter laden with tobacco, brandy, Hollands, and tea. She was called the *Zellow*, which was a fictitious name, and was a vessel of 160 tons with a crew of forty men, copper-bottomed and pierced for fourteen guns. She was painted black, with white moldings round the stern. Her boom also was black, so were her gaff and masthead.

The officers were warned to keep a look-out for her, and informed that she had a large strengthening fish on the upper side of the boom, twenty cloths in the head, and twenty-eight in the foot of the mainsail. It was reported that she was bound for Ballyherbert, Mountain Foot, and Clogher Head in Ireland, but if prevented from landing there she was consigned to Ormsby of Sligo and Burke of Connemara. In the event of her failing there also she had on board two "spotsmen" or pilots for the coast of Kerry and Cork. There was also a lugger at the same time about to proceed from Flushing to Wexford. This vessel was of from 90 to 100 tons, was painted black, with two white moldings and a white counter. She carried on her deck a large boat which was painted white also.

Tobacco was discovered concealed in rather a curious manner on another vessel. She had come from St. John, New Brunswick, with a cargo of timber, and the planks had been hollowed out and filled with tobacco, but it was so cleverly done that it was a long time before it was detected. All sorts of vessels and of many rigs were fitted with places of concealment, and there was even a 50-ton cutter named the *Alborough*, belonging to London, employed in this business, which had formerly been a private yacht, but was now more profitably engaged running goods from Nieuport in Belgium to Hull.

The descriptions of some of these craft sent to the various outports, so that a smart look-out for them might be kept up, are certainly valuable to us, as they preserve a record of a type of craft that has altered so much during the past century as almost to be forgotten. The description of the sloop *Jane*, for instance, belonging to Dumbarton in 1824, is worth noting by those who are interested in the ships of yesterday. Sloop-rigged, and carvel built, she had white moldings over a yellow streak, and her bulwark was painted green inside. Her cross-jack yards,[1] as they are called, her bowsprit-boom, her gaff and studding-sail boom were all painted white, and she had three black hoops on the mast under the hounds. Her sails were all white, but her square topsail and topgallant-yards were black. The *Jane* was a 90-tonner.

The reader will remember considering some time back an open boat which was fitted with hollow stanchions under the thwarts, so that

---

[1] The cro'jack yard was really the lower yard of a full-rigged ship on the mizzen-mast, to the arms of which the clews or lower corners of the mizzen-topsail were extended. But as sloops were fore-and-aft craft it is a little doubtful what is meant here. Either it refers to the barren yard below the square topsail carried by the sloops of those days—the clews actually were extended to this yard's arms—or the word may have been the equivalent of what we nowadays call cross-trees.

The Fine Art of Smuggling:

through these stanchions ropes might pass through into the water below. I have come across a record of a smack registered in the port of London under the singularly inappropriate name of the *Good Intent*. She was obviously built or altered with the sole intention of being employed in smuggling. I need say nothing of her other concealments under the cabin berths and so on, as they were practically similar to those on the Asp. But it was rather exceptional to find on so big a craft as the *Good Intent* a false stanchion immediately abaft the fore scuttle.

Through this stanchion ran a leaden pipe about two inches in diameter, and this went through the keelson and garboard strake, so that by this means a rope could be led through and into the vessel, while at the other end a raft of tubs could be towed through the water. By hauling tightly on to this line the kegs could be kept beautifully concealed under the bilge of the vessel, so that even in very clear water it would not be easy to suspect their presence. The other end of this pipe came up through the ship until it was flush with the deck, and where this joined the latter a square piece of lead was tarred and pitched so as scarcely to be perceived.

There must indeed have been a tremendous amount of thought, as well as the expenditure of a great deal of time and money, in creating these methods of concealment, but since they dared not now to use force, it was all they could do.

CHAPTER SEVENTEEN
Smuggling by Concealment

Second cousin to the method of filling oars and spars with spirits was that adopted by a number of people whose homes and lives were connected with the sea-shore. They would have a number of shrimping nets on board, the usual wooden handles being fitted at one end of these nets. But these handles had been purposely made hollow, so that round tin cases could be fitted in. The spirits then filled these long cavities, and whether they caught many shrimps or not was of little account, for dozens of men could wade ashore with these nets and handles on their backs and proceed to their homes without raising a particle of suspicion. It was well worth doing, for it was calculated that as much as 2-1/2 gallons of spirit could be poured into each of these hollow poles.

Collier-brigs were very fond of smuggling, and among others mention might be made of the *Venus* of Rye, an 80-ton brig which between January and September one year worked three highly profitable voyages, for besides her ordinary cargo she carried each time 800 casks of spirits, these being placed underneath the coals. There was also the brig *Severn* of Bristol, which could carry about five keels of coal, but seldom carried more than four, the rest of the space of course being made up with contraband. In 1824 she worked five voyages, and on each occasion she carried, besides her legitimate cargo, as much as eight tons of tobacco under her coals.

And there was a Danish-built sloop named the *Blue-eyed Lass* belonging to Shields, with a burthen of 60 odd tons, also employed in the coal trade. She was a very suspicious vessel, and was bought subsequently by the people of Rye to carry on similar work to the other smuggling craft. All sorts of warnings were sent to the Customs Board giving them information that *The Rose in June* (needless to say of Rye) was about to have additional concealments added. She was of 37 tons burthen, and had previously been employed as a packet boat. They were also warned that George Harrington, a noted smuggler resident at Eastbourne, intended during the winter months to carry on the contraband trade, and to land somewhere between Southampton and Weymouth. He had made arrangements with a large number of men belonging to Poole and the neighboring country, and had obtained a suitable French lugger.

In 1826 the smacks *Fox* and *Lovely Lass* of Portsmouth were seized at that port with kegs of spirits secreted under their bottoms in a thin contemporary casing. The ingenious part of this trick was that there was no means of getting into the concealed area from the interior of the vessel. Thus any officer coming aboard to search would have little or no reason to suspect her. But it was necessary every time this vessel returned from abroad with her contraband for her to be laid ashore, and at low water the kegs could be got at externally. To begin with there were pieces of plank two inches thick fastened to the timbers by large nails. Then, between the planks and the vessel's bottom the tubs were concealed. The arrangement was exceeding simple yet wonderfully clever. In effect this method consisted of filling up the hollow below the turn of the bilge. It would certainly not improve the vessel's speed, but it would give her an effective means of stowing her cargo of spirits out of the way.

It was because of such incidents as this last mentioned that orders were sent to all ports for the local craft and others to be examined frequently ashore as well as afloat, in order that any false bottom might be detected. And the officers were to be careful and see that the name of the ship and her master painted on a ship corresponded with the names in her papers.

Even open boats were found fitted with double bottoms, as for instance the *Mary*, belonging to Dover. She was only 14 feet long with 5 feet 9-1/2 inches beam, but she had both a double bottom and double sides, in which were contained thirty tin cases to hold 29 gallons of spirits. Her depth from gunwale to the top of her ceiling[1] originally was 2 feet 8-1/2 inches. But the depth from the gunwale to the false bottom was 2 feet 5-3/4 inches. The concealment ran from the stem to the transom. The entrance was made by four cuttles very ingeniously and neatly fitted, with four nails fore and aft through the timbers to secure them from moving. There was one on each side of the keelson, one about a foot forward of the keelson and one under the fore thwart. Even Thames barges were fitted with concealments; in fact there was not a species of craft from a barque to a dinghy that was not modified in some way for smuggling.

The name of the barge was the *Alfred* of London, and she was captured off Birchington one December day in 1828. She pretended that she

---

[1] The ceiling of a ship signified the inside planks.

was bound from Arundel with a cargo of wood hoops, but when she was boarded she had evidently been across to "the other side"; for there was found 1045 tubs of gin and brandy aboard her when she was captured, together with her crew, by a boat sent from the cruiser *Vigilant*. The discovery was made by finding an obstruction about three feet deep from the top of the coamings, which induced the Revenue officer to clear away the bundles of hoops under the fore and main hatchways. He then discovered a concealment covered over with sand, and on cutting through a plank two inches thick the contraband was discovered.

The accompanying diagram shows the sloop *Lucy* of Fowey, William Strugnell master. On the 14th of December 1828 she was seized at Chichester after having come from Portsmouth in ballast. She was found to be fitted with the concealment shown in the plan, and altogether there were 100 half-ankers thus stowed away, 50 being placed on each side of her false bottom. She was just over 35 tons burthen, and drew four feet of water, being sloop rigged, as many of the barges in those days were without the little mizzen which is so familiar to our eyes today.

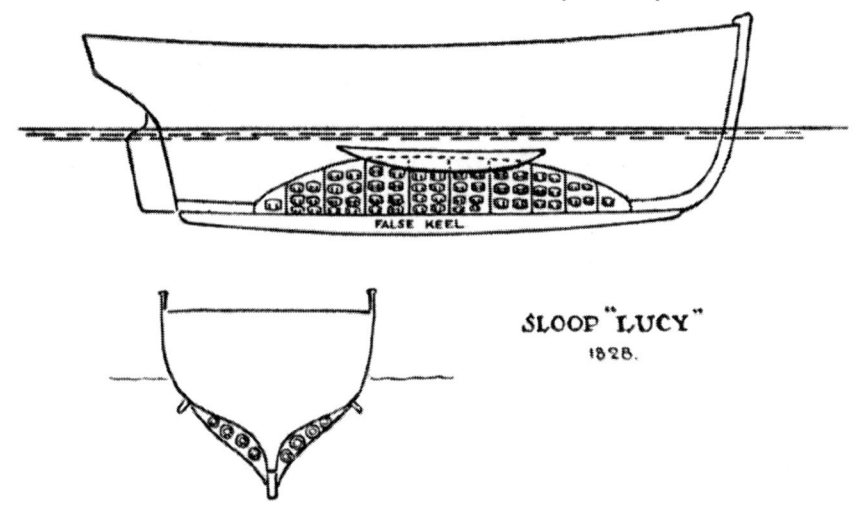

The Sloop Lucy showing Concealments.

Cases of eggs sent from Jersey were fitted with false sides in which silks were smuggled. Trawlers were engaged in sinking tubs of spirits. A dog-kennel was washed ashore from a vessel that foundered off Dungeness, and on being examined it was found to be fitted with a false top to hold 30 lbs. of tobacco. An Irish smack belonging to Cork was specially fitted for the contraband trade, having previously actually been employed as a Coast-Guard watch-boat.

There was a vessel named *Grace* manned by three brothers—all notorious smugglers—belonging to Coverack (Cornwall). This vessel used to put to sea by appointment to meet a French vessel, and having trans-

The Fine Art of Smuggling:

ferred the contraband, she would run the goods ashore somewhere between Land's End and Newport, South Wales. In fact, all kinds of smuggling went on even after the first quarter of that wonderful nineteenth century.

About the year 1831 five casks imported from Jersey was alleged to contain cider, but on being examined they were found to contain something else as well. The accompanying sketch represents the plan of one of these.

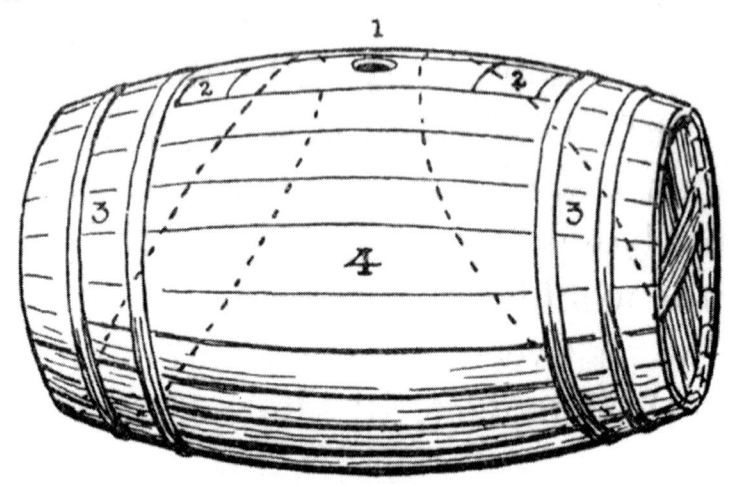

1. BUNG.
2. OPENINGS.
3. TOBACCO.
4. CYDER.

Cask for Smuggling Tobacco.

From this it will be seen that the central space was employed for holding the cider, but the ends were full of tobacco being contained in two tin cases. In this diagram No. 1 represents the bung, No. 2 shows the aperture on each side through which the tobacco was thrust into the tin cases which are marked by No. 3, the cider being contained in the central portion marked 4. Thus the usual method of gauging a cask's contents was rendered useless, for unless a bent or turned rod were employed it was impossible to detect the presence of these side casks for the tobacco.

One may feel a little incredulous at some of the extraordinary yarns which one hears occasionally from people concerning the doings of smugglers. A good deal has doubtless arisen as the result of a too vivid imagination, but, as we have shown from innumerable instances, there is quite enough that is actual fact without having recourse to invention.

I know of a certain port in our kingdom where there existed a legend to the effect that in olden days the smugglers had no need to bring the tubs in with them, but that if they only left them outside when the young flood was making, those tubs would find their own way in to one particular secluded spot in that harbor. A number of amateur enthusiasts debated the point quite recently, and a wager was made that such a thing was not possible. But on choosing a winter's day, and throwing a number of barrels into the water outside the entrance, it was found that the trend of the tide was always to bring them into that corner. But, you will instantly say, wouldn't the Coast-Guard in the smuggling days have seen the barrels as they came along the top of the water?

The answer is certainly in the affirmative. But the smugglers used to do the following, and this I have found in a document dated 1833, at which time the device was quite new—at least to the Customs officials.

Let us suppose that the vessel had made a safe passage from France, Holland, or wherever she had obtained the tubs of spirits. She had eluded the cruisers and arrived off the harbor entrance at night just as the flood tide was making. Overboard go her tubs, and away she herself goes to get out of the sphere of suspicion. These tubs numbered say sixty-three, and were firmly lashed together in a shape very similar to a pile of shot—pyramid fashion. The tops of the tubs were all painted white, but the raft was green. Below this pyramid of tubs were attached two grapnel anchors, and the whole contrivance could float in anything above seven feet of water.

It was so designed that the whole of the tubs came in on the tide below water, only three being partially visible, and their white color made them difficult to be seen among the little waves. But as soon as they came to the spot where there were only seven feet of water the two grapnels came into action and held the tubs moored like a ship. And as the tide rose, so it completely obliterated them. someone was of course on the look-out for his spirits, and when the tide had dropped it was easy enough to wade out and bring the tubs ashore, or else "sweep" them ashore with a long rope that dragged along the bottom of the harbor.

During the year 1834 smuggling was again on the increase, especially on the south and east coasts, and it took time for the officers to learn all these new-fangled tricks which were so frequently employed. Scarcely had the intricacies of one device been learned than the smugglers had given up that idea and taken to something more ingenious still.

Some time back we called attention to the way in which the Deal boatmen used to walk ashore with smuggled tea. About the year 1834 a popular method of smuggling tea, lace, and such convenient goods was to wear a waistcoat or stays which contained eighteen rows well stuffed with 8 lbs. weight of tea. The same man would also wear a pair of drawers made of stout cotton secured with strong drawing strings and stuffed with about 16 lbs. of tea. Two men were captured with nine parcels of lace secreted about their bodies, a favorite place being to wind it round the shins. Attempts were also made to smuggle spun or roll tobacco from

The Fine Art of Smuggling:

New York by concealing them in barrels of pitch, rosin, bales of cotton, and so on. In the case of a ship named the *Josephine*, from New York, the Revenue officers found in one barrel of pitch an inner package containing about 100 lbs. of manufactured tobacco.

The accompanying plan of the smack *Tam O'Shanter* (belonging to Plymouth), which was seized by the Padstow Coast-Guard, will show how spirits were sometimes concealed. This was a vessel of 72 tons with a fore bulkhead and a false bulkhead some distance aft of that. This intervening space, as will be seen, was filled up with barrels. Her hold was filled with a cargo of coals, and then aft of this came the cabin with berths on either side, as shown. But under these berths were concealments for stowing quite a number of tubs, as already explained.

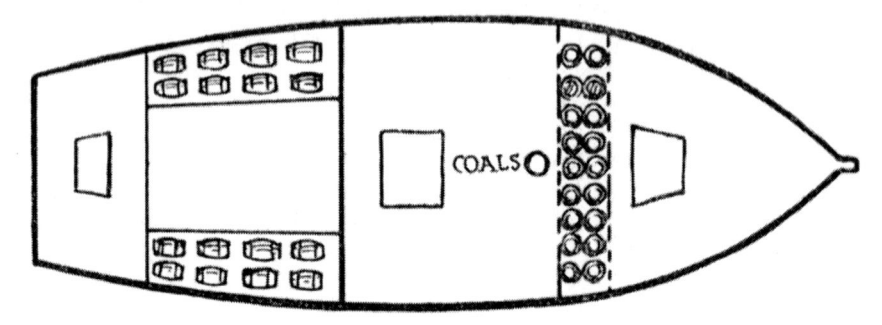

The Smack Tam O'Shanter showing Method of Concealment

A variation of the plan, previously mentioned, for smuggling by means of concealments in casks was that which was favored by foreign ships which traded between the Continent and the northeast coasts of England and Scotland. In this case the casks which held the supplies of drinking water were fitted with false sides and false ends. The inner casks thus held the fresh water, but the outer casks were full of spirits. After the introduction of steam, one of the first if not the very first instance of steamship smuggling by concealment was that occurring in 1836, when a vessel was found to have had her paddle-boxes so lined that they could carry quite a large quantity of tobacco and other goods.

Another of those instances of ships fitted up specially for smuggling was found in the French smack *Auguste*, which is well worth considering. She was, when arrested, bound from Gravelines, and could carry about fifty tubs of spirits or, instead, a large amount of silk and lace. Under the ladder in the forepeak there was a potato locker extending from side to side, and under this, extending above a foot or more before it, was the concealment. Further forward were some loose planks forming a hatch, under which was the coal-hole. This appeared to go as far as the bulkhead behind the ladder, and had the concealment been full, it could never have been found, but in walking over where the coals were, that part of the concealment which extended beyond the locker which was empty sounded hollow: whereupon the officers pulled up one of the planks and discovered the hiding-place.

It was decided in 1837 that, in order to save the expense of breaking up a condemned smuggling vessel, in future the ballast, mast, pumps, bulkheads, platforms, and cabins should be taken out from the vessel: and that the hull should then be cut into pieces not exceeding six feet long. Such pieces were then to be sawn in a fore-and-aft direction so as to cut across the beams and thwarts and render the hull utterly useless. The accompanying sketch well illustrates the ingenuity which was displayed at this time by the men who were bent on running goods.

What is here represented is a flat-bottomed boat, which perhaps might never have been discovered had it not been driven ashore near to Selsey Bill during the gales of the early part of 1837. The manner in which this craft was employed was to tow her for a short distance and then to cast her adrift. She was fitted with rowlocks for four oars, but apparently these had never been used. Three large holes were bored in her bottom, for the purpose which we shall presently explain.

Built very roughly, with half-inch deal, and covered over with a thin coat of white paint, she had a grommet at both bow and stern. She measured only 16 feet long and 4 feet wide, with a depth of 2 feet 2 inches. It

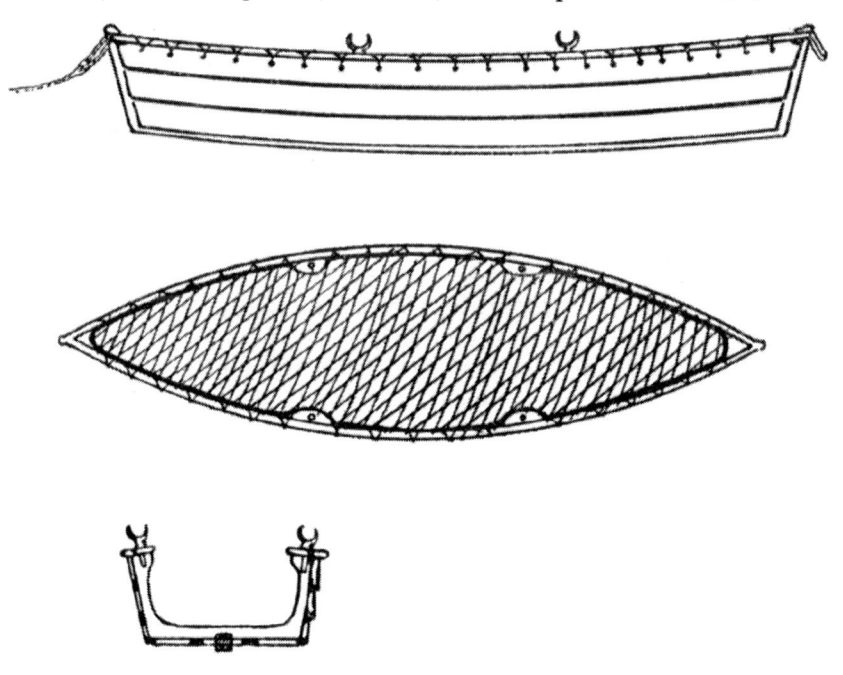

Flat-Bottomed Boat found off Selsey. The sketch shows longitudinal plan, the method of covering with net, and midship section.

The Fine Art of Smuggling:

will be noticed that she had no thwarts. Her timbers were of bent ash secured with common French nails, and alongside the gunwales were holes for lacing a net to go over the top of this boat. Her side was made of three deal planks, the net being made of line, and of the same size as the line out of which the tub-slings were always made. The holes in her floor were made for the water to get in and keep her below the surface, and the net, spreading from gunwale to gunwale, prevented her cargo of tubs from being washed out. It was in order to have ample and unfettered room for the tubs that no thwarts were placed. She would be towed astern of a smack or lugger under the water, and having arrived at the appointed spot the towrope would be let go, and the grapnels attached to both grommets at bow and stern would cause her to catch on the bottom when in sufficiently shallow water. Later on, at low tide, the smugglers' friends could go out in their boats with a weighted line or hawser and sweep along the bottom of the sea, and soon locate her and tow her into the beach.

In order to prevent certain obvious excuses being made by dishonest persons, all British subjects were distinctly forbidden to pick up spirits found in these illegal half-ankers, only officers of the Royal Navy, the Customs, and the Excise being permitted so to do. But it was not always that the Revenue cruisers were employed in catching smugglers. We have pointed out that their duties also included Quarantine work.

In the spring of 1837 it was represented to the Treasury that there was great distress in certain districts of the Highlands and Western Islands of Scotland owing to the failure of the last harvest. Sir John Hill was therefore directed to proceed to Scotland and take such steps as might be necessary for the immediate supply of seed, corn, and potatoes, and the officers and commanders of the Revenue cruisers were directed to afford him every assistance.

In the previous chapter attention was called to the singular inappropriateness of calling a smuggling vessel the *Good Intent*. That was a smack belonging to the year 1824, which was found at Rye. But this name seems to have had a certain amount of popularity among these ingenious gentlemen, for there was a smuggling schooner named the *Good Intent* which was seized in the year 1837. How cleverly and effectively she was fitted up for a smuggling voyage can be ascertained by considering the accompanying longitudinal plan.

She had a burthen of 72 tons, and was captured by the Revenue cruiser *Sylvia* in Mount's Bay on the 14th of March. The plan denotes her principal features, including her sail-room and general store right aft. Immediately forward of this was the first concealment on the port side only. Entrance was gained by means of a slide which was nailed up, and here many casks could easily be stored. Next to this came the after bulkhead, but forward of this was also a false bulkhead, the distance between the real and the false being 2-1/2 feet, and affording a space to contain 138 kegs.

King's Cutters vs Smugglers -1700-1855

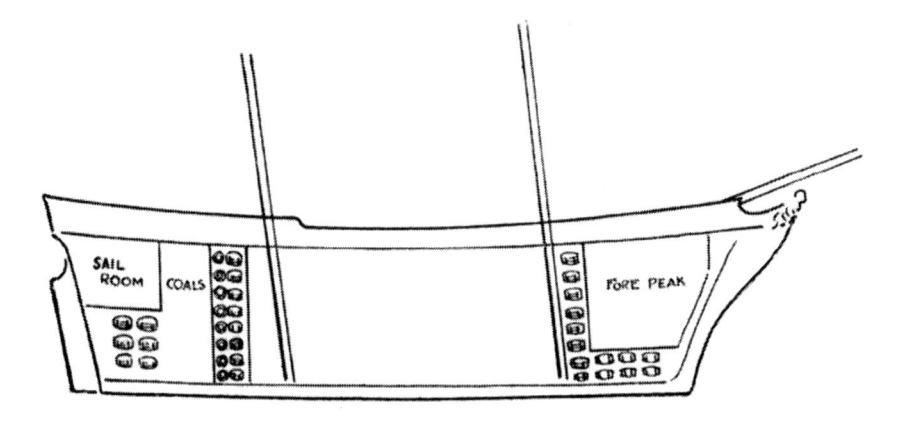

Plan of the Schooner Good Intent showing Method of Smuggling Casks.

Under the cabin were coals, and around the coals under the cabin deck were placed some kegs. The fore bulkhead had also a false bulkhead 2 feet 5 inches apart, and this space held as many as 148 kegs. Under the deck of the forepeak were also 21 kegs. The length of these kegs was 17 inches, and they were nearly a foot in diameter. Each cask contained 4-1/2 gallons of French brandy. This vessel was found to have merely limestone ballast in her hold, but her illicit cargo was more valuable to her than if she had been fully laden with the commodity which she usually and legitimately traded in. Later in the same year, and by the same cruiser *Sylvia*, this time off Land's End, the Jersey schooner *Spartan*, a vessel of 36-1/2 tons, was seized, as she was found to be fitted up with similar concealments (see sketch).

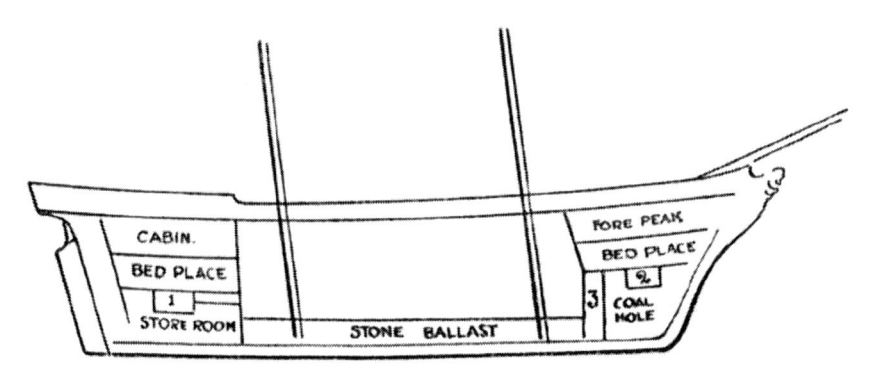

The Schooner Spartan
1. *Hollow beam.*
2. *Opening for entering No. 3.*
3. *Place of concealment.*

The Fine Art of Smuggling:

One day about the middle of the last century a 16-ton Grimsby fishing-smack named *Lord Rivers* left her native port and journeyed south. Her owner and master was in a dismal frame of mind, and complained to his mate that things were pretty bad, and he was becoming remarkably poor. The fishing was not prospering so far as he was concerned, and so after thinking the matter over he was proposing to take the ship over to Boulogne and get a cargo of between thirty and forty gallons of spirits. His mate heard what he had to say and agreed to go with him.

So to Boulogne they proceeded, where they purchased the spirits from a dealer, who brought the spirits on board, not in casks but in skins and bladders, making about fifty in all. These were deposited in the smack's hold, and she then cleared out of harbor and went to the fishing-grounds, where, to make matters appear all right, she remained twenty-four hours, for the purpose of obtaining some oysters by dredging. Whilst on the fishing-grounds the spirits were stowed in a neat concealment at the stern of the vessel on both sides abaft the hatchway. Before long the smack got going and ran into Dover with the oysters and her spirits, lowered her sails, and made everything snug. In due course the bladders of spirits were got out of the hold in small numbers, and placed in baskets and covered over with a sufficiently thick layer of oysters to prevent their presence being detected. These baskets were taken to a neighboring tap-room, the landlord of which bought as much as he wanted, and a local poulterer bought the rest of the spirits and oysters as well.

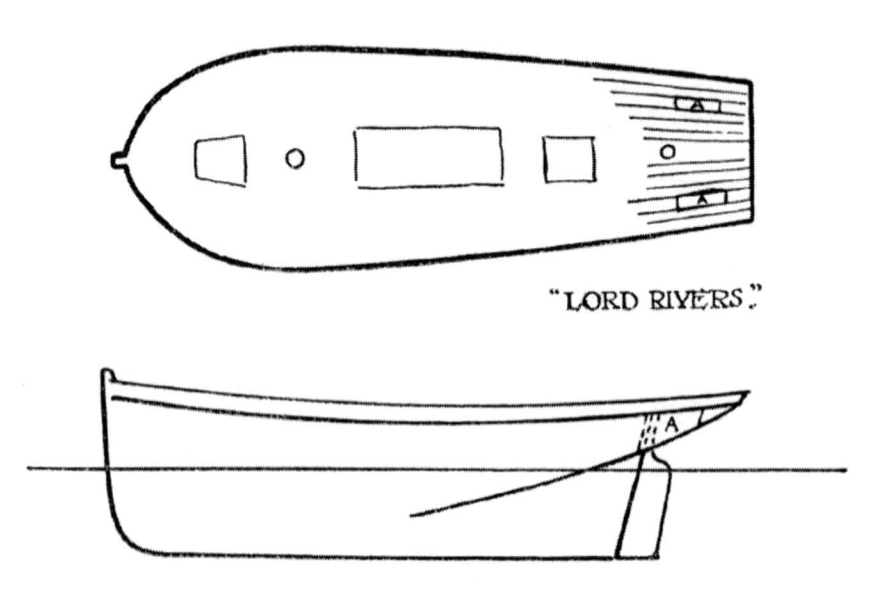

Deck Plan and Longitudinal Plan of the Lord Rivers

But the local Coast-Guard officer had for a long time been suspicious of this vessel, and evidently this was not her first voyage in the smuggling trade. He had watched and followed the man who took the bladders ashore, and now came on board to see what he could find. The deck plan (above) will clearly convey to the reader the way in which the smack was fitted up with concealments. The letters A and A indicate two portions of the deck planking, each portion being about a couple of feet long. These were movable, and fitted into their places with a piece of spun-yarn laid into the seams, and over this was laid some putty blackened on the top.

At first sight they appeared to be part of the solid planking of the deck, but on obtaining a chisel they were easily removed. There was now revealed the entrance to a space on each side of the rudder-case in the false stern capable of containing thirty or forty gallons of spirits. This in itself was conclusive, but when the Coast-Guard also found that the putty in the seams was soft and fresh, and that a strong smell of spirits emanated from this cavity, it was deemed that there was more than adequate reason for arresting the smack even though the hold was quite empty.

Thus the *Lord Rivers* came to a bad end.

CHAPTER EIGHTEEN
By Sea and Land

The evolution of smuggling methods had grown from brute force and superiority of ships to the point where it had become a fine art. With that in mind, we may resume our narrative of the interesting encounters that occurred between the smugglers on the one hand and the Preventive force on the other.

Earlier we dealt with the period up to the year 1822 and discussed various incidents which used to go on around our coast. It is time then to take up some of the notable exploits of cruisers and smugglers in the later period between the years 1822 and 1856. This covers the epoch when improved naval architecture, greater vigilance on the part of the cruisers, and a keener artfulness in the smugglers themselves were at work. Consequently some of these contests represent the best incidents in the whole history of smuggling.

But it was not always that the Revenue cruisers and Preventive boats were in the right. There were occasions when the commanders suffered from too much zeal, though certainly these were quite exceptional.

There is the case of the *Drencher* which well illustrates this. She was a Dutch vessel which had been to Italy, and was now returning home up the English Channel with a cargo of oil, bound for Amsterdam. Being somewhat square and ample of form, with the characteristic bluff bows much beloved by her countrymen, and being very foul on her bottom through long voyaging, she was also a dull sailer.[1] And such being the

---

[1] How slow she was may be guessed by the fact that she took seven hours to go from Dover to the Downs even under the expert handling of MacTavish's crew.

The Fine Art of Smuggling:

case, when she fell in with head winds her skipper and part-owner, Peter Crook, decided to let go anchor under Dungeness, where many a sailing craft then, as today, has taken shelter in similar circumstances.

Whilst she was at anchor waiting for a favorable slant, one of the numerous fishing-boats which are always to be seen hereabouts came alongside the *Drencher*[1] and asked the skipper if he required any assistance. Crook replied that if the wind was still ahead, and he was compelled to remain there until the next day, he would want some fuel for his stove. The fisherman sold some of his catch to the Dutchman, and then went on his way.

But soon after this a boat in the Preventive service, commanded by a Mr. MacTavish, a midshipman, came alongside and boarded the *Drencher*. The midshipman inquired what the Dutchman had had to do with the fishing-boat, and Crook answered that he had done nothing except to purchase some fish. But this did not satisfy Mr. MacTavish, who proceeded now to examine what was on board. Of course he found some casks of spirits, and asked Crook how they came to be there, to which Crook answered that they had been found floating in a former voyage and he had picked them up. This looked doubtful, but it was quite probable, for often the weights of stones from sunken tubs broke adrift and the tubs floated up to the surface. This was especially the case after bad weather.

We can well understand the midshipman's suspicions, and need not be surprised to learn that he felt justified in seizing the ship because of these tubs found on board. He had the anchor broken out, the sails hoisted, and took her first into Dover, and afterwards from Dover to Ramsgate, where most of her cargo was unloaded. But after a time she was ordered to be released and allowed to proceed to Holland, and later still her skipper brought an action against MacTavish for having been wrongfully detained for thirty days, for which demurrage he claimed four guineas a day, besides damage to her cable and other things, amounting in all to £208.

The reader will recollect that in an earlier chapter we saw a couple of sailing craft dodging about suspiciously in West Bay, one of which began to fire signals to the other in order to warn her of the Preventive boat: and we saw that the crew of three men in the offending craft were arrested and found guilty. One of these men, it will be remembered, was John Bartlett, who had at one time been a boy on a Revenue cutter.

From the incident which led to his arrest in 1819 let us pass to the 14th of September 1823. The scene is again West Bay, and the old passion is still strong in Bartlett notwithstanding his sentence. A little to the west of Bridport (Dorset) is Seatown, and just beyond that comes Golden Cape. On the night of the above date one of the Seatown Revenue officers about 1 A.M. noticed flashes coming from the cliff between Seatown and

---

[1] She was officially described as a dogger.

Golden Cape. He proceeded to the cliff, which at high-water runs straight up out of the sea. It was a dark night with no moon, a little breeze, and only slight surf on the shore—ideal conditions for any craft bent on smuggling.

On the cliff the officer, named Joseph Davey, saw a man. He hailed him, thinking it was someone else, and asked him if he were Joey Foss. "Yes," came back the answer, but when the officer seized him he discovered it was not Foss but the notorious John Bartlett. Up came another Revenue man named Thomas Nines to assist Davey, but in a few minutes Bartlett gave a loud whistle, whereupon Nines looked out seaward and exclaimed, "There's a boat."

"I sees him," answered Davey as the craft was approaching the shore. By this time, also, there were ten or twelve men coming towards the officers, and Bartlett managed to run down to the shore, shouting "Keep off!" "Keep off!" as loudly as he could. The officers ran too, but the boat turned round and put off to sea again. In the course of a few minutes there rose up a large fire on the cliff, about a hundred yards from where the officers were. It was another signal of warning to the boat. For Bartlett, having got away from the officers, had doubtless lit this, since it flared up near to where he was seen to run. The officers remained on the coast until daylight, and then launching their boat rowed a little way from the shore, and found a new buoy moored just by the spot where the lugger had been observed to turn round when hailed and warned. It was clear, on examination, that the buoy had not been in the water many hours, and after "creeping" along the sea bottom hereabouts they brought up sixty kegs, which were also quite new, and had evidently only been sunk when Bartlett sung out his warning. The latter was again arrested, and found guilty when subsequently tried. So again Bartlett had to retire from smuggling.

It happened only a few weeks before this incident that a seaman named Willis was on shore with his officer. Willis belonged to H.M.S. *Severn*, which was moored off Dover for the prevention of smuggling. The officer was a naval midshipman named Hope, stationed ashore.

While on duty they began to notice a man, whose name was William Clarke, near Chalk Fall, carrying a basket of nets and fishing lines. For a time both Willis and Hope took shelter under the Chalk Cliff as it was raining, but presently Willis separated from his officer to go to his appointed station. It occurred to him that Clarke appeared to be unnecessarily stout, and he was sure that he was trying to smuggle something. Willis went up to him and said he intended to search him, to which Clarke replied, "Certainly." He admitted he had some liquor there, but he hoped Willis would take no notice of it. The seaman insisted that he must take notice, for if it turned out to be foreign spirits he must seize it: whereupon Clarke flung down a couple of half-crowns and asked him to say nothing about it.

Willis again protested that he must see what the man had beneath his

The Fine Art of Smuggling:

gabardine. But at this Clarke took a knife from his pocket and cut a large bladder which he had under his clothes, containing half a gallon of spirits, and a spirituous liquor poured out on to the ground. Willis put his finger to it and found that it was foreign brandy. But the amusing legal aspect of this incident was that this foreign liquor could not be seized, nor could the man be prosecuted for having it, and it could not be condemned. But Clarke had indeed destroyed that which he had so nearly brought safely home. This was just one instance of the good work which the Coast Blockade was performing, Willis and other seamen being landed every night from H.M.S. *Severn* to act as guard at different points along the coast.

In the annals of smugglers and cruisers there are few more notable incidents than that which occurred on the 13th of January 1823, in the English Channel. On this day the Revenue cutter *Badger* was cruising off the French coast under the command of Lieutenant Henry Nazer, R.N. He was an officer of the Excise, but the cutter at that time was in the service of the Customs, her station being from the South Foreland to Dungeness.

About 7.30 A.M. the officer of the watch came below and told him something, whereupon Nazar hurried on deck and observed a suspicious sail on the starboard tack, the wind being E.S.E. The *Badger* was at that time about nine or ten miles off the French coast, somewhere abreast of Etaples, and about six or seven leagues from the English shore. The craft which was seen was, to use the lieutenant's own language, "a cutter yawl-rigged," which I understand to signify a cutter with a small lug-sail mizzen, as was often found on smugglers. At any rate, he had every reason to believe that this was a smuggling craft, and he immediately made sail after her. At that hour it was just daybreak, and the smuggler was about three or four miles off—to the eastward—and to windward, but was evidently running with sheets eased off in a westerly direction.

But when the smuggler saw the *Badger* was giving chase he also altered his course. It was a fine, clear, frosty morning, and the *Badger* quickly sent up his gaff topsail and began to overhaul the other, so that by nine o'clock the two vessels were only a mile apart. The *Badger* now hoisted his Revenue pendant at the masthead, consisting of a red field with a regal crown at the upper part next the mast, and he also hoisted the Revenue ensign (that is to say "a red Jack with a Union Jack in a canton at the upper corner and a regal crown in the center of the red Jack") at his peak. These signals instantly denoted that the ship was a Revenue cruiser. Lieutenant Nazar also ordered an unshotted gun to be fired as a further signal that the smuggler was to heave-to, but the stranger paid no attention and hoisted no colors.

Ten minutes later, as it was perceived that his signals were disregarded, the *Badger*'s commander ordered a shot to be fired at her, and this was immediately returned by the smuggler with one of her stern guns. From this time a running fire was kept up for nearly three hours, but shortly before midday, whilst the cutter was still chasing her and holding on the same course as the other, the *Badger* came on at such a pace that she ran aboard the smuggler's starboard quarter whilst both ships were still blazing away at each other.

The smuggler's crew then cried out for quarter in English. This was granted by the *Badger*'s commander, who had a boat lowered, but whilst in the act of so doing the treacherous smuggling craft recommenced firing. It was a cowardly thing to do, for Reymas, their own captain, had particularly asked the *Badger*'s commander to forgive them and overlook what they had done, whilst other members of the crew cried out to the same effect. This had caused a cessation of fire for about five minutes, and was only reopened by the smugglers' treachery. One of the *Badger*'s mariners named William Cullum, was in consequence shot dead by a musket aimed at him by one of the smugglers. Cullum was standing by the windlass at the time, and died instantly.

The *Badger*, therefore, again began to fire into the other ship, but in about another five minutes the smuggler again called for quarter, and this was again granted. The cruiser sent her boat aboard her, and brought off the smuggler's crew, amounting to twenty-three men, though two others had been killed in the affray. The *Badger*'s chief mate, on boarding the smuggler, sent away the latter's crew in their own boat, and seven of these men were found to be wounded, of whom one died the following morning.

"The Cruiser's Guns had shot away the Mizzen-Mast."

The Fine Art of Smuggling:

The name of the vessel was seen to be the *Vree Gebroeders*. She was of 119 tons burthen, and had the previous day started out from Flushing with a cargo of 42 gallons of brandy, 186 gallons of Geneva—these all being in the 3-1/2 gallon half-ankers. But there was also a good deal of other cargo, consisting of 856 bales of tobacco which contained 51,000 lbs., thirteen boxes of tea, and six bags of sugar. All these goods were made up in illegal-sized packages and she had nothing on board except what was contraband. The chests of tea were found all ready slung for landing with small ropes.

The *Vree Gebroeders* was provisioned for three months, and was armed with four carronades, 9-pounders, and two swivel muskets, bayonets, and other arms of different kinds. Her destination had been for Ireland. When the chief mate of the *Badger* boarded her he found that the cruiser's guns had shot away the mizzen-mast, but the smuggler's skipper remarked to the chief mate that the spare topmast on deck would serve for a mizzen and that the square-sail boom would make an outrigger, and that the trysail would be found below, but so far, he said, this sail had never been bent. Later on the chief mate found also the deck-log of the *Vree Gebroeders*, which had been kept on two slates, and it was a noticeable fact that these were kept in English. They read thus:

N.W. by N.
Remarks, Monday 13th.
N.W. by W. At 6.30 Ostend
Light bore S.E. distant
12 miles.
At 4 a.m. Calais Light
bore E. by S.

So when the *Badger* first sighted this craft the latter had made her last entry in the log, only three and a half hours before. It was significant that English charts were also found among the ship's papers, though her manifest, her certificate, her bill of lading, and other certificates were all in Dutch. The books found included Hamilton Moore's *Navigation*, another similar work by Norie, the *British Channel Pilot*, and *Navigation of the North Seas*. There was also found a Dutch ensign and a Dutch Jack on board, but there was even an English Prayer-book.

The prisoners remained on board the *Badger* until next day, when they were transferred to H.M.S. *Severn*. The *Vree Gebroeders* was taken into Dover, and was valued, together with her cargo, at the handsome sum of £11,000, which would have been a fine amount of prize money; but in spite of the clear evidence at the trial, the jury were so prejudiced in favor of the smugglers that they found the prisoners not guilty, their contention being that the ship and cargo were wholly foreign, and that more than half of the crew were foreigners.

It had been an unfortunate affair. Besides the death of Cullum and the two smugglers killed and the seven smugglers wounded, Lieutenant Nazer, James Harper, William Poppedwell, Daniel Hannibel, and James

Giles were all wounded on the *Badger*, Nazer being wounded on the left shoulder by a musket ball. The smuggler's crew had made ludicrous efforts to pretend they were Dutch. Dutch names were assumed, but witnesses at the trial were able to assign to them their proper appellations, and it was significant that the crew spoke English without a foreign accent. Her commander insisted his name was Reymas, but his real name was Joseph Wills, and he had been foremost in the calling for quarter. Another of the crew, who pretended his name was Jan Schmidt, was found to be an Englishman named John Smith. The vessel herself had been built by a Kentishman, living at Flushing, the previous year.

And here is another of those occasions when there was displayed an excess of zeal, though under the circumstances who would blame the Preventive officer for what he did?

In February of 1824, a man named Field and his crew of three came out from Rye—that hotbed of smugglers—and intended to proceed to the well-known trawling ground about fifteen miles to the S.W. of Rye, abreast of Fairlight, but about five or six miles out from that shore. Unfortunately it fell very calm, so that it took them some time to reach the trawling ground, and even when with the assistance of the tide they arrived there, the wind was so scant that it was useless to shoot the trawl in the water. Naturally, therefore, it was a long time before they had obtained their cargo of flat fish, and when a little breeze sprang up they had to get back to Rye, as their provisions had run short.

On their way back, when they were only about four or five miles from their harbor, they fell in with a small open sailing-boat named the *Rose*, containing four or five men. Field's bigger craft was hailed by the *Rose* and asked to be taken in tow, as they also had run short of provisions, and were anxious to get back to harbor at once. Field's boat took one of their crew on board, whilst the rest remained in the *Rose* and were towed astern.

It was now about four or five in the morning, and they had not proceeded more than another couple of miles before they were hailed again, but this time by a boat under the command of a Preventive officer named Lipscomb, who had been sent by Lieutenant Gammon, R.N., from the revenue cruiser *Cameleon*. The cutter's boat bumped alongside Field's craft, which was called the *Diamond*. After making fast, Lipscomb and his boat's crew jumped aboard, and announced that they suspected the *Diamond* was fitted with concealments, and he wished to examine her. But after rummaging the ship nothing suspicious was found. Lipscomb then explained that he had been ordered by Lieutenant Gammon to take the *Diamond* and to bring her alongside the *Cameleon* and then to order Field and his crew to go aboard the cruiser as prisoners.

This, of course, did not exactly lead to harmony on board. Lipscomb attempted to seize hold of the tiller, so as to steer the vessel back to Hastings Roads, where the cruiser was lying. But Field turned to him and said: "I don't know about your having the helm. You don't know where the cutter is any more than I do."

With that, Field pushed the man aside, grasped hold of the tiller, and shoved it hard up, and bearing away, ran the vessel out seawards. But after keeping on this course for twenty minutes they fell in with the *Cameleon*, and the two vessels came near to each other. The cruiser's commander shouted to Lipscomb, and ordered him to get into the cruiser's galley, which had been towing astern of the *Diamond* all this time, and to row to the cruiser. This was done, and then Lipscomb received his orders. He was to return to the trawler and seize the hands and bring them to the *Cameleon*. So the galley returned again and brought the *Diamond*'s crew as ordered. It was now 7 A.M., and they were kept as prisoners on the cutter until 9 A.M. the following day. Lipscomb and his boat's crew of four now took charge of the *Diamond*, and began to trim sheets, and before long the two craft got separated.

When Field proceeded on board the *Cameleon* he took with him his ship's papers at the lieutenant's orders. He then ventured to ask how it was that his smack had been detained, to which Gammon replied that he had received information from the Collector of Customs at Rye. Field, however, was incredulous. "I rather doubt your word," he said, whereupon the officer took out of his pocket a letter, doubled the page down one or two lines, and showed the doubting skipper that it was as the lieutenant had stated. Gammon then went below and took Field's papers with him, and there they remained until the following morning.

The *Cameleon* went jogging along, and having arrived abreast of Hastings, Gammon sent one of his crew ashore in the cutter's boat, and later on fetched him back. The object, no doubt, was to send the *Diamond*'s papers ashore to be examined as to their veracity, though nothing was said to Field on the subject. It is clear that the reply from the authorities came back that the papers were found in order, and that Field was not known as a smuggler; for after the man who had been sent ashore returned, the *Cameleon* made sail, and stood out to sea for a distance of eighteen miles. She had lost sight of the *Diamond* and her prize crew, and it was not until about breakfast time the following day that the cruiser found the smack again. When at length the two craft did come together, Lipscomb was called on board the cruiser and summoned below to Gammon. What exactly the conversation was never came out, but from subsequent events it is fairly clear that Gammon asked what opinion Lipscomb had been able to form of the *Diamond*, and that the latter had to admit she was a genuine trawler; for soon after, the lieutenant sent the steward for Field and one of his men to go below. The two men did as they were ordered.

"Good morning," said the cruiser's commander as they came into the cabin, "here are your papers, Field."

Field hesitated for a moment; then answered, "I don't know, sir, as to taking them. I'm not altogether satisfied about being detained so long.

And had I been aboard the smack, and you had refused to let me have the tiller," he continued, getting angrier every moment, "I would have shot you as sure as you had been a man."

"You may do as you please," came the commander's cool reply, "about taking them, but if you do not choose to take them, I shall take you away to Portsmouth and give you up to the Port Admiral, and let him do with you as he thinks proper."

Thinking therefore that it were better to be discreet and hold his tongue, Field took the papers, went up again on deck, collected his men, went back to his smack, and the incident ended—for the present. But the Revenue men had clearly made an error this time. About a year later Field, as a master and part-owner of the *Diamond*, brought an action against Gammon for assault and detention, and was awarded a verdict and £5 damages.

It is curious to find what sympathy the smugglers sometimes received in a section of society where one would hardly have expected this to exist. There are at least three instances of men of position and wealth showing their feelings undisguisedly in favor of these lawless men. There was a Lt. Colonel Chichester, who was called upon for explanations as to his conduct in this respect; there was the case also of the naval officer commanding H.M. sloop *Pylades* being convicted and dismissed the service for protecting smugglers, and, most interesting of all, was the incident which centered round Sir William Courtenay.

The facts of this case may be summarized as follows. On Sunday afternoon, the 17th of February 1833, the Revenue cutter *Lively* was cruising at the back of the Goodwins, when about three o'clock she spotted a vessel about five or six miles off which somehow aroused suspicions. The name of the latter was eventually found to be the *Admiral Hood*. At this time the sloop was about midway between England and France, her commander being Lieutenant James Sharnbler, R.N. The *Admiral Hood* was a small dandy-rigged fore-and-after, that is to say, she was a cutter with a small mizzen on which she would set a lugsail.

The *Lively* gave chase, and gradually began to gain on the other. When the *Admiral Hood* was within about a mile of the *Lively*, the former hauled across the latter, and when she had got on the *Lively's* weather-bow the Revenue craft immediately tacked, whereupon the *Admiral Hood* put about again and headed for the French coast. After vainly attempting to cause her to heave-to by the usual Revenue signals, the *Lively* was compelled to fire on her, and one shot was so well placed that it went clean through the dandy's sail. Thinking that this was quite near enough, the *Admiral Hood* hove-to.

But just prior to this, Lieutenant Sharnbler had ordered an officer and two men to take spyglasses and watch her. At this time they were about fifteen or sixteen miles away from the North Foreland. One of the men looking through his glass observed that the *Admiral Hood* was heaving tubs overboard, and it was then that the first musket was fired for her

The Fine Art of Smuggling:

"The Admiral Hood was heaving tubs overboard."

to heave-to, but as the tubs were still thrown overboard for the next three-quarters of an hour, the long gun and the muskets were directed towards her. The two vessels had sailed on parallel lines for a good hour's chase before the firing began, and the chase went on until about a quarter to five, the tide at this time ebbing to the westward and a fine strong sailing breeze.

There was no doubt at all now that she was a smuggler, for one of the *Lively*'s crew distinctly saw a man standing in the *Admiral Hood*'s hatchway taking tubs and depositing them on deck, whilst someone else was taking them from the deck and heaving them overboard, the tubs being painted a dark green so as to resemble the color of the waves. As the *Lively* came ramping on, she found numbers of these tubs in the wake of the *Admiral Hood*, and lowered a boat to pick them up, and about twenty-two were found a hundred yards from the smuggler, and the *Lively* also threw out a marker buoy to locate two other tubs which they passed. And, in as much as there was no other vessel within six miles distance, the *Admiral Hood* beyond a shadow of doubt was carrying contraband.

After the vessel was at length hove-to, she was seized and ultimately taken into Rochester, and information was duly laid against the persons who had been engaged in this smuggling adventure. But it is here that Sir William Courtenay comes into the story.

This gentleman, who had his seat at Powderham Castle, Devon, came forward and swore positively that the tubs, which the *Lively* was supposed to have picked up, had been seen floating off the coast. He himself was staying on a visit to Canterbury, and on that Sunday afternoon happened to be sailing about off the Kentish coast, and sighted the *Lively* about two o'clock. He kept her in sight, he said, until four o'clock. He also saw the *Admiral Hood*, and witnessed her being chased by the *Lively*, but he had seen the tubs for most of the day, as they had come up with the tide from the westward. With his own eyes, and not through a spyglass, he witnessed the *Admiral Hood* being captured by the cruiser, and followed up this evidence by remarking that "the tubs I saw picked up did not come out of the Lord Hood. I say so sterling and plump."

This was exactly the reverse of the testimony as given by the crew of the *Lively*, so it was evident that someone was lying. But to make a long story short, it was afterwards found that Sir William was not only not afloat that afternoon, did not see the tubs, did not see the two crafts, but was miles away from the scene, and at the time of the chase was in church. He was accordingly brought for trial, found guilty, and sentenced to be imprisoned for three calendar months, and after the expiration of this, he was to be "transported to such a place beyond the seas as his Majesty may direct, for the term of seven years."

He was convicted on unmistakable testimony of having committed perjury; in fact, Mr. Justice Parke, in giving judgment at the time, remarked that it was the clearest evidence in a perjury case that had ever fallen to his lot to try. As to the motive, it was thought that it was done solely with a desire to obtain a certain amount of popularity among the smugglers. Sir William saw that the case would go against the latter unless someone could give evidence for their side. Therefore, abusing his own position and standing, he came forward and perjured himself. It is a curious case, but in the history of crime there is more than one instance of personal pride and vanity being at the root of wrong-doing.

CHAPTER NINETEEN
Action and Counter-Action

It is conscience that makes cowards of us all, and this may be said of smugglers no less than of law-abiding citizens.

A trial was going on in connection with a certain incident which had occurred in Cawsand Bay, Plymouth Sound. It was alleged that, on the night of November 17, 1831, a man named Phillips had been shot in the knee whilst in a boat, trying with the aid of some other men to get up an anchor. The chief officer of the Preventive service at Cawsand was accused by Phillips of having thus injured him and, in due course, the case was brought into court. Among the witnesses was one whom counsel believed to be not wholly unconnected with smuggling. Whether or not this was true we need not worry ourselves, but the following questions and answers are well worth noting.

Cawsand was a notorious smuggling locality, and its secluded bay, with plenty of deep water almost up to the beach, made it highly suitable for sinking tubs well below the surface of the water. There were very few people ashore who had never been connected with this contraband trade. In such villages as this you might usually rely on the local innkeeper knowing as much as anyone in the neighborhood on the subject of smuggling. Such a man, then, from Cawsand, illiterate, but wide-awake, went into the witness-box for counsel to cross-examine, and the following dialogue resulted:

Question. "You are an innkeeper and sailor, if I understand you rightly?"

Answer. "Yes."

Q. "Is that all?"

A. "Mariner and innkeeper."

Q. "Is that all the trades you follow?"

A. "Fishing sometimes."

Q. "What do you fish for?"

A. "Different sorts of fish."

Q. "Did you ever fish for half-ankers?"

A. "Half-ankers?"

Q. "Casks of spirits—is that part of your fishing-tackle?"

A. "No, I was never convicted of no such thing."

Q. "I am not asking you that. You know what I mean. I ask whether it is part of your profession."

A. "No, it was not."

Q. "You never do such things?"

A. "What should I do it for?"

Q. "I cannot tell you. I ask you whether you do it, not what you do it for."

A. "I may choose to resolve whether I tell you or not."

Q. "I will not press you if your conscience is tender. You will not tell me whether you do a little stroke in the fair trade upon the coast? You will not answer me that question?"

A. "I am telling the truth."

Q. "Will you answer that question?"

A. "No."

Q. "Are you or are you not frequently in practice as a smuggler?"

A. "No!"

And that was all that could be got out of a man who probably could have told some of the best smuggling yarns in Cornwall.

The inhabitants so thoroughly loathed the Preventive men that, to quote the words of the man who was chief officer there, "the hatred of the Cawsand smugglers is... so great that they scarcely ever omit an opportunity of showing it either by insult or otherwise."

There was a kind of renaissance of smuggling about the third decade of the nineteenth century, and this was brought on partly owing to the fact that the vigilance along our coasts was not quite so smart as it might have been. But there were plenty of men doing their duty to the service, as may be seen from the account of Matthew Morrissey, a boatman in the Coast-Guard Service at Littlehampton.

About eleven o'clock on the evening of April 5, 1833, he saw a vessel named the *Nelson*, which had come into harbor that day. On boarding her, together with another boatman, he found a crew of two men and a boy. The skipper told him they were from Bognor in ballast. Morrissey went below, got a light, and searched all over the after-cabin, the hold, and even overhauled the ballast, but found nothing. He then got into the Coast-Guard boat, took his boat-hook, and after feeling along the vessel's bottom, discovered that it was not as it ought to have been.

"I'm not satisfied," remarked the Coast Guardsman to her skipper, Henry Roberts, "I shall haul you ashore."

"Getting a firm grip, pushed him ... into the water."

One of the crew replied that he was "very welcome," and the Coast-Guard officer then sent his companion ashore to fetch the chief boatman. The officer himself then again went aboard the *Nelson*, whereupon the crew became a little restless and went forward.

Presently they announced that they would go ashore, so they went forward again, got hold of the warp, and were going to haul on shore by it when the Coast-Guardsman observed, "Now, recollect I am an officer in his Majesty's Revenue duty, and the vessel is safely moored and in my charge; and if you obstruct me in my duty you will abide by the consequences." He took the warp out of their hands, and continued to walk up and down one side of the deck while the crew walked the other.

This went on for about twenty minutes, when Henry Roberts came up just as the Coast-Guard was turning round, and getting a firm grip, pushed him savagely aft and over the vessel's quarter into the water. Heavily laden though the Coast-Guard was with a heavy monkey-jacket, petticoat canvas trousers over his others, and with his arms as well, he had great difficulty in swimming, but at last managed to get to the shore.

The chief boatman and the other man now arrived, and it was found that the *Nelson*'s crew had vanished. The vessel was eventually examined, and found to have a false bottom containing thirty-two tubs of liquor and twenty-eight flagons of foreign brandy. Roberts was later arrested, found guilty, and transported for seven years.

A few pages back we witnessed an incident off Hastings. On the 5th of January 1832, a much more serious encounter took place.

Lieutenant Baker, R.N., was cruising at that time in the Revenue cutter *Ranger* off the Sussex coast, when between nine and ten in the evening he saw a suspicious fire on the Castle Hill at Hastings. Believing that it was a smuggler's signal, he dispatched his four-oared galley, with directions to row between Eccles Barn and the Martello Tower, No. 39. At the same time the *Ranger* continued to cruise off the land so as to be in communication with the galley. About 1 A.M. a report was heard from the Hastings direction, and a significant blue light was seen burning. Baker therefore took his cutter nearer in-shore towards the spot where this light had been seen. He immediately fell in with his galley, which had shown the blue light, and in her he found about two hundred casks of different sizes containing foreign spirits, and also five men who had been detained.

The men of course were taken on board the cruiser, and as the morning advanced, the *Ranger* again stood into the shore so that the lieutenant might land the spirits at the Custom House. Then getting into his galley with part of his crew, the tubs were towed astern in the cutter's smaller boat. But on reaching the beach, he found no fewer than four hundred persons assembled with the apparent intention of preventing the removal of the spirits to the Custom House. Especially notorious among this gang were two men, named respectively John Pankhurst and Henry Stevens. The galley was greeted with a shower of stones, and some of the Revenue men therein were struck, and had to keep quite close to the water's edge. Stevens and Pankhurst came and deposited themselves on the boat's gunwale, and resisted the removal of the tubs. Two carts now came down to the beach, but the mob refused to allow them to be loaded, and stones were flying in various directions, one man being badly hurt. Lieutenant Baker also received a violent blow from a large stone thrown by Pankhurst.

But gradually the carts were loaded in spite of the opposition, and just as the last vehicle had been filled, Pankhurst loosened the bridleback of the cart which was at the back of the vehicle to secure the spirits, and had not the Revenue officers and men quickly surrounding the cart to protect the goods, there would have been a rescue of the casks. Ultimately, the carts proceeded towards the Custom House pursued by the raging mob, and even after the goods had been all got in there was a good deal of pelting with stones and considerable damage done. Yet again, when these prisoners, Pankhurst and Stevens, were brought up for trial, the jury failed to do their duty and convict. But the Lord Chief Justice of that time remarked that he would not allow Stevens and Pankhurst to be discharged until they had entered into their recognisances to keep the peace in £20 each.

But next to the abominable cruelties perpetrated by the Hawkhurst gang related in an earlier chapter, I have found no incident so utterly brutal and savage as the following. I have to ask the reader to turn his imagination away from Sussex, and center it on a very beautiful spot in Dorsetshire, where the cliffs and sea are separated by only a narrow beach.

On the evening of the 28th of June 1832, Thomas Barrett, one of the boatmen belonging to the West Lulworth Coast-Guard, was on duty and proceeding along the top of the cliff towards Durdle, when he saw a boat moving about from the eastward. It was now nearly 10 P.M. He ran along the cliff, and then down to the beach, where he saw that this boat had just landed and was now shoving off again. But four men were standing by the water, at the very spot whence the boat had immediately before pushed off. One of these men was James Davis, who had on a long frock and a covered hat painted black.

Barrett asked this little knot of men what their business was, and why they were there at that time of night, to which Davis replied that they had "come from Weymouth, pleasuring!" Barrett observed that to come from Weymouth (which was several miles to the westward) by the east was a "rum" way. Davis then denied that they had come from the eastward at all, but this was soon stopped by Barrett remarking that if they had any more nonsense they would get the worst of it. After this the four men went up the cliff, having loudly abused him before proceeding. On examining the spot where the boat had touched, the Coast-Guard found twenty-nine tubs full of brandy lying on the beach close to the water's edge, tied together in pairs, as was the custom for landing. He therefore deemed it advisable to burn a blue light, and fired several shots into the air for assistance.

Three boatmen belonging to the station saw and heard, and they came out to his aid. But by this time the countryside was also on the alert, and the signals had brought an angry crowd of fifty men, who sympathized with the smugglers. These appeared on the top of the cliff, so the four coast-guards ran from the tubs (on the beach) to the cliff to prevent this mob from coming down and rescuing the tubs. But as the four men advanced to the top of the cliff, they hailed the mob and asked who they were, announcing that they had seized the tubs. The crowd answered that the coast-guard will not have the tubs, and proceeded to fire at the quartette and to hurl down stones. A distance of only about twenty yards separated the two forces, and the chief boatman ordered his three men to fire up at them, and for three-quarters of an hour this fray continued.

It was just then that the coast guardsmen heard cries coming from the top of the cliff—cries as of someone in great pain. But as soon as the

The Fine Art of Smuggling:

mob left the cliff and went away; the coast guardsmen went down to the beach again to secure and make safe the tubs. There they found that Lieutenant Stocker was arriving at the beach in a boat from a neighboring station. He ordered Barrett to put the tubs in the boat and then to lay a little distance from the shore. But after Barrett had done this and was about thirty yards away, the lieutenant ordered him to come ashore again, because the men on the beach were bringing down Lieutenant Knight, who was groaning and in great pain.

What had happened to the latter must now be told.

After the signals mentioned had been observed, a man named Duke and Lieutenant Knight, R.N., had also proceeded along the top of the cliff. It was a beautiful starlight night, with scarcely any wind, perfectly still and no moon visible. There was just the sea and the night and the cliffs. But before they had gone far they encountered the mob we have just spoken of at the top of the cliff. While the four coast guardsmen were exchanging fire from below, Lieutenant Knight and Duke came upon the crowd from their rear. Two men against fifty armed with great sticks six feet long could not do much. As the mob turned towards them, Lieutenant Knight promised them that if they made use of those murderous-looking sticks they would have the contents of his pistol.

But the mob, without waiting, dealt the first blows, so Duke and his officer defended themselves with their cutlasses. At first there were only a dozen men against them, and these the two managed to beat off. But other men then came up and formed a circle round Knight and Duke, so the two stood back to back and faced the savage mob. The latter made fierce blows at the men, who were warded off by the cutlasses in the men's left hands, two pistols being in the right hand of each. The naval men fired these, but it was of little good, though they fought like true British sailors. Those 6-foot sticks could reach well out, and both Knight and Duke were felled to the ground.

Then, like human panthers let loose on their prey, this brutal, lawless mob with uncontrolled cruelty let loose the strings of their pent-up passion. They kept these men on the ground and dealt with them shamefully. Duke was being dragged along by his belt, and the crowd beat him sorely as he heard his lieutenant exclaim, "Oh, you brutes!" The next thing which Duke heard the fierce mob to say was, "Let's kill the —— and have him over the cliff." Now the cliff at that spot is 100 feet high, and four men then were preparing to carry out this command. Two were at his legs and two at his hands when Duke indignantly declared, "If Jem was here, he wouldn't let you do it."

It reads almost like fiction to have this dramatic halt in the murder scene. For just as Duke was about to be hurled headlong over the side, a man came forward and pressed the blackguards back on hearing these words. For a time it was all that the new-comer could do to restrain the brutes from hitting the poor fellow, while the men who still had hold of his limbs swore that they would have Duke over the cliff. But after being dealt a severe blow on the forehead, they put him down on to the ground and left him bleeding. One of the gang, seeing this, observed complacently, "He bleeds well, but breathes short. It will soon be over with him." And with that they left him.

"Let's... have him over the cliff."

The man who had come forward so miraculously and so dramatically to save Duke's life was James Cowland, and the reason he had so acted was out of gratitude to Duke, who had taken his part in a certain incident twelve months earlier. And this is the sole redeeming feature in a glut of brutality. It must have required no small amount of pluck and energy for Cowland to have done even that much amid the wild fanaticism which was raging. Smuggler and ruffian though he was, it is only fair to emphasize and praise his action for risking his own life to save that of a man by whom he had already benefited.

But Cowland did nothing more for his friend than that, and after the crowd had indulged themselves on the two men they went off to their homes. Duke then, suffering and bleeding, weak and stunned, crawled to the place where he had been first attacked—a little higher up the cliff—and there he saw Knight's petticoat trousers, but there was no sign of the officer himself.

After that he gradually made his way down to the beach, and at the foot of the cliff he came upon Knight lying on his back immediately below where the struggle with the smugglers had taken place. Duke sat down by his side, and the officer, opening his eyes, recognized his man and asked, "Is that you?" But that was all he said. Duke then went to tell Lieutenant Stocker on the beach, who fetched the dying man, put him into Lipscomb's boat, and promptly rowed him to his home at Lulworth, where he died the next day.

It is difficult to write calmly of such an occurrence as this. It is impossible that in such circumstances one can extend the slightest sympathy to a group of men who probably had a hard struggle for existence, especially when the fishing or the harvests were bad. The most one can do is to attribute such unreasoning and unwarranted cruelty to the ignorance and the coarseness which had been bred in undisciplined lives. Out of that seething, vicious mob there was only one man who had a scrap of humanity, and even he could not prevent his fellows from one of the worst crimes in the long roll of smugglers' delinquencies.

The days of smugglers were, of course, coincident with the period of the stage-coach. In the year 1833 there was a man named Thomas Allen, who was master and part-owner of a coasting vessel named the *Good Intent*, which used to trade between Dover and London. In February of that year Thomas Becker, who happened to be the guard of the night coaches running between Dover and London, came with a man named Tomsett to Allen, and suggested that the latter should join them in a smuggling transaction, telling him that they knew how to put a good deal of money into his pocket.

At first Allen hesitated and declined, but the proposal was again renewed a few days later, when Allen again declined, as it was too risky a business. But at length, as "trade was very bad," both he and a man named Sutton, one of his crew, agreed to come into the scheme. What happened was as follows:

The *Good Intent* left Dover on February 23, went as far as the Downs about two miles from the coast, and under cover of darkness took on board from a French vessel, which was there waiting by appointment, about forty bales of silk. In order to be ready to deal with these, the *Good Intent* had been provided with sufficient empty crates and boxes. The silks were put into these, they were addressed to some persons in Birmingham, and, after being landed at one of the London quays as if they had come from Dover, they were sent across to the Paddington Canal, and duly arrived at their destination. Allen's share of that transaction amounted to about £80. He had done so well that he repeated the same practice in April and May; but in June some tea which he brought in was

"Under cover of darkness took on board... forty bales of silk."

seized and, although he was not prosecuted, it gave him a fright. But after being pursuaded by the two tempters, he repeated his first incident, took forty more bales on board, and arrived at the Port of London. But the Custom House officials had got wind of this, and when the *Good Intent* arrived she was searched. In this case the goods had not been put into crates, but were concealed in the ballast, the idea being not to land them in London but to bring them back under the ballast to Dover.

The first remark the Customs officer made was, "There is a great deal more ballast here than is necessary for such a ship," and promptly began moving the same. Of course the goods were discovered, and of course Allen pretended he knew nothing about the forty bales being there concealed. They were seized and condemned.

Becker got to hear of this disaster and that a warrant was out for his own arrest, so he quickly hopped across to Calais. An officer was sent both to Deal and to Dover to find Tomsett, but failed to do so, so he crossed over to Calais, and among the first people whom he saw on the Calais pier were Tomsett and Becker walking about together. The officer had no wish to be seen by Becker, but the latter saw him, and came up and asked him how he was and what he was doing there. The officer made the best excuse he could, and stated that he had got on board the steam-packet and been brought off by mistake.

"Oh, I am here in consequence of that rascal Allen having peached against us," volunteered Becker, and then went on to say that he was as innocent as the child unborn. However, the judge, at a later date, thought otherwise, and imposed a penalty of £4750, though the full penalty really amounted to the enormous sum of £71,000.

CHAPTER TWENTY
Force and Cunning

A smuggling vessel was usually provided with what was called a tub-rail—that is to say, a rail which ran round the vessel just below the gunwale on the inside. When a vessel was about to arrive at her destination to sink her tubs, the proceeding was as follows.

The tubs were all made fast to a long rope, and this rope with its tubs was placed outside the vessel's bulwarks, running all round the ship from the stern to the bows and back again the other side. This warp was kept fastened to the tub-rail by five or seven lines called stop-ropes. Consequently all the smugglers had to do was to cut these stop-ropes, and the tubs and rope would drop into the water, the stone weights immediately sinking the casks.

Bearing this in mind, let us take a look at the Revenue cutter *Tartar*, on the night between the 3rd and 4th of April 1839. She was cruising off Kimeridge, between St. Alban's Head and Weymouth, and a little to the east of where Lieutenant Knight was murdered, as we saw in the last chapter. About 1:40 A.M. Lieutenant George Davies, R.N., the *Tartar*'s commander, was below sleeping with his clothes and boots on, when he heard the officer of the watch call for him. Instantly he went on deck and saw a smuggling vessel. She was then about thirty yards away and within a mile of the shore. Her name was afterwards found to be the French sloop *Diane*.

It was rather a warm, thick night, such as one sometimes gets in April when the weather has begun to get better. By the time that the cruiser's commander had come up on deck, both the cutter and the *Diane* were hove-to, and the vessels were close alongside. When first sighted by the boatswain, the smuggler was standing out from the land. The *Tar-*

The Fine Art of Smuggling:

tar's boat was now launched into the water, and the bo'sun and two men pulled off in her. boarded the *Diane*, and then came back to fetch Lieutenant Davies. The instant the latter boarded the *Diane*, he saw one of the latter's crew throwing something overboard. He stooped down to pick something else up, when Davies rushed forward and caught him round the body as it fell into the water, and a tub-hoop, new, wet, and green, was taken from him. Davies called to his bo'sun to bring a lantern, so that he might identify the seized man and then proceed to search the vessel.

A tub-rail and stop-rope were found on board, and, on going below, the hold was found to be strewn with chips of tub-hoops and pieces of stones for sinking. The upper deck was similarly strewn, while by the hatchway were found sinker-slings. These sinkers were suspended and hitched round the warp at about every sixth tub.

The *Diane*'s master was asked where his boat was since none was found aboard, but there was no satisfactory answer. Tub-boards for fixing on deck so as to prevent the tubs from rolling overboard were also found, so altogether there was sufficient reason for seizing the vessel, which was now done. She was taken into Weymouth and her crew brought before a magistrate. In that port the tub-boat was also found, for the smugglers had doubtless sent most of their cargo ashore in her whilst the *Diane* was cruising about between there and St. Alban's Head.

It was significant that only three men were found on board, whereas smuggling vessels of this size (about twenty to thirty tons) usually carried eight or nine, the explanation being that the others had been sent out with the tub-boat. But the rest of the cargo had evidently been hurriedly thrown overboard when the *Tartar* appeared, and because these casks were thrown over so quickly, fifty-nine of them had come to the surface and were subsequently recovered. Besides these, however, 154 casks were also found on one sling at the bottom of the sea close to where the *Diane* had been arrested, for the *Tartar*'s men had been careful to take cross bearings and so fix their position.

One of the most interesting of these smuggling events was that which occurred in the Medway. About eight o'clock on the evening of March 27, 1839, a smack called the *Mary* came running into the river from outside. At this time it was blowing very hard from the N.E., and the tide was ebbing, so that the wind would be against the tide and a certain amount of sea would be on. But it was noticed by the coast-guard at Garrison Point, which commands the entrance to this river, that the *Mary* had far too much sail up—the whole mainsail as well as gaff-topsail. Considering it was a fair wind and there was a good deal of it, there was far more canvas than was necessary, even allowing for the tide.

It was a rule that all vessels entering the Medway should bring-to off Garrison Point, and allow themselves to be boarded and searched, if required by certain signals. In order to compel the *Mary* so to do, the coast-guard at this point fired a shot and rowed off to meet her. But the smack held on. She was steering straight for the Isle of Grain, and showed no intention of starboarding her helm so as to get on a proper course up the Medway. Another shot was fired, and yet she held on. Now there were some of her Majesty's ships lying near the Grain, which is on the starboard hand as you pass up the river, viz. the *Daedalus* and the *Alfred*. These vessels were of course swung with the tide, and between the *Daedalus* and the Isle of Grain the smack maneuvered.

"Another shot was fired."

A third shot now came whizzing by from the boat that was rowing hard against the tide, and the smack came round between the *Alfred* and *Daedalus*. The coast-guard then boarded the *Mary*, and the master said he was from Brightlingsea. He pretended that he thought the firing was not from the coast-guard, but from a ship at the Little Nore, which is the channel that runs up to Garrison Point from the Nore Lightship. This was curious, for the *Mary* had been in the habit of going up the Medway, and hitherto had always hove-to off Garrison Point for the coast-guard to come aboard. Her skipper excused his action by stating that he was frightened of heaving-to as he might have carried away his mast and gone ashore, if he had hauled up and gybed.

But it was pointed out that it was a foolish and unsafe course for the *Mary* to steer between the *Daedalus* and the Grain Island, especially as it was a dark night without any moon, and blowing very hard. But on going aboard, the coast-guard was not surprised to detect a strong smell of gin, as if spirits had quite recently been removed from the smack. And after making a search there was nothing found on board except that she was in a great state of confusion. None the less it was deemed advisable to place a couple of officers on board her to accompany her up to Rochester. This was on the Friday night, and she arrived at Rochester the same day.

On the Sunday it occurred to the officers to search for the spirits

The Fine Art of Smuggling:

which they were sure the *Mary* had on board, so they proceeded to that spot by the *Daedalus* where the *Mary* had luffed round and met the coast-guard boat. After sweeping for half-an-hour they found 115 tubs slung together to a rope in the usual manner. At each end of the rope was an anchor, and between these anchors was a number of tubs, and in between each pair of tubs were stones. So the *Mary* had gone into that little bight in order that she might throw her tubs overboard, which would be sunk by the stones, and the two anchors would prevent them from being drifted away by the tide. The warp, it was thought, had been in the first instance fastened to the tub-rail in the manner we have already described, and at the third gun the stop-ropes were cut, and the whole cargo went with a splash into the water, and the vessel sailed over the tubs as they sank to the muddy bottom.

Methods employed by Smugglers for Anchoring tubs thrown Overboard

The usual way to get these tubs up was of course by means of grapnels, or, as they were called, "creepers." But the spot chosen by the *Mary* was quite close to the moorings of the *Daedalus*, so that method would only have fouled the warship's cables. Therefore the following ingenious device was used.

A large heavy rope was taken, and at each end was attached a boat. The rope swept along the river-bed as the boats rowed in the same direction stretching out the rope. Before long the bight of this rope found the obstructing tubs, stones, warp, and anchor, and that having occurred, the two boats rowed close together, and a heavy iron ring was dropped over the two ends of the rope, and thus sank and gripped the rope at the point where it met with the obstruction. All that now remained, therefore, was to pull this double rope until the obstruction came up from the bottom of the water. And in this manner the articles which the *Mary* had cast overboard were recovered.

She was obviously a smuggler, as besides this discovery she was found to be fitted with concealments, and fourteen tholes were found on

King's Cutters vs Smugglers -1700-1855

board "muffled" with canvas and spun yarn, so as to be able to row silently. Her skipper, William Evans, was duly prosecuted and found guilty; and it was during the course of this trial that the interesting dialogue occurred between counsel and the coast-guard as to whether the first warning gun fired was always shotted or not. As we have already discussed this point, we need not let it detain us now.

The year 1849 was interesting, as it witnessed the seizing of one of the earliest steam craft on a charge of smuggling.

Very late in the day of May 15 the steam-tug *Royal Charter*, employed in towing vessels in and out of Portsmouth harbor, had been taken to Spithead without the permission of her owner, and information was given to the coast-guard. About midnight she was first discovered steaming towards the port with a small boat attached to her stern, being then about half a mile from the harbor.

Chase was then made and the vessel hailed and ordered to heave-to. She replied that she would round-to directly, but in fact she held on and steamed at full speed, notwithstanding that several shots were fired at her. As she entered Portsmouth harbor she was pursued by the Customs boat, who asked them to shut off steam and be examined. Of course full speed in those days meant nothing very wonderful, and it was not long before she was boarded. She had a crew of three, and there were ten men in the boat towing astern, most of whom were found to have been previously convicted of smuggling. It seems strange to find a steamboat pursuing the old tactics of the sailing smacks, but in her wake there were found 150 half-ankers within about 300 yards of her and where she had passed. The vessel and boat were seized, and the men taken before the magistrates and convicted.

But the following is an instance of steam being employed against smugglers.

One Sunday towards the end of October 1849, about nine o'clock in the morning, the local receiver of duties informed the tide surveyor at St. Heliers, Jersey, that there was a cutter which (from information received) he was convinced was loaded with brandy. This cutter was in one of the bays to the N.W. of the island. But as the wind was then blowing from the W.N.W. and a very heavy surf was rolling in, the consent of the harbormaster was obtained to use the steam-tug *Polka* to go round in search of her, the understanding being that she was to be paid if a seizure were made. The wind and sea were so boisterous that the Revenue boat could not have been used.

Steamer and officers therefore proceeded round the coast until they reached Plemont Bay, about twenty miles from St. Helier, and there they found a small cutter lying at anchor close under the cliff, but with no one on board. The steamer lowered a boat and found the cutter to be the *Lion* of Jersey, five tons, with four hogsheads and seven quarter casks of brandy. The officers then weighed anchor, and by sailing and towing got her round to St. Helier harbor, where she was dismantled, and the

The Fine Art of Smuggling:

brandy and her materials lodged at the Custom House. This little craft had come from Dielette in France, and as Plemont Bay was a very secluded locality, she would have run her goods there with perfect success, had she not been discovered while her crew was on shore, where they had probably gone for the purpose of making arrangements for getting the cargo landed.

But by the middle of the nineteenth century so thoroughly had the authorities gripped the smuggling evil that these men were actually sometimes afraid to take advantage of what fortune literally handed out to them.

The schooner *Walter* of Falmouth was bound on a voyage from Liverpool to Chichester with a cargo of guano on May 30, 1850. Her crew consisted of Stephen Sawle, master, Benjamin Bowden, mate, Samuel Banister, seaman, and George Andrews, boy. On this day she was off Lundy Island, when Andrews saw a couple of casks floating ahead of the schooner and called to the master and mate, who were below at tea. They immediately came up on deck, and the master looked at the kegs through his glass, saying that he thought they were provisions.

The three men then got out the ship's boat, rowed after the casks and slung them into the boat, and brought them on board. In doing so the mate happened to spill one of them, which contained brandy. This gave the skipper something of a fright, and he directed the mate and seaman to throw the casks overboard. They both told him they thought he was a great fool if he did so. He gave the same orders a second time and then went below, but after he had remained there for some time, he said to his crew, "If you will all swear that you will not tell anybody, I will risk it." They all solemnly promised, the master swearing the mate, the seaman, and the boy on the ship's Bible that they would not tell the owner or any living creature.

Presently the mate and Banister removed the hatches and handed up about two tiers of guano, sent the casks of brandy below and placed bags on their top. After the master had been below a couple of hours, he asked whether the casks were out of sight. The mate and Banister replied that they were, whereupon the master took a candle, examined the hold, and afterwards the sleeping-berths, but he could not see anything of the brandy. He then went to the boy and said, "Mind you don't let Mr. Coplin [the owner] know anything about this business, for the world."

The vessel arrived at Falmouth on Sunday morning, the 2nd of June, and brought up off the Market Strand. At six in the morning the boy went ashore and returned about midnight. The mate was on board and addressed him thus, "You knew very well what was going on and ought to have been on board before this." For at that time both the master and Banister were ashore.

On Monday the boy went down to the hold and saw the brandy was gone, and the same night about half-an-hour before midnight the mate and Banister brought four gallons of the brandy to where the boy was lodging, as his share. The youngster complained that it was very little, to which Banister replied that one of the casks had leaked amongst the cargo of guano or he would have had more.

Ostensibly the schooner had put into Falmouth for repairs. Later on the Custom House officers got to hear of it, but it was then the month of July, and the schooner had since sailed and proceeded to Liverpool.

On the 1st of October of this same year a highly ingenious device was discovered through a hitch, which unfortunately ruined the smugglers' chances. In its broad conception it was but a modification of an idea which we have already explained. In its application, however, it was unique and original.

At half-past six on this morning a fore-and-aft-rigged vessel was observed to be sailing into Chichester harbor. When first discovered, she was about a mile from Hayling Island. She was boarded, as smuggled goods were supposed to have been taken by her from a raft at sea. Manned by a master and a crew of two, all English, she was well known in that neighborhood. She was registered at Portsmouth as the *Rival*.

Her cargo was found to consist of a few oysters and thirteen tubs of spirits, but these were attached to the stern in a most ingenious manner.

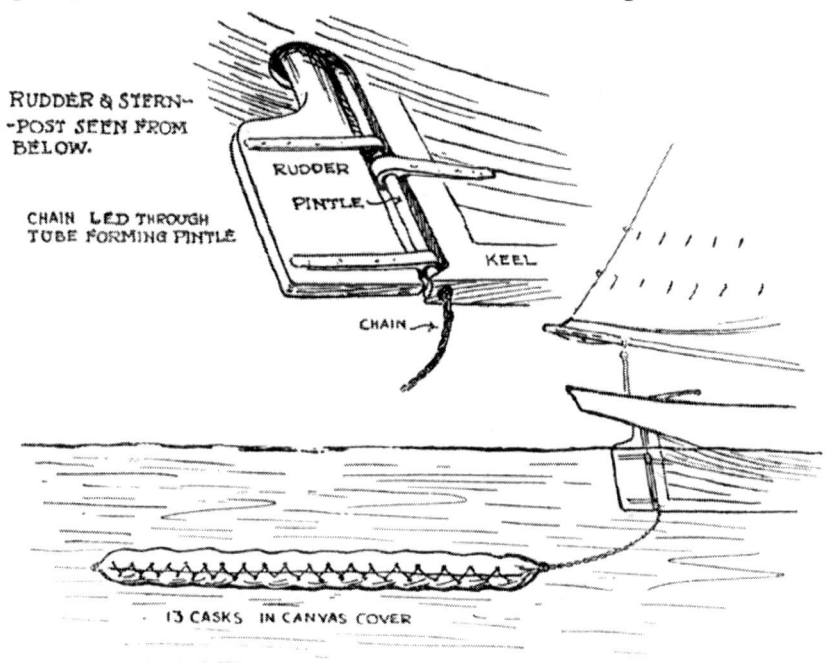

The Rival's Ingenious Device

By her stern-post was an iron pipe, and through this pipe ran a chain, one end of which was secured at the top, close to the tiller, the other end

The Fine Art of Smuggling:

running right down into the water below the ship. Attached to the chain in the water were thirteen tubs wrapped in canvas. The theory was this.

As the vessel sailed along, the chain would be hauled as tight as it would go, so that the casks were kept under the vessel's stern and below water. Now, having arrived in Chichester harbor, the helmsman had suddenly let go the chain, but the latter had unhappily jammed in the pipe, and the tubs were thus dragged with a large scope of chain. The coastguard in coming alongside used his boat-hook underneath, and thus caught hold of the chain and tubs. The vessel was now soon laid ashore, and when her bottom was examined, the whole device was discovered. It had only quite recently been added, but the crew were notorious smugglers, so they got themselves into trouble in spite of their ingenuity.

And now let us bring this list of smuggling adventures to an end with the activities of a very ubiquitous French sloop named the *Georges*, which came into prominent notice in the year 1850. Her port of departure was Cherbourg, and she was wont to run her goods across to the south coast of England with the greatest impudence. In piecing together this narrative of her adventures, it has been no easy task to follow her movements, for she appeared and disappeared, then was seen somewhere else perhaps a hundred miles away in a very short time.

It appears that on April 19 the *Georges*, whose master's name was Gosselin, cleared from Cherbourg. Two days later she was sighted by the commander of the Revenue cutter *Cameleon* off Bembridge Ledge, about one o'clock in the afternoon, about eight or nine miles E.S.E. After she had come up she was boarded by the *Cameleon*, and was found to have one passenger, whom the *Cameleon's* commander described as an Englishman "of a most suspicious appearance." But after being searched she was found perfectly "clean" and free from any appearance of tubs or smell of spirits. The Revenue cutter's commander therefore formed the opinion that the *Georges* was fitted with some concealments somewhere.

In order to discover these, it would be essential for the craft to be hauled ashore. He therefore did not detain her, but, as she was bound for Portsmouth, put an officer and a couple of men aboard her until she should arrive at that port. One thing which had aroused suspicions was the finding on board of exceptionally large fend-offs. These were just the kind which were used by smuggling ships accustomed to be met at sea by smaller craft, into which the casks were transferred and then rowed ashore. And what was more suspicious still was the fact that these fend-offs were found wet; so they had most probably been used recently in a seaway when some tub-boats had been alongside the *Georges*.

Somehow or other, when she arrived at Portsmouth, although the matter was duly reported, it was not thought necessary to haul her ashore, but she was carefully examined afloat. The English passenger found aboard gave the name of Mitchell, but he was suspected of being Robinson, a notorious Bognor smuggler. And it was now further believed that the *Georges* had sunk her "crop" of tubs somewhere near the Owers (just south of Selsey Bill), as on the morning of the day when the *Cameleon* sighted her a vessel answering her description was seen in that vicinity.

On that occasion, then, the *Georges* could not be detained, and we next hear of her on May 3, when again she set forth from Cherbourg. She had no doubt taken on board a fine cargo, for she had a burthen of thirty-one tons, and this she managed in some mysterious manner to land in England. There can be no doubt that she succeeded in hoodwinking the Revenue service for a time, but it is probable that she employed largely the method of sinking the tubs, which were afterwards recovered in the manner already familiar to the reader.

At any rate, Lieutenant Owen, R.N., writing on May 9 from the Ryde coast-guard station to Captain Langtry, R.N., his inspecting commander, reported that this *Georges* had arrived off Ryde pier that morning at seven o'clock. She had five Frenchmen on board besides Gosselin. It was found that her tub-boat was a new one, and when she arrived this was on deck, but it had since been hoisted out, and Gosselin, having been brought ashore, crossed by the Ryde steamer to Portsmouth at 9 A.M.

What business he transacted in Portsmouth cannot be stated definitely, but it is no foolish guess to suggest that he went to inform his friends as to where he had deposited the casks of spirits a few hours previously. However, Gosselin did not waste much time ashore, for he had returned, got up anchor and sails, and was off Bembridge Ledge by five in the afternoon, at which time the *Georges* was sighted by Captain Hughes, commanding the Revenue cutter *Petrel*.

The *Georges* was boarded and searched, there was a strong smell of brandy noticed, and it was clear that her tub-boat had been recently used. Somewhere—somehow—she had recently got rid of her "crop," but where and when could not be ascertained. The *Georges*' master protested that he was very anxious to get back to Cherbourg as quickly as possible. Because there was nothing definite found on board, Captain Hughes decided to release her.

That was on May 9; but exactly a week later this same *Georges* came running into Torbay. On arrival she was found to have no tub-boat, although in her inventory she was said to have a boat 21 feet long and 9 feet broad. Some of her crew were also absent, which looked even more suspicious. Still more, she was found to have battens secured along her bulwarks for the purpose of lashing tubs thereto. This made it quite certain that she was employed in the smuggling industry, and yet again there was no definite reason for arresting this foreign ship.

We pass over the rest of May and June until we come to the last day of July. On that date the lieutenant in charge of the coast-guard at Lyme (West Bay) reported that he had received information from Lieutenant Davies of the Beer station that a landing of contraband goods was likely to be attempted on the Branscombe station, which is just to the west of Beer Head. It was probable that this would take place on either the 1st or

The Fine Art of Smuggling:

2nd of August, and at night. Orders were therefore given that a vigilant look-out should be kept in this neighborhood. Nothing occurred on the first of these dates, but about twenty minutes past eleven on the night of August 2 reports and flashes of pistols were heard and seen on the Sidmouth station as far as Beer Head.

These were observed by Lieutenant Smith and his crew, who were in hiding; but, unfortunately, just as one of the coast guardsmen was moving from his hiding-place he was discovered by a friend of the smugglers, who instantly blazed off a fire on the highest point of the cliff.

Lieutenant Smith, however, did not waste much time, and quickly had a boat launched. They pulled along the shore for a distance of a mile and a half from the beach, and continued so to do until 2:30 A.M., but no vessel or boat could be seen anywhere. But as he believed a landing was taking place not far away, he sent information east and west along the coast. As a matter of fact a landing did occur not far away, but it was not discovered.

An excise officer when driving along the Lyme road, actually fell in with two carts of tubs escorted by fifteen men. This was somewhere about midnight. He then turned off the road and proceeded to Sidmouth as fast as he could, in order to get assistance, as he was unarmed. From there the chief officer accompanied him, having previously left instructions for the coast-guard crew to scour the country the following morning. But the excise and chief officer after minutely searching the cross-roads found nothing, and lost track of the carts and fifteen men.

"Taken completely by surprise."

King's Cutters vs Smugglers -1700-1855

That time there had been no capture, and the smugglers had got clean away. But the following night Lieutenant Smith went afloat with his men soon after dark, and about half-past ten observed a signal blazed off just as on the previous evening. Knowing that this was a warning that the smuggling vessel should not approach the shore, Smith pulled straight out to sea, hoping, with luck, to fall in with the smuggling craft. Happily, before long he discovered her in the darkness.

She appeared to be cutter-rigged, and he promptly gave chase. At a distance of only two miles from the shore he got up to her, for the night was so dark that the cutter did not see the boat until it got right alongside, whereupon the smugglers suddenly slipped a number of heavy articles from her gunwale. Taken completely by surprise, and very confused by the sudden arrival of the coast-guard boat, Lieutenant Smith was able to get on board their ship and arrest her. It was now about 11.15 P.M.

But, having noticed these heavy splashes in the water, the lieutenant was smart enough instantly to mark the place with a buoy, and then was able to devote his attention entirely to his capture. He soon found that this was the *Georges* of Cherbourg. She was manned by three Frenchmen, and there were still hanging from the gunwale on either quarter a number of heavy stones slung together, such as were employed for sinking the tubs. There can be no doubt that the *Georges'* intention had been to come near enough to the shore to send her tubs to the beach in her tub-boat, as she had almost certainly done the night before. But hearing the coast-guard galley approaching, and being nervous of what they could not see, the tubs were being cast into the sea to prevent seizure.

Although no tubs were found on board, yet it was significant that the tub-boat was not on board, having evidently been already sent ashore with a number of casks. There was a small 12-feet dinghy suspended in the rigging, but she was obviously not the boat which the *Georges* was accustomed to use for running goods. Lieutenant Smith for a time stood off and on the shore, and then ran along the coast until it was day, hoping to fall in with the tub-boat.

Just as he had captured the *Georges* another coast-guard boat, this time from the Beer station, came alongside, and so the officer sent this little craft away with four hands to search diligently up and down the coast, and to inform the other coast guardsmen that the tub-boat had escaped. When it was light, Smith took the *Georges* into Lyme Cobb, and her crew and master were arrested. She had evidently changed her skipper since the time when she was seen off the Hampshire shore, for the name of her present master was Clement Armel. They were landed, taken before the magistrates, and remanded. But subsequently they were tried, and sentenced to six months' hard labor each in Dorchester jail, but after serving two months of this were released by order of the Treasury.

On the 5th of August the boats from Lieutenant Smith's station at Branscombe went out to the spot where the *Georges* had been captured and the marker-buoy with a grapnel at the end of it had been thrown.

The Fine Art of Smuggling:

There they crept for a time and found nothing. But it had been heavy weather, and probably the tubs had gone adrift without sinkers to them. At any rate no landing was reported along the shore, so it was doubtful if the tub-boat had managed to get to land. As to the *Georges* herself, she was found to be almost a new vessel. She was described as a handsome craft, "and very much the appearance of a yacht, and carries a white burgee at her masthead with a red cross in it, similar to vessels belonging to the Yacht Club."

The reference to the "Yacht Club" signifies the Royal Yacht Squadron, which was originally called the Royal Yacht Club. In those days the number of yachts was very few compared with the fleets afloat today. Some of the Royal Yacht Club's cutters were faster than any smuggler or Revenue craft, and it was quite a good idea for a smuggler built with yacht-like lines to fly the club's flag if he was anxious to deceive the cruisers and coast-guards by day.

Some years before this incident there was found on board a smuggling lugger named the *Maria*, which was captured by the Revenue cruiser *Prince of Wales* about the year 1830, a broad red pendant marked with a crown over the letters "R.Y.C.," and an anchor similar to those used by the Royal Yacht Club. One of the *Maria*'s crew admitted that they had it on board because they thought it might have been serviceable to their plans. The point is not without interest, and, as far as I know, has never before been raised.

But to conclude our narrative of the *Georges*. As it was pointed out that she was such a fine vessel, and that Lyme Cobb (as many a seafaring man today knows full well) was very unsafe in a gale of wind, it was suggested that she should be removed to Weymouth "by part of one of the cutters' crews that occasionally call in here." So on the 7th of September in that year she was fetched away to Weymouth by Lieutenant Sicklemore, R.N. She and her boat were valued at £240, but she was found to be of such a beautiful model that she was neither destroyed nor sold, but taken into the Revenue service as a cutter to prevent the trade in which she had been so actively employed.

And so we could continue with these smuggling yarns; but our limit has been reached, and we must draw to a close.

If the smuggling epoch was marred by acts of brutality, if its ships still needed to have those improvements in design and equipment which have today reached such a high mark of distinction, if its men were not altogether admirable characters, at any rate their seamanship and their daring, their ingenuity and their exploits, cannot but incite us to the keenest interest in an exceptional kind of contest.

APPENDIX I
Sloops or Cutters

The reputed difference between a sloop and cutter in the eighteenth century is well illustrated by the following, which is taken from the Excise Trials, vol. xxx., 1st July 1795 to 17th December 1795, p. 95.

In Attorney-General v. Julyan and others there was an action to condemn the vessel *Mary* of Fowey, brought under the provisions of sec. 4, c. 47, 24 Geo. III, as amended by sec. 6, c. 50, 34 Geo. III There were several counts, including one with regard to the vessel being fitted with "arms for resistance," but the case turned on the question whether she was cutter-rigged or sloop-rigged. Counsel for the prosecution defined a cutter as "a thing constructed for swift sailing, which, with a view to effect that purpose, is to sink prodigiously at her stern, and her head to be very much out of water... built so that she should measure a great deal more than she would contain."

Such a definition, however satisfactory it may have been to the legal mind, was one that must have vastly amused any seafaring man. The judge, quoting expert evidence, explained the difference between a cutter and a sloop as follows:A standing or running bowsprit is common to either a sloop or a cutter, and a traveler, he said, was an invariable portion of a cutter's rig, so also was a jib-tack. The jib-sheet, he ruled, differed however; that of a cutter was twice as large as that of a sloop and was differently set. It had no stay. A sloop's jib-sheet was set with a fixed stay. Furthermore, in a cutter the tack of the jib was hooked to a traveler, and there was a large thimble fastened to a block which came across the head of the sail. There were two blocks at the mast-head, one on each side. "A rope passes through the three blocks by which it is drawn up to the halliards." The jib of a cutter "lets down and draws in a very short time." A cutter usually had channels and mortice-holes to fix legs to prevent oversetting.

APPENDIX II
A List of Cruisers Employed in the Customs Service for the Year 1784

Name	Crew	Stationed	Remarks
Lively and Vigilant	14	London	These vessels were the property of the Crown. The Lively cruised in the winter half-year, but in the summer her crew did duty on board the Vigilant.
Defence	16	Gravesend	On the Establishment.
Success	23	Rochester	On the Establishment.
Otter	13	Rochester	Moored in Standgate Creek to guard the Quarantine.
Active	18	Eaversham	On the Establishment.
Sprightly	30	Sandwich	Employed by Contract from May 27, 1784.
Greyhound	17	Sandwich	Employed by Contract from January 27, 1784.
Scourge	30	Deal	Employed by Contract from January 27, 1784.
Nimble	30	Deal	Employed by Contract from April 23, 1784.

The Fine Art of Smuggling:

Name	Crew	Stationed	Remarks
Tartar	31	Dover	On the Establishment.
Assistance	28	Dover	Employed by Contract.
Alert	16	Dover	Employed by Contract from April 22, 1784.
Stag	24	Rye	On the Establishment.
Hound	30 & 24	Rye	Contract. Crew reduced to 24 on October 9, 1784.
Surprise	28	Newhaven	Contract. Crew reduced to 24 on October 9, 1784.
Enterprise	18	Shoreham	Establishment in 1784, but afterwards on Contract.
Falcon	18 & 28	Chichester	Establishment.
Roebuck	21	Portsmouth	Establishment.
Antelope	11	Portsmouth	Establishment.
Rose	30	Southampton	Establishment.
Speedwell	31	Weymouth Cowes	She was on Contract at Weymouth but was removed to Cowes on June 10, 1784.
Swan	23	Cowes	Contract from March 6, 1784
Laurel	20	Poole	Contract from March 6, 1784
Diligence	32	Poole Weymouth	Contract. Removed from Poole to Weymouth, March 2, 1784.
Alarm	26	Exeter	Contract. Removed from Poole to Weymouth, March 2, 1784.
Spider	28	Dartmouth	Contract. Removed from Poole to Weymouth, March 2, 1784.
Ranger	21	Plymouth	Establishment.
Wasp	20	Plymouth	Contract.

King's Cutters vs Smugglers -1700-1855

Name	Crew	Stationed	Remarks
Squirrel	20	Looe	Contract.
Hawke	18 & 26	Falmouth	Contract.
Lark	20	Falmouth	Contract.
Lurcher	30	Penryn	Contract.
Tamer	25	Scilly	Contract.
Brilliant	30	St. Ives	Contract.
Dolphin	26	St. Ives	Contract.
Brisk	19	Milford	Contract.
Repulse	33	Colchester	Establishment.
Argus	24	Harwich	Establishment.
Bee	16	Harwich	Contract.
Hunter	25	Yarmouth.	Establishment.
Experiment	18	Boston	Establishment.
Swallow	24	Hull	Establishment.

APPENDIX III
A List of Cruisers Employed in the Customs Service for the Year 1797 (up to June 27th)

Vessel	Commander	Tons	Guns	Men	Station
Vigilant Yacht	Richard Dozell	53	6	13	To attend the Honourable Board. In the winter season the cutter with ten additional hands cruised on the coasts of Essex, Kent, and Sussex
Vigilant Cutter		82	8	+10	
Diligence	William Dobbin	152	14	32	Milford to Solway Firth, or as the Board should direct.
Swallow	Thomas Amos	153	10	32	As the Board should direct.
Lively	Du Bois Smith	113	12	30	As the Board should direct.
Defence	Geo. Farr (Acting)	76	6	18	Gravesend to Dungeness.
Ant	Thomas Morris	58	4	15	Gravesend to the Nore.
Fly	Thomas Gibbs	52	4	15	Gravesend to the Nore.
Success	William Broadbank	74	6	24	Rochester to North Sand Head.

The Fine Art of Smuggling:

Vessel	Commander	Tons	Guns	Men	Station
Otter	John Matthews	68	—	13	Rochester to the Buoy of the Woolpack.
Active	Thomas Lesser	75	8	18	Mouth of Medway to N. Foreland, round the Longsand and up the Swin to Leigh.
Swift	J. Westbeech (Tide Surveyor)	52	—	8	Downs to the Longsand.
Nimble	William Clothier (Acting)	41	2	15	Between the Forelands.
Tartar	B.J. Worthington	100	10	23	The Gore to Beachy Head.
Stag	John Haddock	153	14	32	Dover to Brighton, but extended on special circumstances.
Hound	J.R. Hawkins	111	12	30	N. Foreland to Isle of Wight.[Pg 408]
Falcon	Charles Newland	131	12	33	Beachy Head to Isle of Wight.
Roebuck	John Stiles	104	12	27	Round the Isle of Wight.
Antelope	John Case	97	10	26	Round the Isle of Wight, and from Needles to Swanage.
Rose	William Yeates	114	12	32	From Lool to Lyme.
Swan		[Building at this date]			Beachy Head to Lyme
Greyhound	Richard Wilkinson	200	16	43	Beachy Head to the Start.
Alarm	Andrew Dealey	130	12	36	Between Portland and the Start.

King's Cutters vs Smugglers -1700-1855

Vessel	Commander	Tons	Guns	Men	Station
Ranger	Nathaniel Cane	80	8	25	Land's End to Cape Cornwall.
Busy	Alexr. Fraser (mate)	46	—	11	Plymouth Sound and Lawsand Bay.
Hinde	Gabriel Bray	160	12	41	Portland to St. Ives and Scilly.
Dolphin	Richard Johns (Junr.)	139	14	32	St. Ives to Padstow, round Scilly; Land's End to Helford.
Racer	James Wood (mate)	40	—	9	Chepstow to Ilfracombe.
Speedwell	John Hopkins	\[Building at this date\]			Holyhead, Bristol Channel, and to the Land's End.
Endeavour	Thomas Peregrine	34	—	11	The whole port of Milford.
Repulse	G.G.H. Munnings	143	14	43	North Yarmouth to Portsmouth.
Argus	John Saunders	135	14	32	Buoy of the Middle[25] to Lowestoft.
Hunter	Thomas Ritches	143	14	32	Harwich to Cromer.
Bee	A. Somerscalls (mate)	28	—	9	Humber, York, and Lincoln, and to guard Quarantine.
Eagle	George Whitehead	\[Building at this date\]			Tynemouth to Yarmouth.
Mermaid	John Carr	112	10	30	Berwick to the Spurn.
Viper	John Hudson (mate)	28	—	9	Isle of Anglesea to St. Bee's Head occasionally.

APPENDIX IV
A List of Revenue Cruisers Built Between July 18, 1822 and October 1, 1838

Name of Cruiser	When Built	Tons	Builders	Where Built	Draft Fwd	Draft Aft	Speed Knots
Fly (late New Charter)	Jul 18, 1822	44	Thos. White	Cowes	5 × 6	7 × 4	—
Lion	Jul 18, 1822	82	Th. Inman	Lymington	—	—	—
Arrow (late Seaflower)	Jul 18, 1822	43	Ransom & Ridley	Hastings	4 × 6	9 × 3	9
Cameleon (lost)	Jul 18, 1822	85	Wm. Hedgcock	Dover	—	—	—
Dolphin	Jul 18, 1822	68	J.B. Good	Bridport	5 × 3	9 × 0	10
Ranger	Jul 18, 1822	71	Chas. Golder	Folkestone	4 × 6	9 × 6	8
Tartar	Jul 18, 1822	82	Ransom & Ridley	Hastings	5 × 2	10 × 2	8
Repulse	Jul 18, 1822	82	W. Good & Son	Ealing	—	—	—
Nimble	Jul 18, 1822	65	Rd. Graves	Sandgate	5 × 0	10 × 0	10
Sprightly	Jul 18, 1822	63	Chas. Miller	Cowes	5 × 6	8 × 6	7

The Fine Art of Smuggling:

Name of Cruiser	When Built	Tons	Builders	Where Built	Draft Fwd	Draft Aft	Speed Knots
Sealark	Oct. 10, 1823	42	Th. White	Cowes	—	—	—
Scout	Aug. 15, 1823	84	Th. White	Cowes	5 × 11	8 × 4	8
Fox	Oct. 10, 1823	85	Th. White	Cowes	6 × 6	10 × 0	10
Endeavour	Jul 16, 1823	45	N. Harvey	Rye	5 × 6	9 × 6	—
Adder (sold)	Oct. 10, 1823	73	T. White	Cowes	—	—	—
Vigilant	Feb. 10, 1824	99	T. White	Cowes	6 × 8	9 × 4	9
Kite	Mar. 21, 1825	164	Ransom & Ridley	Hastings	6 × 8	12 × 10	11
Hound (lost)	Mar. 21, 1825	169	T. White	Cowes	—	—	—
Experiment	Apr 16, 1825	43	T. White	Cowes	5 × 0	7 × 4	—
Racer	Aug. 10, 1825	53	Ransom & Ridley	Hastings	4 × 4	9 × 8	8
Viper (late Mermaid)	Aug. 23, 1825	43	T. White	Cowes	—	—	—
Stag	Feb. 20, 1827	130	T. White	Cowes	6 × 9	10 × 9	10
Diligence (lost)	Feb. 4, 1828	171	Ransom & Ridley	Hastings	6 × 9	12 × 4	12
Bee	Aug. 18, 1828	69	Ransom & Ridley	Hastings	6 × 0	10 × 0	—
Stork	Jan. 5, 1830	160	Ransom & Ridley	Hastings	7 × 4	12 × 6	11
Liverpool (now Speedwell)	Jul 1, 1830	28	T. White	Cowes	—	—	—

King's Cutters vs Smugglers -1700-1855

Name of Cruiser	When Built	Tons	Builders	Where Built	Draft Fwd	Draft Aft	Speed Knots
Victoria	Aug. 31, 1831	22	Ransom & Ridley	Hastings	—	—	—
Chance	Apr 2, 1832	58	T. White	Cowes	6 × 6	9 × 6	9 ½ to 10
Squirrel	Jun 21, 1832	36	T. White	Cowes	—	—	—
Amphi-trite	Jul 4, 1832	30	Th. Inman	Lyming-ton	—	—	—
Victoria	Apr 2, 1832	114	Th. Inman	Lyming-ton	6 × 6	11 × 0	11
King George	Aug. 3, 1832	36	Ransom & Ridley	Hastings	—	—	—
Wickham	Apr 2, 1832	150	T. White	Cowes	7 × 3	11 × 3	11
Adelaide	Apr 2, 1832	143	Ransom & Ridley	Hastings	7 × 1 ½	12 × 2 ½	10
Dolphin	Apr 2, 1832	84	Ransom & Ridley	Hastings	7 × 0	10 × 3	9
Liverpool (tender to Kite)	Aug. 10, 1832	36	T. White	Cowes	—	—	—
Hornet	Jul 6, 1832	143	Ransom & Ridley	Hastings	7 × 0	12 × 0	7.6 to 8
Prince George	Nov. 3, 1832	70	Ransom & Ridley	Hastings	—	—	—
Provi-dence	Dec. 10, 1832	20	N. & E. Edwards	Scilly	—	—	—
Margaret	Dec. 10, 1832	22	T. Inman	Lyming-ton	5 × 2	8 × 4	9
Asp	Apr 22, 1833	32	T. White	Cowes	—	—	—
Lady of the Lake	Apr 25, 1833	22	T. Inman	Lyming-ton	—	—	—
Hind	May 25, 1833	41	Ransom & Ridley	Hastings	—	—	—

The Fine Art of Smuggling:

Name of Cruiser	When Built	Tons	Builders	Where Built	Draft Fwd	Draft Aft	Speed Knots
Caroline	Jan. 31, 1834	36	Ransom & Ridley	Hastings	—	—	—
Frances	Feb. 3, 1834	40	T. White	Cowes	4 × 6	7 × 8	8
Royal George	Mar. 27, 1834	149	T. Inman	Lymington	6 × 8	11 × 3	11
Maria	Sept. 10, 1834	36	T. Inman	Lymington	—	—	—
Vulcan (steamer)	Oct. 30, 1834	325	T. White	Cowes	—	—	—
Hamilton	Jan. 11, 1835	59	T. White	Cowes	5 × 6	9 × 6	9
Cameleon	Feb. 21, 1835	89	T. Inman	Lymington	6 × 6	10 × 6	10
Kingstown	May 4, 1835	21	T. Inman	Lymington	—	—	—
Bat	Nov. 20, 1835	37	T. White	Cowes	—	—	—
Tiger	Mar. 8, 1836	18	T. Inman	Lymington	—	—	—
Onyx	Sept. 1, 1836	36	T. White	Cowes	—	—	—
Flying Fish	Sept. 1, 1836	41	T. White	Cowes	5 × 3	8 × 3	8
Gertrude	Oct. 26, 1836	37	T. White	Cowes	—	—	—
Royal Charlotte	Oct. 27, 1836	130	T. White	Cowes	6 × 5	10 × 9	10
Active	Oct. 29, 1836	101	T. Inman	Lymington	6 × 2	11 × 1	10
Vixen	Feb. 11, 1837	56	T. White	Cowes	5 × 3	8 × 4	10

Name of Cruiser	When Built	Tons	Builders	Where Built	Draft Fwd	Draft Aft	Speed Knots
Ferret	Mar. 18, 1837	39	T. Inman	Lymington	—	—	—
Desmond	Jun 10, 1837	68	T. Inman	Lymington	4 × 9	8 × 6	9
Harpy	Oct. 10, 1837	145	T. White	Cowes	6 × 7	11 × 3	11
Asp	Feb. 20, 1838	46	T. Inman	Lymington	—	—	—
Rose	Feb. 20, 1838	53	T. Inman	Lymington	5 × 6	9 × 3	10
Adder	Feb. 20, 1838	53	T. White	Cowes	5 × 2	8 × 3	[Never Tried]
Neptune	Jun 19, 1838	42	T. White	Cowes	—	—	—
Kingstown	Oct. 1, 1838	35	Pinney & Adams	Poole	6 × 4	9 × 4	—

N.B. There is no information to show how the rate of sailing was assessed. We know not (a) whether the vessel was sailing on a wind or off; whether close-hauled or with the wind abeam; (b) whether the distance was taken from a measured mile reckoned between two fixed objects ashore; (c) what sail was set; whether reefed or not; (d) whether the speed was estimated by means of the old-fashioned log.

It is probable that the last mentioned was the method employed, but in any one of these cases the rate given can only be approximate unless we know the force and angle of the wind at each trial trip. The non-nautical reader may be reminded in considering the rates given above that a knot is equivalent to 1000 fathoms or, more exactly, 6086 English feet.

APPENDIX V
Specification for Building a Cutter for the Revenue Service of Thirty-Five Tons
(As built in the Year 1838)

LENGTH.—From Stem to Sternpost, 44 feet. Keel for tonnage, 41 feet.

BREADTH.—Extreme from outside the Plank, 14 feet 5 inches.

DEPTH.—From the upper-part of the Main Hatch-Beam to the Ceiling alongside the Keelson, 7 feet 8 inches.

KEEL.—The Keel to be of good sound Elm, in not more than two pieces, with Hook and Butt Scarphs 6 feet long, sided 6-1/2 inches. Depth aft 12 inches, forward 14 inches, with a false Keel.

STEM.—To be of sound English Oak, clear of Sap and all other defects, sided 5-1/2 inches, and to be sufficiently thick at the head to admit of a hole for the Main Stay.

STERN POST.—To be of sound English Oak, clear of Sap and all other defects, sided 5-1/2 inches.

DEAD WOOD.—The Dead Wood both forward and aft to be of Oak, clear of Sap and all defects, except the two lower pieces which may be Elm, and secured by a Knee well bolted through the Sternpost, and Dead Wood aft, and Stem and Dead Wood forward.

FLOORS AND FUTTOCKS.—To be sided 5-1/2 and not more than 6 inches apart. The lower Futtocks sided 5-1/2 inches, second Futtocks 5, third Futtocks 5, and Toptimbers 4-1/2, Stantions 4 inches. The heels of the lower Futtocks to meet on the Keel, all the Timber to be well grown and seasoned, clear of Sap and other defects;—of English Oak.

KEELSON.—The Keelson to run well forward and aft, of sound Oak, clear of Sap, sided 7 inches and moulded 9 inches Midships. The ends moulded 7 inches and sided 6 inches. To be bolted through the floors and Keel with 3/4 inch Copper Bolts well clenched on a ring, under the Keel.

STANTIONS.—Stantions sided 4 inches at the Gunwale and 3-1/2 inches at the Head, and so spaced as to form 4 ports, each side 20 inches in the clear, and the port lids hung with composition hooks and hinges to roughtree rail and one Stantion between each port, or more if necessary.

COUNTER-TIMBERS.—To be sided from 4-1/2 to 4 inches and the Transoms well kneed.

BREAST-HOOKS.—To have 3 Breast-Hooks, one under the Bowsprit sided 4 inches, the others sided 4-1/2 inches, all of the best English Oak, with arms not less than 3 feet long, clear of Sap and other defects; the two lower ones to be bolted with Copper Bolts. The Throat Bolt to be 3/4 inch diameter, to go through the stem and clenched, and three in each arm of 5/8, all well clenched on a ring.

BEAMS.—The Beams to be good sound Oak, clear of all defects, to round up 5-1/2 inches. The Beam before and the Beam abaft the Mast to be sided 6 inches, and moulded 6 inches, and not more than 4 feet apart, and to have two Wood lodging Knees to each, also one Iron hanging Knee to each; the remainder of the Beams to be sided 5 inches, and moulded 5 inches, and regularly spaced, and not more than three feet from Center to Center, with two 1 inch dowels in each end, instead of dovetailing into the shelf-piece, with a 5/8 inch bolt through each dowel, and an inch and quarter hole bored in the end of all the Beams 10 inches in, and another from the under side to meet it, then seared with a hot Iron to admit Air.

CARLINGS AND LEDGERS.—To have 2 fore and aft Carlings between each Beam 4 inches by 3-1/2, and a Ledge 3-1/2 by 3 inches between the Beams where required. The Mast Carlings to be good English Oak, 4 inches thick, and 10 inches broad.

WALES AND BOTTOM PLANK.—The Wales to be of English well-seasoned Oak, 3 inches thick, clear of all defects, with one strake of 2-1/2 inches thick next under the Wales, and one bilge strake of 2-1/2 inch each side. The remainder of the Bottom to be full 2 inches thick when worked, all of sound English Oak, except the Garboard and one next to it which may be of Elm; Plank to work 16 feet long with 6 feet shifts, and two strakes between each Butt: the first strake above the Wales to be 2 inches thick, the remainder 2 inches, paint strake 2 inches.

SPIRKETTING.—The Spirketting to be 2 inches thick.

WATERWAYS.—The Waterways to be of English Oak, 3 inches thick, clear of Sap and strakes, and not less than 6 inches broad in any part.

PLANSHEER.—The Plansheer of good English Oak, full 2 inches thick when worked, and to form the lower Port Sills.

SHELF PIECES.—The Shelf Pieces to be fitted to the Timbers instead of working it over the Clamp, as heretofore, to be of good sound English Oak, 6 inches broad, 3-1/2 inches thick, and bolted with 5/8 inch bolts, two feet apart, well clenched.

CLAMPS.—The Clamps to be of good sound Oak, 8 inches broad and 2 inches thick, fitted up to the under side of the Shelf Pieces.

CEILING.—To have two strakes of 2 inch Oak on the Floor and lower Futtock Heads, both sides, and the Ceiling to be of 1-1/4 inch Oak, all English, as high as one foot above the lower Deck; the remainder as high as the clamp, to be of Red Pine, clear of Sap and other defects, 3/4 inch thick.

CHANNELS.—The Main Channels to be of the best English Oak, of sufficient breadth, to convey the rigging clear of the Weather Cloth Rail, and 3-1/2 inches thick with 4 substantial Chainplates with Iron bound Dead-eyes complete, on each side. The two lower bolts in each plate to be 1 inch in diameter. No Bolt in the Chainplate through the Channel as usual. The Chainplates to be let their thickness into the edge of the Channel, and an Iron plate 3 inches broad, and 3/8 inch thick, secured over all by Small Bolts 4-1/2 inches long.

PORTS.—To have 4 Ports on each side properly spaced, and the Port Lids hung with Copper Hooks and Hinges.

BULWARK.—The Bulwark to be of Baltic Red Pine 1 inch thick, to be worked in narrow strakes about 5 inches broad. The edges grooved and tongued together, and not lined as usual, except from forward to bow port.

ROUGHTREE RAIL.—To be of good clean, straight grained Oak 4-1/2 inches broad, and 2-1/4 deep, to be fitted with a sufficient number of Iron Stantions 2-6/8 inches long, with Oak Rail 2 inches square for Weather Cloths. The Roughtree Rail to be 2 feet high from Deck.

DECK.—The Upper Deck to be of the best Baltic Red Pine, full 2 inches thick when worked, clear of Sap, strakes, etc., and not more than 5 inches broad each plank. The plank under, and between the Bitts Knees, to be English Oak 2-1/2 inches thick, the whole to be fastened with Copper Nails of sufficient length.

BITTS.—The Bowsprit Bitts to run down to the Ceiling, with a Bolt in the Keel of each, and so placed that the Bowsprit may be run aft clear of the Mast Larboard Side. Size of the Bitts at the head fore and aft 7 inches, thwartships 6 inches, and to be the same size at lower part of Deck, with a regular taper to heel. The Windlass Bitts to be sided 7 inches, and left broad and high enough above the Deck to admit of a Patent Pinion Cog, and Multiplying Wheels to be fitted to Windlass, with Crank, Handles, etc. To have good and sufficient Knees to all the Bitts. The Bowsprit Bitt Knees sided 6 inches, Windlass Bitt Knees sided 5 inches.

WINDLASS.—The Barrel of the Windlass to be of good sound English Oak, clear of all defects, diameter in the middle 10 inches, and fitted with Patent Iron Palls, with two hoops on each end, and seasoned Elm Whelps 2-1/2 inches thick, hollowed in the middle for Chain Cable 14 inches long, taking care that it leads far from the Hawse Holes, to have 6 Iron Plates let into the Angles of the Whelps. The Iron Spindle to be 2 inches Diameter, and to let into the Barrel of the Windlass 12 inches, and

The Fine Art of Smuggling:

to be fitted with Pinion, Cog, and Multiplying Wheels and Crank Handles, to have two Windlass ends not more than a foot long each; care must be taken not to cut the Handspike holes where the Chain Cable works.

SCUPPERS.—To have 2 oval Lead Scuppers, each side, 3 by 1-3/4 inch in the clear.

EYE PLATES.—To have two stout Iron Eye Plates, both sides forward for Bowsprit, Shrouds, etc. with two Bolts in each, and three Plates both sides for Runners and Tackles aft, the Eyes to reach up to the top of Roughtree Rail, and to have a good strong Iron Hanging Knee each side to the Beams abreast the Runners.

HATCHWAYS.—The Main Hatchway to be 4 feet broad and 3 feet fore and aft in the clear. The Combins 3 inches thick and 11 inches broad, let down on Carlings 3 inches thick and 4-1/2 inches broad.

SKYLIGHTS.—To be fitted with two Skylights with Plate Glass and Copper Guard, Commanders to be 3 feet long and 2 feet broad; Mates Skylight 2 feet square, with Plate Glass, Copper Bars 3/8 diameter.

ILLUMINATORS.—To have 10 oblong 4 inch Illuminators let into the Deck where most required, and a 5 inch Patent one over the Water Closet.

WINCH.—To have a Patent Winch round the Mast, and the Mast to be wedged in the partners.

PUMPS.—To be fitted with two Metal Bilge Pumps 3-1/2 inch chamber and everything complete; also one Metal Pump amidships with 6 inch chamber, and two sets of Brass Boxes, and everything requisite; also a Wash Deck Pump fitted aft.

RUDDER.—To have a good and sufficient Rudder with two sets of Metal Pintles and Braces, and one Iron Pintle and Brace at the head of the Sternpost above the Deck, and to be fitted with two good Tillers.

COMPANION.—To be fitted with a Companion and Bittacle complete.

HAWSEPIPES.—To have two stout cast Iron Hawsepipes for Chain Cable 4 inches in the clear, also two Cast Iron Pipes in the Deck with Bell Mouth, to conduct the Chain Cable below.

LOWER DECK.—The Lower Deck Beams to be regularly spaced and not more than 4 feet apart, the Deck to be 1-1/4 inches thick, of good Red Pine, the Midships part 3 feet broad, to be fastened to the Beams, also some of the side plank, the remainder made into Hatches, the edges bolted together with 1/2 inch Iron, the Deck and Cabin Floor abaft, Main Hatch to be 1 inch thick, and made into Hatches where required.

MAGAZINE.—To have a Magazine abaft, properly fitted and lined on the inside with 5 lb. Lead, and Double Doors with Copper Hinges and Lock to the outside Door.

BREAD ROOM.—To have Bread Rooms and Flour Bins lined with Tin as usual.

GALLEY.—The Galley under the Fire Hearth to be coppered with 32 oz. Sheet Copper 5 feet square, and the under part of the Upper Deck, Beams, etc.; over the Boilers 4 feet square, to be leaded with 6 lb. Lead.

LOCKERS AND BINS.—To be fitted with Store Bins and Lockers from the Bows to the Cabin Bulkheads between Decks.

BULKHEADS.—To have Bulkheads between Decks for Commander's Cabin, State Room, and all other Bulkheads, as is customary for a Revenue Cruiser of the 3rd class, with all Drawers, Cupboards, Bed-places, Tables, Wash-stands, etc. complete. The Cabin Bulkheads to be framed in Panels, all Hinges to be Brass with Brass Pins.

BULKHEADS, HOLD.—To have Bulkheads in the Hold, for Coals, Stores, Casks, Chain Cables, etc., and an opening of one inch left between each Plank to give air, except the Coal-hole which must be close.

LADDERS.—To have a Main Hatch, Fore Hatch, and Cabin Ladder complete.

CLEATS.—To be fitted complete, with all Cleats, Cavels, Snatch Cleats with Shieves, Brass coated Belaying Cleats, and Racks with Belaying Pins, etc., and an Iron Crutch on Taffrail for the Boom.

FASTENINGS.—The whole of the Plank to be fastened with good well seasoned Treenails, and one 1/2 inch Copper Bolt in every Butt from the Keel up to the Wales, to go through and clench on a Ring on the Ceiling, and the Treenails drove through the Ceiling, wedged on the inside and caulked outside.

RING AND EYE BOLTS.—To be fitted with all necessary Ring and Eye Bolts, as customary for a Revenue Cruiser.

LEGS.—To have 2 substantial Oak Legs properly fitted.

PAINT.—The whole of the Wood Work inside and out to have three coats of the best Paint, well put on.

HULL.—The Hull to be completed in every respect as a Revenue Cruiser of the 3rd Class, and all Materials found by the Contractor, except Copper Sheathing for the Bottom and Water-Closets, with all Shipwrights', Caulkers', Joiners', Blacksmiths', Copper-smiths', Braziers', Glaziers', Plumbers' and Painters' work.

CATHEAD.—To have an Iron Cathead with two Shieves strong enough to cat the Anchor, and fitted both sides.

COCK.—To have a Stop Cock fitted forward under the Lower Deck, to let in Water occasionally.

WATER-CLOSET.—To have a Patent Water-Closet of Danton's fitted below, and a Round-house on Deck, aft Starboard side complete, with a Pantry for meat, the Larboard side to correspond with the Round-house, and a Poop Deck between both, nailed with Copper Nails; also a seat of ease on the Larboard side forward for the Crew, with Lead Pipe to water edge; the whole of the Locks throughout to be Brass and Brass Works.

AIR OPENINGS.—An inch opening to be left all fore and aft under the Clamp both sides, also in the Ceiling between the Lower Deck Beams, and another in the upper part of the Bins, and one inch auger hole bored between the Timbers in the run aft and forward where lists cannot be left out, also a hole of one inch in all the Timbers, fore and aft, to admit air, and those holes seared with a hot iron; all Chocks for securing the frame Timbers together are to be split out before the bottom Plank is worked.

The Cutter to remain in frame for one Month before closed in, then when the outside Plank is worked and all the Sap taken off the Timbers, and before the Ceiling is worked, to give the Timbers a good coat of Stockholm Tar.

Should there be any omission or want of more full statement in this Specification, the Contractor is to understand that the Hull of the said Vessel is to be fitted and completed fit for Sea in every respect as is usual for a Revenue Vessel of her Class, the Board finding the Copper Sheathing and Water-Closet.

DEFECTS TO BE AMENDED.—Any defects discovered in the Timbers or Plank, etc., by the Officer or Overseer appointed by the Honorable Board of Customs to survey and inspect the same, or insufficient workmanship performed to the said Cutter during her building, the said defect or deficiency both in the one and in the other, shall upon notice thereof to the Contractor be forthwith amended, and the said Overseer shall not at any time have any molestation or obstruction therein.

Note.—For a 150-ton Revenue Cutter the following dimensions were employed:

> Length.—(Stem to Sternpost) 72 feet.
> Keel for Tonnage, 68 feet.
> Breadth.—(Extreme) 22 feet 10 inches.
> Depth.—10 feet 3 inches.
> Beams to be 7 inches.
> Deck to be 2 inches thick.
> Four Oak Legs to be supplied

APPENDIX VI
Dimensions of Spars of Revenue Cutters

The following list shows the length and thickness of mast, boom, bowsprit, gaff, topmast, and spread-yard [i.e. the yard on which the square-sail was set] as used in the Revenue Cutters of different sizes from 150 to 40 tons. The dimensions given below were those in vogue in the year 1838.

Spar	150 Tons	130 Tons	100 Tons	90 Tons	80 Tons	70 Tons	60 Tons	50 Tons	40 Tons
	ft. ins.	ft. ins.	ft. ins.	ft. ins.	ft. ins.	ft. ins.	ft. ins.	ft. ins.	ft. ins.
Mast	75 × 20	72 × 18	68 × 17	65 × 16½	63 × 15¾	60 × 15	56 × 14	55 × 13½	50 × 12
Boom	61 × 13¼	59 × 13	54 × 12	51 × 11½	49 × 10¾	47 × 10½	45 × 10	43 × 8¾	42 × 8½
Bowsprit	55 × 16¾	53 × 15½	49 × 14	47 × 13¼	44 × 12½	43 × 12	38 × 11¼	37 × 10¾	32 × 10
Gaff	45 × 8¾	40 × 8½	38 × 7¾	33 × 7½	32 × 7¼	31 × 7	28 × 6¾	30 × 6½	26 × 6
Topmast	52 × 9¾	48 × 8½	45 × 7¾	42 × 7½	40 × 7¼	39 × 7	35 × 6¾	35 × 6½	30 × 6
Spread-Yard	58 × 9¼	56 × 8½	48 × 8¼	47 × 7¾	46 × 7½	44 × 7	42 × 6¾	38 × 6¼	32 × 6

APPENDIX VII
A List of the Cruisers in the Revenue Coast Guard of the United Kingdom in the Year 1844

Name of Cruiser	Number	Name of Cruiser	Number
Shamrock	45	Badger	16
Kite	34	Skylark	16
Swift	34	Petrel	16
Prince of Wales	34	Racer	15
Wickham	33	Hamilton	23
Greyhound	33	Chance	16
Prince Albert	33	Harriett	14
Royal George	33	Rose	14
Mermaid	33	Adder	14
Adelaide	30	Rob Roy	14
Wellington	33	Eliza	13
Harpy	30	Jane	13
Royal Charlotte	29	Experiment	10
Stag	29	Albatross	13

The Fine Art of Smuggling:

Name of Cruiser	Number	Name of Cruiser	Number
Defence	29	Asp	10
Eagle	29	Frances	10
Lapwing	29	Arrow	10
Sylvia	29	Viper	10
Victoria	27	Neptune	10
Lively	23	Sealark	10
Vigilant	23	Hind	10
Active	23	Liverpool	10
Cameleon	21	Maria	12
Fox	21	Sylph	8
Dolphin	21	Gertrude	8
Scout	21	Governor	8
Tartar	21	Nelson	7
Hawke	21	Princess Royal	7
Ranger	20	Ann	7
Nimble	17	Fairy	7
Desmond	17	Ferret	7
Sprightly	17	Lady of the Lake	5
Lion	16	Vulcan (steamer)	31

Note.—The size of the above varied from 25 tons to 164 tons. But the ss. Vulcan was of 325 tons.

APPENDIX VII
The Relationship between the Royal Navy and the Revenue Service

No better instance of the strained relationship existing between the Royal Navy and the Revenue Service could be found than the following. It will be seen that the animosity had begun at any rate before the end of the seventeenth century and was very far from dead in the nineteenth.

The first incident centers round Captain John Rutter, commander of "one of the smacks or sloops in the service of the Customs about the Isle of Wight." He stated that on April 24, 1699, about eight o'clock in the evening, he went on board to search the ship *Portland* at Spithead, the latter having arrived from France with a cargo of wine. At the same time there put off the long boat from Admiral Hopson's *Resolution* demanding four hogsheads and four tierces, which (said Rutter) "I denied, but however they took it out by force and carried it on board." Rutter then went on to the *Resolution* and there found the wine lying on deck. The Admiral sent for him aft, and said that he would see the wine forthcoming, for he would write to the Commissioners of Customs.

Some time afterwards Rutter was ashore at Portsmouth in company with Captain Foulks, who was one of the officers stationed on land. The latter informed Rutter that he was a rogue for having informed against the Admiral. Foulks drew his sword, and, had he not been prevented, would have murdered Rutter. Apparently Admiral Hopson never forgave Rutter. For, some months later, Rutter was riding off Portsmouth "with my Pendent and Colors flying, rejoicing for the happy arrival of His Maty."

Hopson was being rowed ashore, and when near "my yacht ordered my pendent to be taken down. I being absent, my men would not do it without my order, whereon he sent his boat on board and one of his men took it down. I coming on board to goe upon my duty ordered it to be hoysted again and imediately he sent his boat with one of his Lieutenants to take it down again with a verball order which I refused to lett him do, but by strength overpowered me and my company and took it down by force, and beat us to ye degree yat I know not whether it may not hazard some men's lives, which I acknowledge I did not wear it in contempt, and if he had sent another time I would readily have obeyed his Order. Now I humbly conceive that it was merely out of malice as I can prove by his own mouth."

Arising out of this incident, a letter was sent from the Admiralty to the Portsmouth Custom House and signed by "J. Burchett." The latter opined that it was not a fault for the Custom House smacks to wear a pendant, but pointed out that the Proclamation of 1699 obliged the Custom House smacks to wear such a pendant as was distinct from the King's "as well as their Jacks and Ensigns." Furthermore he suggested that it had always been customary to strike such pendant when in sight of an Admiral's flag, especially if demanded.

The second incident occurred on February 4, 1806. The commanding officer of H.M. Armed vessel *Sentinel* was lying in Shields harbor. He sent word to a man named Stephen Mitchell, who caused the watch of the Revenue cutter *Eagle* to hoist the *Eagle*'s pendant half-mast. Mitchell naturally replied that he dared not do so without his captain's orders. Mitchell, therefore, sent to his captain, George Whitehead, but before the latter's arrival the pendant was hauled down and carried on board the *Sentinel* with threats that Whitehead should be prosecuted for wearing a pendant.

Whitehead accordingly wrote to the Collector and Controller of the Customs at Newcastle to lodge a complaint. The latter, in turn, wrote to Lieut. W. Chester, R.N., commanding this *Sentinel* gun-brig asking for an explanation. The naval officer replied by referring them to Articles 6 and 7 of the Admiralty Instructions regarding ships or vessels in the service of any public office, by which it was ordered that they should wear the same Ensign and Jack as ships having Letters of Marque, except that in the body of the Jack or Ensign there should be likewise described the seal of the office they belonged to. All vessels employed in the service of any public office were forbidden to wear pendants contrary to what was allowed, and officers of ships-of-war were permitted to seize any illegal colors.

Chester contended that the *Eagle* was hailed and requested to lower her colors half-mast, as an officer of the Navy was being interred at South Shields, and all the other vessels in the harbor "had their colors half staff down" except the *Eagle*. Because the latter refused, Chester requested her mate to come on board the *Sentinel*, as the former wished to explain why the colors should be lowered. An officer was thereupon sent on board the *Eagle* to haul them down. Chester demanded an apology for the disrespect to the deceased officer.

And one could easily quote other similar instances between H.M.S. *Princess* and the Revenue cutter *Diligence*: and H.M. gun-brig *Teazer* and the Revenue cruiser *Hardwicke*.

For the Finest in Nautical and Historical Fiction and Nonfiction

www.FireshipPress.com

Interesting • Informative • Authoritative

All Fireship Press books are now available directly through www.FireshipPress.com, amazon.com and via leading bookstores from coast-to-coast

Breinigsville, PA USA
February 2011
996BV00004B/21/P